VITAL I

VITAL
NEW TESTAMENT
ISSUES

THE VITAL ISSUES SERIES

VITAL ISSUES SERIES

VITAL NEW TESTAMENT ISSUES

Examining New Testament Passages and Problems

ROY B. ZUCK
GENERAL EDITOR

kregel
RESOURCES

Grand Rapids, MI 49501

Vital New Testament Issues: Examining New Testament Passages and Problems by Roy B. Zuck, general editor

Copyright © 1996 by Dallas Theological Seminary

Published by Kregel Resources, an imprint of Kregel Publications, P.O. Box 2607, Grand Rapids, MI 49501. Kregel Resources provides timely and relevant resources for Christian life and service. Your comments and suggestions are valued.

Cover design: Sarah Slattery
Book design: Alan G. Hartman

Library of Congress Cataloging-in-Publication Data
Roy B. Zuck
Vital New Testament issues: examining New Testament issues and problems / Roy B. Zuck, gen. ed.
p.   cm. (Vital Issues Series; v. 8)
1. Bible. N.T.—Criticism, Textual. 2. Bible. N.T.—Language, style. I. Zuck, Roy B. II. Series.
BS2325.V57   1996   225.6—dc20   96-10339
                                                    CIP

ISBN 0-8254-4074-2 (paperback)

1 2 3 4 5 Printing / Year 00 99 98 97 96

Printed in the United States of America

Contents

5

Contributors

Andrew D. Chang
  Academic Dean, Korea Baptist Bible College, Seoul, Korea

Charles H. Dyer
  Assistant to the President and Professor of Bible Exposition, Dallas Theological Seminary, Dallas, Texas

D. Edmond Hiebert
  Late Professor Emeritus of New Testament, Mennonite Brethren Biblical Seminary, Fresno, California

H. Wayne House
  Academic Dean and Professor of Theology, Michigan Theological Seminary, Ann Arbor, Michigan

Gordon E. Kirk
  Pastor, First Congregational Church, Pasadena, California

Robert M. Lewis
  Teaching Pastor, Fellowship Bible Church, Little Rock, Arkansas

Curtis C. Mitchell
  Professor Emeritus of Biblical Studies and Theology, Talbot School of Theology, La Mirada, California

John D. Reaume
  Lecturer, Biblical Studies Department, United Missionary Theological College, Ilorin, Nigeria

Cleon L. Rogers, Jr.
  Missionary, Huettenberg/Weidenhausen, Germany

Walter B. Russell
  Associate Professor of New Testament, Talbot School of Theology, La Mirada, California

Charles C. Ryrie
  Professor of Systematic Theology, Emeritus, Dallas Theological Seminary, Dallas, Texas

7

Robert C. Swift
   Computer Programmer, American Airlines, Flower Mound, Texas

Tom Thatcher
   Instructor in Biblical Studies, Cincinnati Bible Seminary, Cincinnati, Ohio

Allison A. Trites
   Librarian and Professor of New Testament, Acadia Divinity College, Wolfville, Nova Scotia

Kenneth T. Wilson
   Assistant Professor of Bible and Theology, Colorado Christian University, Morrison, Colorado

Preface

No one can read the New Testament without being impressed with its accurate reporting of the beginning and rapid growth of Christianity, its practical guidance for Christian living, and its predictions of events yet to come. Yet within these twenty-seven books—books that record Jesus' life, death, and resurrection; that report the apostles's witness of Him in their ministries; and that give reported calls to godly behavior—numerous questions are raised.

The chapters in *Vital New Testament Issues* address some of those issues, including the following: What is the significance of the Day of Pentecost? How does the Holy Spirit intercede for believers? Should women wear headcoverings? What is the meaning of the phrase "baptized for the dead"? Do the "mystery religions" of the Greco-Roman world relate in any way to the misguided practice of tongues-speaking in Corinth?

Who were Paul's opponents in Galatia? Can a single theme be detected in the multifaceted book of Philippians? Were the women in 1 Timothy 3:11 deaconesses? Does Christ's death have value only for the elect or for all humankind? What is the identity of the city of Babylon in Revelation 17–18?

The writers of these chapters, reprinted from *Bibliotheca Sacra*, Dallas Seminary's theological journal, discuss these and other provocative questions and propose thoughtful answers. Read the chapters, ponder the issues, and deepen your understanding of the life-giving truths of God's enriching Word.

Roy B. Zuck

About *Bibliotheca Sacra*

A flood is rampant—an engulfing deluge of literature far beyond any one person's ability to read it all. Presses continue to churn out thousands of journals and magazines like a roiling, raging river.

Among these numberless publications, one stands tall and singular—*Bibliotheca Sacra*—a strange name (meaning "Sacred Library") but a journal familiar to many pastors, teachers, and Bible students.

How is *Bibliotheca Sacra* unique in the world of publishing? By being the oldest continuously published journal in the Western Hemisphere—1993 marked its 150th anniversary—and by being published by one school for more than six decades—1994 marked its diamond anniversary of being released by Dallas Seminary.

Bib Sac, to use its shortened sobriquet, was founded in New York City in 1843 and was purchased by Dallas Theological Seminary in 1934, ten years after the school's founding. The quarterly's one-hundred-and-fifty-three-year history boasts only nine editors. Through those years it has maintained a vibrant stance of biblical conservatism and a strong commitment to the Scriptures as God's infallible Word.

Each volume in the Kregel *Vital Issues Series* includes carefully selected articles from the thirties to the present—articles of enduring quality, articles by leading evangelicals whose topics are as relevant today as when they were first produced. The chapters have been edited slightly to provide conformity of style. We trust these anthologies will enrich the spiritual lives and Christian ministries of many more readers.

ROY B. ZUCK, EDITOR
Bibliotheca Sacra

For *Bibliotheca Sacra* subscription information, call Dallas Seminary, 1-800-992-0998.

CHAPTER 1

Do the Synoptics Depend on Each Other?

Charles H. Dyer

What is the literary relationship between the Synoptic Gospels? How does one explain the many similarities of content and wording within the Gospel accounts while at the same time accounting for the numerous differences between the individual records? This chapter examines the theories that have been proposed in an attempt to arrive at an acceptable solution to the question of literary dependence in the Synoptic Gospels.

Much of the discussion in this regard is hypothetical, and some might question the validity of engaging in such a study. However, as Scroggie points out, a problem does exist and it should not be overlooked.

> That there is such a problem is a fact, and everyone who is interested in the Gospels should know something about it. In detail it is a matter for the scholars, but the average student of these Records cannot afford to overlook it. . . .
>
> We are in possession of three Gospels, Matthew, Mark, and Luke, which are called Synoptic, because they survey the life of Christ from a common viewpoint. . . . In these Gospels are resemblances and differences, and the problem consists in the harmonizing of these, and so of determining the relation of the Synoptics to one another.[1]

The Synoptic Problem

What exactly is the problem between the Synoptic Gospels that raises the question of literary dependence? Actually there are four aspects to this problem which must be understood. Guthrie presents a helpful summary of the four points.

> Arising out of a detailed study of the three Synoptic Gospels is the important question of their relationship to each other, and this is affected by the following main considerations.

a. Similarity of arrangement

All these Gospels are based on the same general historical structure. . . . Moreover, there is a high proportion of the Gospel material common to all three Gospels.

b. Similarity of style and wording

In many sections of the Gospels not only is there similarity of contents but also of vocabulary. . . .

c. Similarities in two Gospels only

(1) There are some cases where sections recorded in all three Gospels agree more closely in style and wording in two as compared with the third. . . . (2) But the more important data under this heading relate to Matthew and Luke, which contain a considerable amount of material common to both but omitted from Mark. . . .

d. Divergences

The problem would be less difficult to solve were it not for the considerable differences both in arrangement and vocabulary over many points of detail. Some sections of common material have little verbal similarity, while others are placed in different historical settings. . . . In addition to the differences just mentioned, each of the three Synoptics has certain sections peculiar to it.[2]

Each of these problems mentioned by Guthrie needs to be examined in more detail.

SIMILARITY OF ARRANGEMENT

The first problem is the similarity of arrangement. A glance at any harmony of the Gospels shows that the three agree in the general outline of materials.[3]

1. Ministry of John the Baptist
2. Baptism of Christ
3. Temptation of Christ
4. Ministry of Christ in Galilee
5. Last public ministry of Christ in Jerusalem
6. Betrayal and arrest of Christ
7. Trial and crucifixion of Christ
8. Burial of Christ
9. Resurrection of Christ

Any explanation of the relationship between the Gospels must explain this unity of arrangement.

SIMILARITY OF STYLE AND WORDING

The second problem is the similarity between the style and

wording. In many instances two or more of the Gospels present strikingly parallel accounts for extended passages. One example among many is the account of Christ receiving little children and speaking to the rich young ruler (Matt. 19:14–20; Mark 10:14–20; Luke 18:16–21). It is obvious that these accounts are closely related, and any explanation must be able to account for these similarities.

SIMILARITIES IN TWO GOSPELS ONLY

While all three Synoptics have much in common, large sections of material are found in two of the Gospels but not in the third. To compound the problem, these additions usually consist of Christ's words which are found in Matthew and Luke but not in Mark. A list of some of these sections can be quickly gained through examining a harmony of the Gospels.[4]

1. Genealogy of Christ (Matt. 1:1–17; Luke 3:23–38)
2. Preaching of John the Baptist (Matt. 3:7–10; Luke 3:7–14)
3. Explanation of Christ's temptations (Matt. 4:3–11; Luke 4:3–13)
4. Sermon on the Mount (Matt. 5–7, Luke 6:17–49)
5. Christ's healing of the centurion's servant (Matt. 8:5–13; Luke 7:1–10)
6. Exhortation to follow Christ (Matt. 8:19–22; Luke 9:57–62)
7. Eulogy for John the Baptist (Matt. 11:2–19; Luke 7:18–35)
8. Christ's lament over Jerusalem (Matt. 23:37–39; Luke 13:34–35)

In addition to these major passages which are entirely lacking in Mark, the other two Synoptic writers, Matthew and Luke, often "flesh out" Mark's basic statements with additional material. Once again, any explanation of the relationship between these Gospels must take into account the large amount of material common to just two of the three.

DIVERGENCES

The problem of divergences within the Synoptics seems to cause the most difficulty for those who attempt to arrive at a unified explanation of the relationship between the Gospels. One problem is the use of parallel materials in different settings. For example, Matthew's account of Christ's lament over Jerusalem occurs in the temple in Jerusalem *after* His triumphal entry into the city (Matt. 21:9–10; 23:37–24:1). However, Luke's account of Christ's lament over Jerusalem occurs somewhere on the road to Jerusalem before His triumphal entry into the city (Luke 13:22, 31–35; 19:28–40).

A second problem with the differences between the Gospels concerns the materials that are unique to one Gospel. Since so much of the material is similar, these unique sections must be accounted for. Scroggie lists twenty-two such sections for the Gospel of Luke. He concludes that just over half of the Book of Luke is unique to itself.[5] The same phenomenon is repeated in both Matthew and Mark though to a lesser degree. Each of these Gospels has material peculiar to it alone, and any solution to the problem must account for this material.

Basically the problem comes down to this: Why are these three Gospels so similar and yet so distinct? Did the Gospels draw on some common source or sources; and if so, can the content of these sources and the order of borrowing be determined? These are the questions that need to be answered.

The Proposed Solutions

Suggestions on possible solutions to the Synoptic problem are abundant. In fact if the many different variations are considered separately, the field is crowded with suggested hypotheses. It would be a waste of time to examine many of these variations which have long since been rendered improbable. For the sake of conciseness this section will present only the three major views which currently hold sway in this debate: the oral tradition theory, the mutual dependence theory, and the documentary hypothesis.

THE ORAL TRADITION THEORY

The first major theory to gain some measure of acceptance is the oral tradition theory. Iverach detailed the essence of this view. "It assumes that each of the evangelists wrote independently of the others, and derived the substance of his writing, not from written sources, but from oral narratives of sayings and doings of Jesus, which, through dint of repetition, had assumed a relatively fixed form."[6]

The idea behind this theory is the belief that a fixed oral tradition soon developed in the early church. Christ's words were repeated verbatim by the apostles and their followers and were committed to memory by those who heard them. Much as someone today might memorize the Preamble to the United States Constitution or the Gettysburg Address, the words of Christ were memorized by His followers. This would account for the striking similarity among the Gospel accounts.

A second concept inherent within the oral tradition theory is the belief that Christ repeated His teachings in a stereotyped form, that is, Christ delivered the same message in nearly the same form on different occasions.

> But can we say something more about the character, especially the form, of this old oral tradition? Indeed we can. The written Gospels themselves allow us to do so. The Gospels inform us that the oral tradition had two peculiarities: (1) it was the custom of the preachers to repeat their teachings, especially the sentences in which the greater part of their instruction was given. (2) Their teaching assumed a stereotyped form, the words were almost always the same. . . .
>   We cannot give full details in this paper. But we believe there is but one good interpretation of the facts we have named, and it is: Jesus had the habit of teaching in a stereotyped form.[7]

Grosheide's point is well taken. There are indications that Christ gave the same message on different occasions (e.g., Christ's lament over Jerusalem in Matt. 23:37–39 and Luke 13:34–35). These different settings could account for the differences between some of the Gospel accounts.

THE MUTUAL DEPENDENCE THEORY

The mutual dependence theory was first propounded by Augustine. It was reconsidered following the work of Griesbach in the 18th century.[8] This theory holds that one Gospel was used by the others and thus accounts for the similarities.

The problem comes when one tries to decide which of the Gospels was written first and which two borrowed from the original source. Iverach has given a brief synopsis of the confusion which has developed. "There have been many variations of the theory. Each of the 3 Gospels has been put first, each second, and each third, and each in turn has been regarded as the source of the others. In fact, all possible permutations (6 in number) have been exhausted."[9]

By the early part of the 20th century the hypothesis as revived by Griesbach had largely fallen into disfavor.[10] However, it has shown signs of recovery during the past decade.

> At first, reaction to the re-emergence of the Griesbach hypothesis was almost wholly negative. But within a few years its merits began to be noted. During the past twelve years certain major developments of the

Griesbach hypothesis have taken place, so that today a new situation exists. We are actually living between two epochs.[11]

Farmer feels that the position is now gaining in ascendancy.

There are basically two reasons why the Griesbach hypothesis is receiving favourable attention. The first has to do with the rediscovery of its central and essential strength—viz. that it offers a credible explanation for the order of the episodes in the synoptic gospels.

The second reason has to do with certain new developments in synoptic criticism. These developments are three in number. The first has to do with the characteristics of textual conflation. The second concerns the cultural context in which the evangelists did their work. And the third has to do with the use Luke may have made of Matthew.[12]

Farmer's technical explanation is far too long to reproduce here, but he does offer much proof for his position. It is safe to say that the foundation stone for the reemergence of this theory is the denial of Marcan priority among the Gospels.[13] This relates closely to the next theory, but the essence of the argument is this: The next theory developed from the mutual dependence theory by assuming that Mark was written first. If the priority of Mark is denied, that theory falls and the mutual dependence theory again becomes dominant.

Farmer's order of priority is probably the one that will become dominant in this theory. He basically repeats the ideas first presented by Griesbach.

On the Griesbach hypothesis Luke omits much of Matthew, and adds a great deal from his special source material. Mark omits most of this same material from Matthew which Luke has omitted while taking very little of what Luke has added. The result is that Mark is shorter than either Matthew or Luke, but not because he has "abbreviated" either one of them. The fact that his text of individual episodes is generally fuller than that of Matthew and Luke suggests that Mark may not have cherished brevity for its own sake.[14]

Thus the basic idea behind this theory is that one of the Gospels (probably Matthew) was written first. The other Gospels then used that first Gospel as a source to guide them in their composition. However, while the second Gospel (Luke) only used the first Gospel as his source, the third Gospel (Mark) used both of the earlier Gospels as sources. The literary dependence in this type of scheme is rather obvious.

THE DOCUMENTARY HYPOTHESIS

At the present time the theory which holds the greatest sway in the study of the Synoptic Gospels is the documentary hypothesis. This theory in all its varied forms holds that the writers of the Gospels used various *sources* in their composition of the Gospels, The similarities in the Gospels occurred when the writers copied from the same sources, and the differences resulted when they used different sources. There are two main schools of thought regarding the documentary hypothesis—the two-source theory and the four-source theory.

The two-source theory. The two-source theory of the documentary hypothesis is actually an outgrowth of some of the initial conclusions developed by the mutual dependence theory. One of those early results was the acceptance of the priority of Mark. Mark was considered to be the Gospel on which Matthew and Luke were dependent.

> One of the stable findings of synoptic criticism has been the priority of Mark. It is a striking fact, that whereas the order of Mark and Matthew may agree against Luke and that the order of Mark and Luke may agree against Matthew, the order of Matthew and Luke never agrees against Mark. In other words, Mark is the stable factor. Most prob[ably], Mark was the source common to the other two, which they generally followed, but sometimes altered. This common material is almost entirely narrative.[15]

Once the priority of Mark was accepted, though, the mutual dependence theory was hard pressed to explain the material common to Matthew and Luke but not found in Mark. The obvious answer was to postulate a second source that was available to Matthew and Luke in addition to Mark. That source is commonly called Q.

> *Q* is a hypothetical source. Modern man has never seen it, but a careful study of Matthew and Luke has caused many scholars to assume its existence. These two Gospels have in common about 207 verses that are missing in Mark. . . . The hypothetical document is commonly called *Q* after *Quelle* which means "source.". . .
>
> *Q* was not a gospel, which is a literary form in which the good news of Jesus' life, death, and resurrection was narrated. *Q* consisted largely of a collection of miscellaneous sayings arranged topically. . . . The fact that these Gospels relied so heavily on *Q* testifies to the high esteem in which this document was held in the early church. *Q* probably ceased to circulate independently after it was incorporated in Matthew and Luke.[16]

The two-source theory rests on two foundational pillars—the priority of Mark and the existence of Q. Both of these have gained a wide acceptance as attested by Marxsen.

The Two-Source theory has been so widely accepted by scholars that one feels inclined to abandon the term "theory" (in the sense of "hypothesis"). We can in fact regard it as an assured finding—but we must bear in mind that there are inevitable uncertainties as far as the extent and form of Q and the special material are concerned.[17]

In spite of Marxsen's optimistic appraisal, the "inevitable uncertainties" of the two-source theory continued to plague scholars who accepted the basic premises of the documentary hypothesis. They accepted the conclusions of the two-source theory as far as those conclusions went, but they still felt that this theory failed to account for all of the evidence. More specifically, it failed to account for the extensive material which was unique to Matthew or Luke. Scroggie quotes Westcott who estimated that 42 percent of Matthew and 59 percent of Luke are unique to their respective books.[18] The origin of this material is not explained by the two-source theory.

The four-source theory. Because of the inability of the two-source theory to account for all the relevant facts, Streeter proposed a basic expansion of the theory. He posited a four-source theory to account for the unique material in Matthew and Luke.[19] Connick gives a detailed explanation of these two additional sources.

L stands for another hypothetical source. There are about 300 verses in the Gospel of Luke, excluding the first two chapters, which have no parallel elsewhere. The supposition is that they came from an independent source. They contain both narrative and teaching material and include such memorable parables as the Good Samaritan and the Prodigal Son. Incidents in the ministry of Jesus from the preaching of John the Baptist to the ascension of Jesus are related with little concern for chronology. . . .
    M stands for a . . . hypothetical source, the material peculiar to Matthew. It contains about a dozen quotations from Hebrew Scripture, a like number of narratives (Nativity, Peter walking on the water, etc.), and many parables and sayings. Its spirit is markedly Jewish, and it exhibits a keen interest in Jesus' relation to Judaism. Jesus is pictured as a second Moses. This characteristic has fostered speculation that Jerusalem was the birthplace of the collection.[20]

The four-source theory thus seeks to explain the similarities and distinctions between the Gospels through the use of three hypothetical sources (Q, L, M) and through the acceptance of Marcan priority. However, this multiplicity of sources also poses its own problems, and thus the four-source theory is not widely accepted today. As Hobbs notes, "Streeter's M and L will not do, for they are simply further props to the Q hypothesis."[21]

Several variations of these theories have been proposed to

explain the origin of the similarities and differences in the Gospel accounts. However, the three which have just been examined are the most popular. The others are generally modifications of these basic presentations. The remainder of this chapter examines these three theories in an attempt to arrive at the best solution to the question of literary dependence.

A Suggested Solution

The underlying presuppositions of the three theories already presented must be examined to see if the theories correspond to reality.

THE PRIORITY OF MARK

The cornerstone of the documentary hypothesis is the priority of Mark. Both the two-source and four-source theories are built on the presupposition that Matthew and Luke used Mark as a written source. But what proof is given to support this assumption? Guthrie gives an excellent summary of the major arguments which have been presented.

(i) *The proportion of Mark reproduced.* Almost the whole of Mark is paralleled in Matthew (about 90 percent). . . . About half of Mark also appears in Luke. . . .

(ii) *The primary order of Mark.* In the main the three Gospels keep to the same general outline, but where they diverge in matters of detail it is more rare for Matthew and Luke to agree against Mark than for Mark to be in the majority. . . .

(iii) *The literary characteristics.* There are a number of ways in which Mark's language and style appear to give a more primitive account. First, Mark's amplification of details and even of whole sections are made more concise in Matthew and Luke. . . . Secondly, Mark's style is polished by Matthew and Luke. . . .

(iv) *The greater historical candour.* Because Mark often records evidences of Jesus' human emotions where Matthew and Luke in parallel passages either omit or modify, it is supposed that he must represent an earlier tradition. The modifications are regarded as signs of increasing reverence. . . .

(v) *The least explicit account.* In the narrative of Peter's confession at Caesarea Philippi Mark has only "Thou are the Christ," but both Matthew and Luke add further descriptions. . . .[22]

It is the opinion of this writer that these arguments are not as solid as many scholars believe. Each of the "proofs" is capable of an alternative interpretation. For example, it can be argued that the order of Mark is followed more closely because his is the Gospel with the greatest percentage of narrative material. He is seeking to present the life of Christ with a minimal amount of discourse material (parables, sermons, etc.). When the other Gospels also present their narratives of Christ's life, one would expect them to parallel Mark. It is when they add additional discourse material that they would tend to differ from Mark's order.

Closely related to this argument on the order of events was the argument based on the percentage of Marcan material reproduced. Basically this argument holds that Mark must have been written first because so much of it is reproduced in Matthew and Luke. However, this argument is not so strong as it might seem. This writer would like to postulate two literary "rules" which seem self-evident and which can explain the phenomena without assuming literary dependence.

1. Multiple accounts of the same event will exhibit striking similarities.
2. The shorter version of two or more parallel accounts will generally have a greater percentage of its material included in the other accounts.

The basic idea in these two "rules" can be explained rather easily. First, if several people write an account of the same event (whatever that event might be so long as it was observable), one would expect their accounts to be similar. Second, the shortest of the multiple accounts would be expected to have the greatest percentage of its words and phrases repeated in the other accounts since its brevity would force it to focus on the major events which would be the most likely items to be included by the others.

These "rules" can explain the high proportion of Mark which appears in Matthew and Luke. If each Gospel is faithfully recounting the events of Christ's life, then similarities in arrangement and content should be expected. Moreover, if the shorter account is detailing only the main events, then a greater percentage of that account should appear in the longer versions.

Another error in the arguments for Marcan priority can be noted. According to those arguments, if Mark's account were *more detailed* than Matthew's or Luke's it supposedly proves Mark's priority because he has the more primitive account. "Mark's amplification of details and even of whole sections are made more concise in Matthew and Luke."[23] However, if Mark's account was *less detailed* than Matthew's or Luke's it supposedly proves Mark's priority since the "least explicit account" must be the earliest.[24] Thus the proponents of this view use opposing arguments to prove the same point. They are inconsistently applying their assumptions to make the evidence fit their preconceived conclusions.[25]

The arguments for Marcan priority from literary characteristics and greater historical candor must also be rejected because they attribute to Mark an inferiority that the later writers supposedly had to correct. If the Gospels are viewed synthetically, the "historical candor" of Mark is no problem. Each writer emphasized a different aspect of the person of Christ. If Mark emphasized Christ's humanity it was *not* to the exclusion of His deity.

The presupposition of Marcan priority cannot be proven by a careful study of the three Gospels. Such a presupposition is based primarily on an evolutionary bias which believes the shortest and least extensive Gospel *must* be first with the other Gospels being later embellishments of that early account. This is a tenuous assumption.

THE REALITY OF SOURCES

Both the mutual dependence theory and the documentary hypothesis depend on the concept of sources (though in varying degrees). Each theory holds that the individual writers borrowed their material to some extent from an earlier source. Actually there is some validity to this basic concept. Unless one believes that the Gospels are a product of divine dictation to human scribes, he seems bound to accept the necessity of sources. For example, Matthew and Luke obtained their genealogical records from some source (e.g., perhaps temple records, oral tradition from Christ's family, etc.). In Luke's report that Mary "treasured up" all the events that surrounded Christ's birth and "pondered them in her heart" (Luke 2:19), this writer sees no problem in attributing these thoughts to Mary whom Luke might have interviewed and used as a "source" for his Gospel.

These examples could be multiplied, but most conservative scholars have no problem seeing the Gospel writers employing outside sources in gathering material about incidents they had not witnessed—all the while being guided by the Holy Spirit who was guaranteeing the accuracy of the completed documents. Luke himself acknowledges his familiarity with other written accounts of Christ's life and states that he has "carefully investigated everything from the beginning" (Luke 1:1–4).

The problem is that what conservative scholars mean by "sources" is *not* what the critical scholars mean. The word has different meanings to the two groups. Many critical scholars see the sources not as independent eyewitnesses or isolated records employed by the Gospel writers, but rather they view the sources as extensive writings which provided the majority of the material in the present Gospels. The writers of the Gospels were then no more than skilled editors who utilized and combined these available sources to produce their own accounts. Thus if any material is common to Matthew and Luke it must have been copied from Q. If any material is unique to Matthew alone it must first have existed in M. Connick shows how this concept of sources is used to explain the origin of Matthew's Gospel.

> Matthew's principal source was Mark. He reproduced about 90 percent of the earliest Gospel, making his own writing a second edition of Mark, revised and enlarged. . . . He abbreviated it, added to it, omitted from it, and corrected it to suit his purposes. In addition to Mark he used Q, M (material found only in Matthew), a list of Old Testament quotations, a genealogy of Jesus' ancestors, and a nativity narrative. From these diverse and sometimes discordant parts he fashioned an artistic and memorable whole.[26]

This writer rejects the critical view of sources for at least two reasons. First, no objective evidence for these sources can be found. No one has yet produced a copy of Q, M, or L. If these sources were so well known and highly respected that they were used by the original Gospel writers, one can well wonder why no trace of them can be found while other apocryphal gospels (which are far inferior) managed to survive. A theory that rests on such extensive invisible evidence should immediately be suspect.

Second, the critical view of sources fails to account for the present structure of the Gospels. It is one thing to speak of the percentage of Mark reproduced in Matthew; it is quite another to see *how* that material is "reproduced." The impression one gets is that vast sections of the Gospels are often reproduced word for word. However, a study of the texts reveals a far different picture.

Farmer has produced the *Synopticon* which is a color-coded text of the three Synoptic Gospels showing the extent of verbal relationship between them.[27] A detailed examination of even a single pericope shows that the writers would have had to perform literary gymnastics with their sources to produce their final product. Often the verbal agreement involves isolated words separated by other words unique to that one Gospel. If the Gospel writers were copying from each other, one would expect more consistency. Also much of the alleged "literary dependence" involves words that must appear due to the nature of the story. For example, it would be difficult for any writer to describe the baptism of Christ without using words such as "Jesus," "John the Baptist," "Jordan River," "baptize," "water," "Holy Spirit," "dove," and others.

The Gospel writers did employ sources, but not in the sense proposed by the critics. They did not resort to wholesale copying of some earlier (now lost) texts, nor did the later writers edit, adapt, or plagiarize the accounts of the earlier writers. Rather, they selectively gathered information from various sources (including eyewitness accounts) which they used to compose their records. God superintended the process to insure that the final product as it came from the authors' pens was without error.

THE NECESSITY OF LITERARY DEPENDENCE

This presupposition was dealt with in the preceding discussion. There is no need to posit literary dependence. The similarities between the records can be explained by seeing the accounts as accurate witnesses of actual events. Parallel accounts of the same occurrence are bound to be similar.

Davidson made an observation that is important to the discussion of literary dependence. He noted that "the verbal coincidences are more numerous in reciting the words of Jesus, and in the reports of words spoken by others in connection with his language, than in the narrative parts."[28] Davidson is saying that the greatest areas of verbal agreement occur in the discourses rather than in the narratives. Literary dependence cannot explain this phenomenon, but the Bible does offer an explanation. Just before Christ was arrested and crucified He gave His disciples a promise. "All this I have spoken while still with you. But the Counselor, the Holy Spirit, whom the Father will send in my name, will teach you all things *and will remind you of everything I have said to you*" (John 14:25–26). Christ was promising a supernatural work of the Holy Spirit which would enable the disciples to recall all of Christ's words. Thus one would expect close verbal agreement in the discourses since Christ promised this very thing. In contrast, the narratives have less verbal agreement since each Gospel writer tends to use his own words to describe events as they transpired. The similarities in accounts do not demand literary dependence. The unity in the discourses can reflect the supernatural working of the Holy Spirit to guarantee an accurate account of the words which were spoken. The similarities and differences in the narratives can be explained by understanding that each author described the same events in his own words.

THE UNIFORMITY OF ORAL TRADITION

This is another area that has some basis in fact. It Is well known that extensive memorization was common among the Jews of Christ's day.[29] To understand the extent of their memorization, one need only remember the vocalization of the unpointed Hebrew text which was accurately passed from generation to generation. If such care were taken to preserve accurately the sacred text given by God, how much more would the early Jewish Christians seek to preserve accurately the words and deeds of God Incarnate?

> The words of Jesus would be regarded as sacred and committed to memory because of their intrinsic worth and because of the regard in which the Christians held their Lord. This surpassed any rabbinical teacher-pupil relationship. They recognized His divine nature which invested His words with such authority that every effort would be made to retain as far as possible the very words in which He taught. This accounts for the fact that fewer deviations occur in parallel accounts of His sayings than in the narratives of His doings.[30]

The one objection to the idea of oral tradition is the presence of variations within the sayings of Christ. Sometimes the sayings *are* different, and sometimes the sayings are the same but the settings are different. One obvious answer is that Christ often repeated His message. He probably delivered the same message or used the same illustration or parable on numerous occasions. Guthrie notes, "The probability that He repeated His teaching material many times would in itself account for some of the differences in the Synoptic record."[31]

Conclusion

After viewing the above data it is this writer's opinion that there is no evidence to postulate a tradition of literary dependence among the Gospels. The dependence is rather a parallel dependence on the actual events which occurred. The Gospels are similar because they are all recording the same events. And yet they are different because each writer under the guiding hand of the Holy Spirit carefully chose the material which accorded best with the purpose of his book. Matthew based a good portion of his work on his eyewitness account as a disciple. Mark based his on the testimony of Peter, and Luke wrote after consulting several authorities which he met in his travels with Paul through Palestine and the rest of the Roman world.

One need not postulate an extensive scheme of literary dependence or hypothetical sources in order to account for the similarities and differences in the Gospels. There are other options that accord with the facts and that restore the authors to their rightful places as God's chosen servants who composed accurate accounts that are divinely inspired.

CHAPTER 2

A New Look at Asides in the Fourth Gospel

Tom Thatcher

In 1960, Merrill C. Tenney noted a general failure of Bible students to analyze the numerous asides in the Gospel of John. He said a thorough treatment was needed, as "some of [these notes] are quite important to [the book's] structure and interpretation." Rising to the occasion, Tenney produced "The Footnotes of John's Gospel" as a supplement to the "occasional notes in the major commentaries."[1] After defining "footnote," Tenney identified 59 footnotes in the Fourth Gospel and grouped them in 10 categories. He explained each category, noted difficult cases, and included a helpful summarizing chart.[2]

Almost 20 years later John O'Rourke observed that a number of recent English commentaries had acknowledged the significance of asides in the Gospel of John, including commentaries by Raymond E. Brown, Rudolf Bultmann, Barnabas Lindars, and Leon Morris. O'Rourke sought to clarify the subject by revising Tenney's work, which he said was "the most systematic study" available.[3] O'Rourke described Tenney's categories, then reshuffled Tenney's asides, while increasing the list to 109. The "theological discussions" category underwent the most notable expansion, from Tenney's three asides to O'Rourke's 27. O'Rourke also provided a tabular compilation of his findings and a chart tracking chapter frequency.[4]

After presenting his revised table, however, O'Rourke made the critical observation that "unfortunately, the different classifications [in Tenney's system] are not altogether mutually exclusive."[5] This is because Tenney's concept of a "footnote" or "aside" is vague. Tenney began his article by referring to a "great deal of explanatory material [in the Fourth Gospel] which is not directly involved in the progress of the narrative . . . but is parenthetical."[6] He then stated that "most of the footnotes in John

26

are more nearly 'glosses' or 'asides' which the writer introduced to make his story more lucid, or to explain the cause or motive for some act."[7] This sentence encompasses three distinct functions of the asides: to increase lucidity, to define cause, and to define the motives of individuals. Tenney added that John's "footnotes" are "sentences or paragraphs of explanatory comment interjected into the running narrative of the story."[8] Here he combined function ("explanatory") with formal features. Little wonder that Tenney prefaced his study with the warning, "not all of these are indisputably clear."[9]

The use of content to define some categories (5 of 10) leaves Tenney's analysis, and O'Rourke's revision, subjective and open to dispute. This is especially the case with "theological notes"— what makes narrative material "theological"? Tenney's "notes explanatory of *situations or actions*" apparently define events "in terms of cause or of consequence,"[10] including motives of characters. This category covers a broad range of content types, and some of his samples have competing functions. For example he said John 2:9 "distinguishes" the fact of the Cana miracle from the method; 6:23 is a clarification evidencing "a desire for historical accuracy"; 7:5 explains a person's actions; 20:30–31 states "the whole purpose of the Gospel."[11] Such broad, mixed categories are too indistinct to be helpful.

Tenney's observation that the asides of the Gospel of John have "a definite value for understanding the meaning of the Gospel"[12] warrants a reconsideration of this issue. Since Tenney's essay and O'Rourke's revision, narrative criticism has further specified the nature and value of asides. This chapter seeks to define and categorize the asides of the Fourth Gospel more precisely in light of such research.

An aside is a direct statement that *tells* the reader something. Asides are never observable events, but are interpretive commentary on observable events, commentary that reveals information "below the surface" of the action. This builds on Wayne Booth's acclaimed distinction between telling and showing. Readers may receive information by observing what the author shows them, or by listening to what the author tells them.[13] Asides are always what the author tells.

Because they are not events, asides do not advance the plot. Rather, the author uses them to guide the reader's interpretation of and response to events. Asides thus have a rhetorical function.

Different kinds of content may serve the same function, and similar contents may serve different functions in various contexts. For example in John 6:19 the narrator noted that Jesus came to the disciples on the Sea of Galilee when they had rowed 25 to 30 stadia; here the spatial note heightens the miraculous significance of Jesus' sudden appearance. But in 11:18, John indicated that Bethany is 15 stadia from Jerusalem to explain why so many Jews were present at Lazarus' wake. The same type of content, a measure of distance, has served different functions in these two contexts. On the other hand in John 2:17 the narrator "told" that the disciples later realized that Jesus' words fulfilled Psalm 69:9, indicating the significance of Jesus' remark about the temple. But in John 4:54 the significance of the healing of the official's son is stressed with a note that this was Jesus' "second sign." Here two distinct content types, a memory and a sign, serve a similar function. Because asides of all content types explain what is happening in the narrative, any attempt at categorization must give priority to function over content.

The asides in John's Gospel may be organized under four broad functions, with subcategories based on content (see the table, pp. 31–35). Some asides function to *stage* an event by defining the physical context in which it occurs. Other asides function to *define* or specify something. Still other asides *explain discourse,* telling why something was said (or was not said, e.g., 7:13, 30). Parallel to these are others that function to *explain actions,* noting why something happened (or did not happen).

Staging asides may include references to space (Sp), time (Ti), objects (O) available for use, or climate (C).[14] The Gospel of John is remarkable for qualitative notations of space, time, and climate. Qualitative markers situate events in symbolic contexts that define their significance. The spatial note in 18:5 emphasizes Judas' treachery by noting that he stood "with them," the mob, during Jesus' arrest. Of 22 time references, 12 situate Jesus' activity in reference to a Jewish festival, particularly the Passover (2:13, 23; 6:4; 11:55; 12:1; 13:1; 19:14). John 19:14 stages Pilate's condemnation of Jesus at the sixth hour of the Day of Preparation, the hour of sacrifice. Notations of climate specify light (day or night), season (e.g., winter), and temperature (cold or warmth). "Night" and "cold" are not good places to be in John's Gospel: Nicodemus went to Jesus at night, apparently symbolizing his inability to grasp the truth (3:2); Judas went from the Upper Room into the night to betray Jesus (13:30); just before denying Jesus, Peter sought the dim light and warmth of a charcoal fire in the "cold" courtyard (18:18). Thus in the Gospel of John a wide variety of content types may function to stage an action by situating it in a particular, often symbolic, context.

Defining asides include translations (Tr) from Aramaic to Greek or vice versa; preliminary character labels (PL), which introduce characters to the reader; and reminiscent character labels (RL), which reintroduce characters who have already appeared. Eight of the 10 translations indicate the Greek meaning of Hebrew (Aramaic) terms, but two move from Greek to Hebrew (19:13, 17). Character labels establish identity or personal qualities, pointing out the significance of an individual or explaining his or her behavior. Thus the man at Bethesda had been sick 38 years (5:5); the blind man of 9:1 was "blind from birth"; Nicodemus went to Jesus at night because he was a Pharisee and ruler of the Jews (3:1); Joseph of Arimathea had been a secret disciple because he feared the Jews (19:38). John's Gospel opens with a cluster of five labels (1:1–14) that precisely identify Jesus (and John the Baptist) before the story begins. Judas is never referred to in the Fourth Gospel without the epithet "betrayer" (6:71; 12:4; 13:2); so the reader is little surprised when Judas finally left the Upper Room to hand Jesus over. Preliminary labels introduce a character by some distinguishing feature; when that person appears later in the story, a reminiscent label is often used to remind the reader about that individual. After 3:1, Nicodemus is the one who "came to Jesus before" and "by night" (7:50; 19:39). Labels clue the reader that a character will be significant in a particular, sometimes symbolic, way; thus they function to "define" the character for the reader.

Asides that *explain discourse* may include the reason (R) for what a speaker said or its significance (Si). When characters did not speak openly about their belief in Jesus, it was often because they feared the Jews or the Pharisees (7:13; 9:22; 12:42), which means, to the narrator, that they "loved the approval of men rather than the approval of God" (12:43). Jesus' associates often made unperceptive statements about Him because they lacked proper understanding (10:6; 11:13; 13:22; 20:14; 20:15; 20:24). John 12:41 is particularly interesting, as the narrator wrote that Isaiah spoke of Israel's blindness because Isaiah "saw His [Jesus'] glory." Asides stating the significance of discourse appear for a variety of reasons. In 4:9 and 27, the woman's surprised remark and the disciples' silence indicate that Jesus' discourse with the Samaritan woman violated normal social convention. The majority of these asides, however, interpret Jesus' enigmatic statements. John, apparently concerned that the reader might misunderstand Jesus' words, explicitly decoded them (2:21–22; 7:39; 8:27; 12:33; 18:9; 19:28; 21:19, 23), thereby giving the reader a marked advantage over characters in the story. On one occasion even the speaker, Caiaphas, did not realize the true significance of his own words (11:51). Both categories of asides that explain discourse seek to limit the reader's interpretation of what characters in the narrative said.

Those *asides that explain actions* may again provide the reason (R) or motive for an act or indicate its significance (Si).[15] Tenney's "explanation of custom" falls under the reason category, as content about Jewish customs generally explains why individuals were doing something (11:55; 18:28; 19:40; 19:42). John was concerned that the reader understand the reasons and significance behind what Jesus did. Five reasons explain Jesus' actions, and 19 of the 24 explanations of events indicate the significance of His activity. Significance is frequently stated as signs or fulfillment of Scripture (2:11, 17; 4:54; 12:15; 12:38; 19:24, 36–37; 20:9). Four statements of significance cluster around the cross (19:23–37); three assure the reader that Scripture was fulfilled in Jesus' death; and the fourth (19:35) indicates the value of John's testimony as he claimed to be an eyewitness of these events. Most of the Gospel's "theological notes" are in fact given in asides that specify the significance of some event.

The following table shows that John included 191 "telling" asides, far more than Tenney and O'Rourke supposed. Divided into functional categories, 44 asides stage, 46 define, 48 explain discourse, and 53 explain actions or events. Without reverting to O'Rourke's chapter summary, it is notable that 61 asides (32 percent) occur in the last four chapters to influence the reader's perception of Jesus' death and resurrection.

Two controls have been imposed in the table to help increase objectivity. First, each aside is assigned only one function. Verses that receive two listings contain two distinct asides. For example the first aside in 7:39 explains the significance of Jesus' words by indicating that He spoke of the coming Spirit, while the second aside explains why the Spirit had not yet come. Second, "significance" is an admittedly difficult category. The table notes three asides in John 10:22–23: the time is the Feast of Dedication, the climate is winter, the space is Solomon's portico. All three may explain the significance of Jesus' words. In such cases the table indicates the most immediate narrative function, and does not comment on the possibility of a deeper, secondary function such as "explain significance." Specific interpretive conclusions of this sort were reserved for the discussion above.

Two asides, 11:33 and 11:38, both of which reveal Jesus' inner emotions, are absent from the table because their primary function is unclear. If added, the list would increase to 193. The present assignments may be subject to reinterpretation, but it is hoped that these functional categories will help direct further inquiry in the proper direction.

Asides in the Fourth Gospel

John		Stage				Define			Explain Discourse		Explain Actions	
	Sp	Ti	O	C	Tr	PL	RL	R	Si	R	Si
1:1						•					
1:4						•					
1:6						•					
1:7							•				
1:8						•		•			
1:14						•					
1:18											•
1:28	•										
1:38					•						
1:39										•	
1:40						•					
1:41					•						
1:42					•						
1:44						•					

Legend

Sp = Space	PL = Preliminary Character Labels
Ti = Time	RL = Reminiscent Character Labels
O = Objects	R = Reasons
C = Climate	Si = Significance
Tr = Translations	

John	Stage				Define			Explain Discourse		Explain Actions	
	Sp	Ti	O	C	Tr	PL	RL	R	Si	R	Si
2:6			•								
2:9									•		
2:11											•
2:13		•									
2:17											•
2:21									•		
2:22									•		
2:23		•									
2:25										•	
3:1						•					
3:2				•							
3:23										•	
3:24		•									
4:1, 3										•	
4:5	•										
4:6	•	•									
4:8								•			
4:9									•		
4:25					•						
4:27									•		
4:45										•	
4:46							•				
4:50										•	
4:53										•	
4:54											•
5:1–4	•	•									
5:5						•					
5:9		•									
5:16										•	
5:18										•	
6:1					•						
6:2										•	
6:4		•			•						
6:6								•			
6:8							•				
6:10	•										
6:15										•	
6:16				•							
6:19								•			•
6:59	•										

John	Stage				Define			Explain Discourse		Explain Actions	
	Sp	Ti	O	C	Tr	PL	RL	R	Si	R	Si
6:61								•			
6:64									•		
6:71					•						
7:1										•	
7:2		•									
7:5								•			
7:13								•			
7:14		•									
7:30										•	
7:37		•									
7:39									•	•	
7:50							•				
8:2		•									
8:6								•			
8:20	•									•	
8:27									•		
9:1						•					
9:7					•						
9:14		•									
9:18								•			
9:22								•			
10:6								•			
10:22		•									
10:23	•			•							
11:1						•					
11:2						•					
11:5										•	
11:13								•			
11:16						•					
11:18	•										
11:30	•										
11:31										•	
11:39							•				
11:49						•					
11:51									•		
11:52											•
11:55		•								•	
11:56	•										

John	Stage				Define			Explain Discourse		Explain Actions	
	Sp	Ti	O	C	Tr	PL	RL	R	Si	R	Si
12:1		•					•				
12:4							•				
12:6								•			
12:9							•			•	
12:15											•
12:16											•
12:18										•	
12:21							•				
12:33									•		
12:38											•
12:39										•	
12:41								•			
12:42								•			
12:43								•			
13:1		•									•
13:2						•					•
13:3											•
13:11								•			
13:21								•			
13:22								•			
13:27											•
13:29									•		
13:30				•							
14:22						•					
16:19								•			
18:2								•		•	
18:4											•
18:5	•						•				
18:9									•		
18:10			•			•					
18:13						•					
18:14								•			
18:15										•	
18:18				•							
18:26						•					
18:28		•								•	
18:32									•		
18:40									•		
19:8								•			

John	Sp	Stage			Define			Explain Discourse		Explain Actions	
		Ti	O	C	Tr	PL	RL	R	Si	R	Si
19:13					•						
19:14		•									
19:17					•						
19:20										•	
19:23								•			
19:24											•
19:28									•		
19:29			•								
19:31								•			
19:35											•
19:36											•
19:37											•
19:38						•					
19:39							•				
19:40										•	
19:41	•										
19:42										•	
20:1		•									
20:8											•
20:9											•
20:14								•			
20:15								•			
20:16					•						
20:19		•								•	
20:24							•	•			
20:26		•									•
20:31								•			
21:2							•				
21:4		•							•		
21:7										•	
21:8	•										
21:12								•			
21:14											•
21:17								•			
21:19									•		
21:20							•				
21:23									•		
21:24											•
21:25											•

CHAPTER 3

The Significance of Pentecost

Charles C. Ryrie

B y anyone's standards Pentecost, as recorded in Acts 2, was a significant day. It is the purpose of this chapter to discuss the significant aspects of the events of that day in relation to certain major areas of theology.

Significance in Relation to Typology

Typology has suffered at the hands of both its friends and its enemies, since for many the study of types is still an uncertain science. Some, it is true, have found types in almost everything in the Scriptures, while others in their reaction against this give little or no place for typological studies. My own definition of a type is that it is a divinely purposed illustration which prefigures its corresponding reality. This definition not only covers types expressly so designated by the New Testament (e.g., 1 Cor. 10) but also allows for types not so designated (e.g., Joseph as a type of Christ). Yet in the definition the phrase "divinely purposed" should guard against an allegorical or pseudospiritual interpretation of types which sees chiefly the resemblances between Old Testament events and New Testament truths to the neglect of the historical, geographical, and local aspects of those events. While all things are in a sense divinely purposed, not all details in all stories were divinely purposed illustrations of subsequently revealed truth. Pentecost is a good example of this, for although there is a clear type-antitype relationship, not all the details of the Old Testament feast find a corresponding reality in the events recorded in Acts 2.

As the antitype of one of the annual feasts of the Jews Pentecost has significance. This feast (Lev. 23:15–21) was characterized by an offering of two loaves marking the close of harvest. The corresponding reality of this ceremony was the joining on the day of Pentecost by the Holy Spirit of Jews and Gentiles as one loaf in the one body of Christ (1 Cor. 12:12). Pentecost is sometimes called the feast of weeks because it fell seven (a week of) weeks after the Feast of Firstfruits. No date could be set for the observance of Firstfruits, for the depending on the ripening of the grain for harvest. However, when the time did arrive a small amount of grain was gathered, threshed, ground into flour, and presented to the Lord as a token of the harvest yet to be gathered. The corresponding reality is, of course, "Christ the firstfruits" (1 Cor. 15:23). The 50–day interval between the two feasts was divinely purposed in the Old Testament type and finds exact correspondence in the New Testament antitype.

SIGNIFICANCE IN RELATION TO THEOLOGY

The theological significance of the day of Pentecost pertains chiefly to the doctrine of the Holy Spirit. The third Person of the Trinity, not Peter, played the leading role in the drama of that day. The Holy Spirit is the power of Pentecost, and in a very special sense the era which followed is His age. Obviously the Spirit of God has always been present in this world, but He has not always been a resident as one who permanently indwells the church. This was a new relationship which did not exist even during the days of Jesus' earthly ministry, for He said to His disciples concerning the Spirit, "He abides with you, and will be in you" (John 14:17).

THE EVIDENCES OF HIS COMING (ACTS 2:1–4)

Wind. A sound as of a rushing mighty wind was the first evidence of the Spirit's coming. It came suddenly so that it could not be attributed to any natural cause, and it came from heaven, which probably refers both to the impression given of its origin and also to its actual supernatural origin. It was not actually wind but rather a roar or reverberation, for verse 2 should be literally translated "an echoing sound as of a mighty wind borne violently." It filled all the house, which means that all 120 people there would have experienced the sensation since so many people would of necessity have been scattered throughout the house. This was a fitting evidence of the Spirit's coming, for the Lord had used this very symbol when He spoke of the things of the Spirit to Nicodemus (John 3:8).

Fire. The audible sign, wind, was followed by a visible one, fire. Actually the tongues that looked like fire divided themselves over the company, a tongue settling on the head of each one. This too was an appropriate sign for the presence of the Holy Spirit, for fire had long been to the Jews a symbol of divine presence (Ex.

3:2; Deut. 5:4). The form of the Greek makes one doubt the presence of material fire, though the appearance of the tongues was as if they had been composed of fire.

Languages. Each person present began to speak in a real language which was new to the speaker but which was understood by those from the various lands who were familiar with them. This was the third piece of evidence, and although some have assumed that this miracle was wrought on the ears of the hearers, this certainly forces the plain and natural sense of the narrative. These tongues were evidently actual languages (Acts 2:6–8) which were spoken, and the imperfect tense, "was giving" (v. 4), indicates that they were spoken in turn, one after another.

THE EFFECTS OF HIS COMING (ACTS 2:5–13)

Baptism. The most important effect of the Spirit's coming at Pentecost was the placing of men and women into the body of Christ by His baptism. The Lord spoke of this baptizing work of the Holy Spirit just before His ascension (Acts 1:5), and it is clear from His words that this was a ministry of the Spirit thus far unknown even to those to whom He had said, "Receive the Holy Spirit" (John 20:22). If the baptism of the Holy Spirit was not something new until the day of Pentecost, then the Lord's words in Acts 1:5—and especially the future tense of the verb "you shall be baptized"—mean nothing. Although Acts 2 does not specifically record that the baptism of the Spirit occurred on the day of Pentecost, Acts 11:15–16 states that this happened then, and that what happened at Pentecost was the fulfillment of the promise of Acts 1:5. However, Paul explained what this baptism (not to be confused with what is meant in Acts 2:38) accomplishes when he wrote, "For by one Spirit we were all baptized into one body, whether Jews or Greeks, whether slaves or free, and we were all made to drink of one Spirit" (1 Cor. 12:13). In other words, on the day of Pentecost believers were first placed into the body of Christ and that by the baptism of the Holy Spirit. Since the church is the body of Christ (Col. 1:18), the church *could not* have begun until Pentecost. Furthermore, since no reference to the baptism of the Spirit is found in the Old Testament, since all references in the Gospels are prophetic, and since the prophecies of the future kingdom include no reference to the Spirit's baptism, one may conclude that this work of His is peculiar to this dispensation and peculiar to the church (which, it follows, must also be limited to this dispensation) in forming it and uniting the members to the body of Christ forever.

Bewilderment. Certain visible effects of the Spirit's coming were evident in the crowd that gathered as a result of the phenomena connected with His coming. At first the people (including Eastern or Babylonian Jews, Syrian Jews, Egyptian Jews, Roman Jews, Cretes, and Arabians) were amazed (Acts 2:7). Literally the text says they stood out of themselves (ἐξίστημι) and were astonished (θαυμάζω). This is a mental reaction showing that their minds were arrested by what they observed. Next they were perplexed (v. 12). This verb διαπορέω means "to be wholly and utterly at a loss." This was mental defeat. "The amazement meant that they did not know. The perplexity meant that they knew they did not know."[1] Not knowing is always a blow to man's pride; consequently this crowd, driven to find an answer to what they had seen and heard, replaced their ignorance with criticism (v. 13). These are merely normal reactions of satanically blinded minds to which the things of God are foolishness (2 Cor. 4:4; 1 Cor. 2:14).

Significance in Relation to Homiletics

THE SERMON (ACTS 1:14–36)

Introduction: Explanation. Peter, spokesman for the Eleven, seized the opportunity for a witness by answering the charge of drunkenness that had been leveled at the apostles. He thus wisely introduced his sermon by using the local situation, and taking what was uppermost in his hearers' thoughts He formulated his introduction as an explanation of what they had just seen and heard (v. 15). He did not introduce his message with a story or a joke. Peter's mind was full of Scripture, not stories; Peter's concern was for the people, not pleasantries. The disciples could not be drunk, he told them, for it was only nine o'clock in the morning. Pentecost was a feast day, and the Jews who were engaged in the services of the synagogues of Jerusalem would have abstained from eating and drinking until at least 10 o'clock and more likely noon.

From this categorical denial of the charge of drunkenness Peter passed easily and naturally to the explanation of what the phenomenon was. It was not wine but the Holy Spirit who was causing these things, and to prove this Peter quoted Joel 2:28–32. This Old Testament passage presents a definite prophecy of the Holy Spirit's being poured out when Israel will again be established in her own land. The problem here is not one of interpretation but of usage only. Clearly Joel's prophecy was not fulfilled at Pentecost, for (a) Peter did not use the usual scriptural formula for fulfilled prophecy as he did in Acts 1:16 (cf. Matt. 1:22; 2:17; 4:14); (b) the prophecy of Joel will clearly not be fulfilled until Israel is restored to her land, converted, and enjoying the presence of the Lord in her midst (Joel 2:26–28); and (c) the events prophesied by Joel simply did not come to pass. If language means anything Pentecost did not fulfill this prophecy nor did Peter say it did. Peter's quotation of this passage in Joel need not raise theological questions at all, for the matter is primarily homiletical and any problems should be solved in that light. Peter's point was that the Holy Spirit and not wine was responsible for what these Jews had seen. He quoted Joel to point out that as Jews who knew the Old Testament Scriptures they should have recognized this as the Spirit's work. In other words, their own Scriptures should have reminded them that the Spirit was able to do what they had just seen. Why then, someone may ask, did Peter include the words from Joel recorded in Acts 2:19–20? Why did he not stop with verse 18? The answer is simple. Peter not only wanted to show his audience that they should have known from the Scriptures that the Spirit could do what they had seen, but he also wanted to invite them to accept Jesus as their Messiah by using Joel's invitation, "whosoever shall call on the name of the Lord shall be saved" (v. 21). Thus what is recorded in Acts 2:19–20 is simply a connecting link between the two key points in his argument. "The remainder of the quotation from Joel, verses 19, 20, has no bearing on Peter's argument, but was probably made in order to complete the connection of that which his argument demanded."[2]

Theme: Jesus is the Messiah. It does not mean much to modern-day audiences today to say that Jesus is Christ or the Messiah. However, to Jews of that day this was an assertion that required convincing proof, and it was the theme of Peter's sermon. Peter's proof was built along very simple lines. First, he painted a picture of the Messiah from the Old Testament Scriptures. Second, from contemporary facts he presented a picture of Jesus of Nazareth. Third, he superimposed these two pictures on each other to prove conclusively that Jesus is Messiah. The focus of each picture is the resurrection. In verses 22–24 Peter proclaimed the resurrection of Jesus of Nazareth. Then there follows (vv. 25–31) the prediction of resurrection from Psalm 16:8–11 which Peter applied to the Messiah. Then Peter identified the Messiah as Jesus whom they crucified and of whose resurrection they were witnesses. Significantly the truth of Jesus' resurrection was not challenged but was well attested by the conviction of these thousands of people who were in the very city where it had occurred less than two months before.

Conclusion: Application. Peter now challenged his hearers to decide about Jesus, and yet there was really no choice, so conclusive had been his argument. How gracious of God to appeal once again to the very people who had crucified His Son. The application was personal. Peter did not say "someone" but "you."

THE RESULTS (ACTS 2:37–41)

Conviction. Peter's sermon brought conviction of heart. The word κατανύσσαμαι, translated "pierced," is a rare verb (occurring only here in the New Testament), which means "to pierce, stun, or smite." Outside the Scriptures it is used of horses dinting the earth with their hoofs. In like manner the hearts of his hearers were smitten by Peter's message as the Spirit of God applied it.

Conversion. To the group of 120 (which included men and women, Acts 1:14) were added three thousand souls (Acts 2:41). They repented or changed their minds, for that is the meaning of repentance. It is not merely the emotion of sorrow, for one can be sorry for sin without being repentant. Neither is repentance mere mental assent to certain facts, for genuine repentance involves the heart as well.[3] For the Jews gathered at Pentecost it involved a change of relationship toward Him whom they had considered as merely the carpenter's son of Nazareth and an impostor by receiving Jesus as Lord and Messiah.

The Spirit of God must always do the work of enlightening and converting, but people are still His method of heralding the message. Peter's sermon was doctrinally sound, homiletically excellent, filled with and explanatory of the Word of God, and directed specifically toward those to whom he spoke.

Significance in Relation to Practical Theology

In practical theology two things command attention from among the many events of Pentecost and the days that immediately followed.

THE ORDINANCE OF BAPTISM

To the question "What shall we do?" Peter replied, "Repent and be baptized." That this refers to the new converts' being baptized by the Spirit is untenable for several reasons. (1) It is doubtful that Peter or his hearers understood yet the truth concerning the baptism of the Spirit even though it did first occur at Pentecost. (2) If this were referring to that automatic ministry of the Spirit, then there would be no need for the report in verse 41, "So then, those who had received his word was baptized." (3) What would this audience have understood by Peter's answer? His words meant that they were to submit to a rite performed with water, which would be a sign of their identification with this new group. They would have thought immediately of Jewish proselyte baptism which signified entrance of the proselyte into Judaism.[4] They would have thought of John's baptism, submission to which meant identification with John's message in a very definite way; for John was the first person to baptize other people (all proselyte baptisms were self-imposed), which was a striking way to ask people to identify themselves with all he stood for. They would have realized that they were being asked to identify and associate themselves with this new group who believed Jesus is the Messiah, and Christian baptism at the hands of these disciples signified this association as nothing else could.[5] Even today for a Jew it is not his profession of Christianity nor his attendance at Christian services nor his belief in the New Testament but his partaking of water baptism that definitely and finally excludes him from Judaism and sets him off as a Christian. And there is no reason why it should not be the same line of demarcation for all converts to Christianity, signifying the separation from the old life and association with the new.[6]

THE ORGANIZATION OF BELIEVERS

Its commencement. As already noted, the church as an organism, the body of Christ, began on the day of Pentecost, but the church as an organization also began that day as the Lord added three thousand souls.

Its continuance. The power of the early church, humanly speaking, was due largely to the facts recorded in Acts 2:42. There was no rapid falling away from the newly embraced faith. Just the opposite was true, for membership in the early church involved persevering adherence. They continued in the apostles' doctrine. Teaching had always had a prominent place among the Jews, and it is not strange to find the Christian group appearing as a school. The apostles were the first teachers, and the bulk of their teaching is in the Gospels. It consisted of the facts of the Lord's life as well as His doctrine and teaching. The church today could well afford to emulate the early church in this. Instead of capitalizing on new converts and exploiting them, churches should teach them even if that means keeping them in the background for awhile.

Furthermore the new believers continued steadfastly in fellowship, and this is evidently to be understood in the broadest sense of the word, for the Greek says "the fellowship." This means partnership with God, partnership with others in the common salvation and in the sharing of material goods. They also continued in the "breaking of bread," which refers to the Lord's Supper though not isolated but as the climax of the love feast. At first this was evidently observed daily (v. 46) though afterward it seemed to form the great act of worship on the Lord's Day (20:7). The early church remembered her Lord with great frequency and with great freedom, for it was observed in homes without distinction between ordained clergy and laity (no service of ordination having yet occurred in the church).

Also they continued in "prayers." Again the definite article is used with this word and probably indicates definite times for prayer. This word is used exclusively for prayer to God and indicates the offering up of the wishes and desires to God in a devotional frame of mind.[7]

Its characterization. The early organization was characterized by fear (v. 43), favor (v. 47), and fellowship (vv. 44–46). Fear kept coming on this new group as signs and wonders were being done through the apostles (both verbs are in the imperfect tense). This fear was not alarm or dread of injury but a prevailing sense of awe in the manifest presence of the power of God. Favor was also their portion with the people at this time although times changed very quickly. Also fellowship in spiritual things demonstrated itself in fellowship of goods and worship. No doubt many of the pilgrims to the feast of Pentecost lingered in Jerusalem after their conversion to learn more of their new faith, and this created a pressing economic need. Providing for them through the sale and distribution of goods was God's way of meeting this emergency. The necessity for this was probably short-lived though the saints in Jerusalem remained a poor group.

This is the significance of Pentecost—the type fulfilled, the Holy Spirit baptizing individuals for the first time into the body of Christ, the sermon built on the fact of Jesus' resurrection and bringing conviction and conversion, and the young church marked off and established in the Word and ways of the Lord.

CHAPTER 4

Church Growth in the Book of Acts

Allison A. Trites

F rank Stagg has described the Book of Acts as "the story of an unhindered gospel."[1] He takes his cue from the unusual adverb ἀκωλύτως ("unhindered," Acts 28:31) with which the book ends. He sees the whole book focusing on the remarkable growth of the church under the guidance of the Lord and in the power of the Holy Spirit. While many scholars would posit other themes as the author's main concern, Luke certainly punctuated his account with many summary statements about church expansion (2:43–47; 5:14; 6:7; 9:31; 12:24; 16:5; 19:20). There is no better place to examine the factors that made the early church grow than the Acts of the Apostles.

This brief study of church growth in Acts discusses the fact of church growth, the kinds of church growth, and the characteristics of church growth.

The Fact of Church Growth

Beyond question church growth was a remarkable feature of first-century Christianity. In this connection it is profitable to note that the Greek verb "grow" (αὐξάνω) occurs several times in the Book of Acts. In only three places does the Bible state that "the word of God grew" or "the word of the Lord grew," and all of them are in Acts. In the first passage the Word of God spread in spite of internal problems (Acts 6:7). When the issues that divided the Christian community were squarely faced and constructive action taken, church growth resulted. The choosing of the seven leaders to meet the needs of the Greek-speaking Jews was important in settling a contentious matter within the life of the church. Then the growth of the fellowship of believers could continue unimpeded.

The second passage is set against the background of idolatry. Herod Agrippa made an impressive speech to the people of Tyre and Sidon, to which they responded, This is "the voice of a god and not of a man" (12:22). He was immediately struck down and died, "but the Word of the Lord continued to grow and to be multiplied" (12:24). Evidently the cult of personality and the impact of idolatry were not sufficient to overcome the gospel's advance.

The third passage is equally striking. Paul and his fellow workers met hard-nosed opposition in Ephesus. When they had confounded the Jewish exorcists there, the Jews and Greeks living in Ephesus were all seized with fear "and the name of the Lord Jesus was being magnified" (19:17). The upshot of this encounter was that many repented of their sins, confessing their deeds, and "the Word of the Lord was growing mightily and prevailing" (19:20).

In these three instances church growth was the result. The gospel is clearly presented in Acts as "the power of God for salvation to everyone who believes" (Rom. 1:16). It is able to overcome linguistic differences between Christians, it can conquer idolatry, and it can successfully face opposition. Luke most emphatically stressed the fact of church growth in his account of the development of the early church.

The Kinds of Church Growth

Luke highlighted at least three kinds of church growth—numerical, geographical, and spiritual.

NUMERICAL GROWTH

Luke wrote of the small numbers at the beginning of the church era. He named the eleven remaining apostles and described the believers in the first prayer meeting as numbering 120 (Acts 1:13–15). After the mighty movement of the Spirit on the day of Pentecost, those who accepted the message and were baptized numbered about three thousand (2:41). As Christians were "devoting themselves to the apostles' teaching and to fellowship, to the breaking of bread and to prayer" (2:42), they experienced real blessing and happiness. Often the gospel spread through entire families, villages, and towns (e.g., 16:11–34), a process described by church-growth authorities today as "homogeneous grouping." In this way the Christian message reached people who shared a common background, culture, or geography.

The striking church growth in the Book of Acts is not easily dismissed as an initial "flash in the pan." After Peter and John had been arrested in Jerusalem for preaching the good news of Christ, "many of those who had heard the message believed; and the number of the men came to be about five thousand" (4:4). Other indications of growth are mentioned: "more believers in the Lord, multitudes of men and women, were constantly added to their number" (5:14); "the disciples were increasing in number" (6:1); "the church throughout Judea and Galilee and Samaria . . . continued to increase" (9:31). A remarkable testimony to this growth is given by James and the other leaders of the Jerusalem church, who informed Paul "how many thousands [of] Jews . . . have believed" (21:20), not to mention the host of Gentile converts. Acts strongly underscores the fact of numerical growth. While Luke did not worship numbers, he certainly did not ignore them! Like the modern church-growth movement, he used statistical analysis "to discern the response to the gospel in a given situation."[2]

This numerical growth is all the more remarkable when contrasted with the modern-day church situation. Churches today grow usually by *biological* growth (when the children within a local church family make a personal profession of faith) or by *transfer* growth (when a newcomer transfers his or her membership from another local church). In Acts, however, the growth was *conversion* growth, for the church was just beginning its work in the world and therefore could not rely on the other forms of growth at all.

GEOGRAPHICAL GROWTH

The second kind of church growth in the Book of Acts is geographical. The gospel spread not only from one individual to another, but also from place to place. This development is clearly observable in Acts, which records in broad terms the spread of the Christian message from Jerusalem to Rome as suggested by several of its key texts (Acts 1:8; 9:15). It was not restricted to Jerusalem; it spread to Lydda, Sharon, and Joppa (9:35, 42). The message of salvation moved out from its Jewish matrix into Samaria (8:5, 12), then farther afield into Phoenicia, Cyprus, and Antioch (11:19–26). The gospel, in other words, is for everyone. As Peter declared to the household of Cornelius, "I most certainly understand now that God is not one to show partiality, but in every nation the man who fears Him and does what is right, is welcome to Him" (10:34–35). This means that the geographical expansion of the Christian message was undergirded by the strong conviction that the gospel is for every person. Jesus Christ is relevant to the religious needs of the whole world, and therefore the whole world must be given an opportunity to hear the good news of "peace through Jesus Christ" (10:36). In the Book of Acts the geographical spread of the gospel was God's plan.[3] The missionary extension of the faith is no optional extra; it is in harmony with the gracious purpose of a loving God who does not want "any to perish but for all to come to repentance" (2 Peter 3:9).

SPIRITUAL GROWTH

The early church's growth was not simply quantitative; it was also qualitative. There was not just an increase in numbers and in geographical outreach; there was also a definite deepening of spiritual life in the developing Christian communities throughout the Mediterranean basin and the Roman Empire. Wherever the gospel was preached, there was an increase in godly living.

Luke's use of the "fear" motif, for example, highlights the reverent awe the Christian faith stimulated both in those who received it and in those influenced by it (φόβος is used in Acts 2:43; 5:5, 11; 9:31; 19:17; cf. Luke 5:26; 7:16, where fear is also used positively). A striking instance of this godly fear is apparent in Luke's summary of church activity in Judea, Galilee, and Samaria, given in Acts 9:31, which speaks not only of the church's numerical growth but also of its spiritual encouragement by the Holy Spirit and its dynamic lifestyle "in the fear of the Lord."

The Book of Acts faithfully records the spiritual growth of the early church. Acts 2:42–47 is a beautiful cameo of the inner life of the church. The spiritual growth of the fellowship is reflected in the boldness of the believers' prayer in a time of crisis (4:23–31). Also the voluntary, generous way in which Christians willingly shared their possessions showed the depth of the change Christ was effecting in their lives (4:32–37). The saintly way Stephen died (7:59), the faithful manner in which Philip preached (8:4–40), and the courage of the early Christians in facing persecution (5:27–33, 40–42; 16:19–25) all bear witness to their growth in grace. Indeed the leaders of the church gave attention to this nurturing process, "strengthening . . . the disciples, encouraging them to continue in the faith, and saying, 'Through many tribulations we must enter the kingdom of God'" (14:22; cf. 15:32, 35, 41; 18:23).

Teaching thus played a decisive part in church growth. New converts must be discipled and trained not only to bear witness to their Lord, but also to face the possibility of persecution (διωγμός:

8:1; 13:50; θλίψις: 11:19; 14:22; 20:23; cf. 2 Tim. 3:12). Hence teaching with a view to discipleship became an essential feature of the church's ministry. This priority is evident in the decision to appoint seven leaders in the Jerusalem church to assume administrative and welfare responsibilities so that the apostles could devote themselves to "prayer and to the ministry of the Word" (6:4).

The Jewish authorities were anxious to stop the Christian faith from "spreading" any further (διανέμω, 4:17). Despite the authorities' repeated warnings against teaching in the name of Jesus (4:18; 5:28), the apostles continued to do so, accepting the suffering that inevitably followed (5:40).

Teaching is an important aspect of Christian leadership (cf. 1 Tim. 3:2, "able to teach"). The apostles persisted in it with enthusiasm and faithfulness: "And every day, in the temple and from house to house, they kept right on teaching and preaching Jesus as the Christ" (Acts 5:42). The same concern for teaching and discipleship is evident in the ministry of Paul and Barnabas at Antioch (11:26; 15:35; cf. 13:1) and in Paul's lengthy teaching stints in Corinth (18:11) and Ephesus (19:8–10; 20:31). Philip and Apollos are also cited as effective teachers (8:26–39; 18:27–28). The strengthening of the churches was important to Luke,[4] and absolutely indispensable to genuine long-term church growth.

Luke presented a balanced picture of church growth that included numerical, geographical, and spiritual growth. To Luke, the Christian faith was truly an evangelistic faith, in which believers are to reach out to others and draw them to Jesus Christ. The Christian faith is also a missionary faith, attempting to cross national and cultural barriers to bring the gospel to every individual. And certainly the Christian faith is concerned with the edification and spiritual development of God's people. Luke's symmetrical picture of the early church gives careful attention to each of these factors.[5]

The Characteristics of Growth

What were the features of the early church that help explain its remarkable growth? Seven characteristics may be noted.

A WITNESSING CHURCH

The first Christians shared their faith with others.[6] Just before Christ left His apostles, He challenged them to be His witnesses

(Acts 1:8). They were equipped by the Holy Spirit for this task and began to speak boldly for Christ (4:13, 29–31). Unlike many modern believers, they did not think they could delegate the task of witness-bearing to professionals. While the apostles continued to testify "to the resurrection of the Lord Jesus" (4:33), so did Stephen, Philip, Apollos, Aquila, and Priscilla. These leaders were helped and encouraged by lay people, who shared in the task of reaching out for Christ.

The impressive story of Christian growth in Acts shows repeatedly the role of the rank and file in the church. Ordinary men and women planted churches in such places as Damascus, Phoenicia, Cyprus, Antioch, and Rome (9:10; 11:19; 28:13–14). They did not wait for an important person or a mission board to initiate a new work. After great persecution arose against the church in Jerusalem, "those who had been scattered went about preaching the word" (8:4). The early Christians had a compulsive desire to bear witness to Christ. "We are witnesses of these things," declared the apostles, "and so is the Holy Spirit, whom God has given to those who obey Him" (5:32; cf. v. 42). While the apostles had a unique role as the original eyewitnesses of Christ (1:21–22), every believer without exception was expected to share his or her faith in Christ with others. These ordinary church members were active partners in the Christian mission. They included John Mark's mother (12:12), Lydia the businesswoman from Thyatira (16:14), the Greeks Gaius and Aristarchus (19:29), and other traveling companions of Paul (20:4).

A PRAYING CHURCH

Prayer was a regular, characteristic feature of these growing Christian communities (Acts 2:42; cf. 3:1).[7] The church had issued from a prayer meeting in an upper room in Jerusalem, when 120 faithful people looked to God for the promised outpouring of the Holy Spirit (1:12–15; cf. 2:1–4). Prayer was certainly important to the leaders of the church, who pledged to give their attention "to prayer, and to the ministry of the Word" (6:4). And the church faced its crises with frank, earnest prayer (1:24; 4:24–31; 12:5). A striking example of the power of prayer occurred in the experience of Paul and Silas at Philippi. Imprisoned, stripped, and beaten, the two men at midnight were overheard "praying and singing hymns of praise to God" (16:25). As a result the Philippian jailer was converted and the first church in Europe was eventually established.

In Luke's eyes the evangelistic task of the church was undergirded by the believing prayers of God's people.

A UNITED CHURCH

A wonderful bond of unity was evident in the early church. Believers experienced in full measure the benediction described in Psalm 133:1, "How good and how pleasant it is for brothers to dwell together in unity!" Luke used a rather remarkable adverb to describe this unity (ὁμοθυμαδόν, "with one mind, by common consent, together"). He noted that the believers were united in worship (Acts 2:46; 5:12), in prayer (4:24), and in decision-making (15:25). They "continued steadfastly" in their Christian discipleship as a community (Acts 2:42, KJV; cf. 1:14). Luke stressed the fact that the believers came together frequently, both in his summaries of church life (2:42–47; 4:32–37; 5:12–16) and in his fondness for the quasi-technical phrase ἐπὶ τὸ αὐτό (1:15; 2:1, 44; cf. Luke 17:35), which Metzger suggests refers to being "in church fellowship."[8] They lived in close fellowship with each other and spent quality time "together" (ὁμοῦ, Acts 2:1).

A SPIRIT-FILLED CHURCH

The work of the Holy Spirit has already been mentioned, but its importance to church growth calls for special attention. Jesus had promised His disciples that the Spirit of God would empower them for their task as witnesses. "You shall receive power when the Holy Spirit has come upon you; and you shall be My witnesses both in Jerusalem, and in all Judea and Samaria, and even to the remotest part of the earth" (Acts 1:8). Everything that marked the early church's effectiveness in witness was due to the inflow of the Spirit into their lives. The Spirit made Peter and John so bold in the face of their opponents that "they were marveling, and began to recognize them as having been with Jesus" (4:13). This same boldness (παρρησία) was also characteristic of the other leaders, who spoke for Christ quite openly and frankly (e.g., Stephen, Philip, Apollos). God was clearly working in their lives by His mighty Spirit.

The Holy Spirit was at work in guiding the church in response to the faithful prayers of God's people. On one occasion they sensed the Spirit's guidance so keenly that the Jerusalem Council could dispatch its letter to Gentile believers with the preamble, "It seemed good to the Holy Spirit and to us" (15:28). On another unforgettable occasion after believers had prayed, "the place where they had gathered was shaken, and they were all filled with the Holy Spirit, and began to speak the Word of God with boldness" (4:31). In choosing leaders for the missionary task during a time of worship and prayer, the church was plainly aware of the Holy Spirit's directive: "Set apart for Me Barnabas and Saul for the work to which I have called them" (13:2). Also an individual Christian worker like Philip was conscious of the Spirit's direct guidance: "Go up and join this chariot" (8:29; cf. Ananias in 9:15). And Paul's ministry from the very start of his Christian life was that of a person "filled with the Holy Spirit" (9:17).[9] Clearly in Luke's thinking there was no genuine church growth without the guidance and power of the Holy Spirit.

A CHRIST-CENTERED CHURCH

One of the most obvious features of the early church was its focus on the Person and work of Christ. The Christian community had taken its origin from Jesus of Nazareth. It proclaimed that "God anointed Him with the Holy Spirit and with power, and how He went about doing good and healing all who were oppressed by the devil; for God was with Him" (10:38). But that was not all, for the early church bore witness to the unique place of Jesus Christ as the one and only Savior of a lost world: "Salvation," Peter declared, is found "in no one else; for there is no other name under heaven that has been given among men, by which we must be saved" (4:12).

The living Christ was the heart and soul of the life of the church, and the church grew as the Lord Jesus was lifted up. Through Jesus a new way of access had been opened for people to enjoy fellowship with the living God. When God raised up Jesus, His Servant and Son, God the Father sent the Son "to bless you by turning every one of you from your wicked ways" (3:26). At the very center of this early community was an emphasis not only on repentance toward God but also on faith in the Lord Jesus Christ (2:38; cf. Luke 24:47; Acts 16:31).

The Christocentric character of church life is indicated in the speeches of the early Christian leaders (e.g., Peter, 2:22–24; 3:6, 16; 10:36–38; Philip, 8:5, 35; Stephen, 7:56, 59). This is also strongly suggested by the warm, loving, unselfish lifestyle of the early Christian community (2:42–47).

A SACRIFICIAL CHURCH

The growth of the Christian church was not cheap. It was not based on gimmicks or tricks (cf. Acts 8:9–24). Faithfulness to the gospel often brought the apostles persecution (4:3; 5:18; 12:1–4). Other leaders of the church faced the same hostility (e.g., Stephen, 7:54–60). Luke was perfectly aware that persecution served to purify the church and must be handled with patience and perseverance. In describing the signs of the end of the age Jesus Himself had predicted as much: "They will lay their hands on you and will persecute you, delivering you to the synagogues and prisons, bringing you before kings and governors for My name's sake. . . .You will be delivered up even by parents and brothers and relatives and friends, and they will put some of you to death, and you will be hated by all on account of My name" (Luke 21:12, 16–17). Certainly Christ had taught His followers to expect hard times and opposition, and the Book of Acts is full of such encounters with hostile forces. Stephen and James were martyred, the apostles frequently arrested, and the early disciples scattered after persecution broke out against the church in Jerusalem. Christianity was not simply a comfortable pew in those days! Some of its leaders, namely, Barnabas and Paul, "risked their lives for the name of our Lord Jesus Christ" (15:26). This sacrificial spirit has been copied from time to time throughout the history of the church, but never has the primitive church been surpassed.

A CARING CHURCH

Also the early church grew because it was a caring church. This loving attitude of concern shines through the Book of Acts. It shows itself in the wonderful way Christians shared their possessions with each other: "Those who believed were of one heart and soul; and not one of them claimed that anything belonging to him was his own; but all things were common property to them. . . . For there was not a needy person among them, for all who were owners of lands or houses would sell them and bring the proceeds of the sales, and lay them at the apostles' feet; and they would be distributed to each, as any had need" (Acts 4:32, 34–35). This sharing was voluntary, temporary, and spontaneous, but it speaks volumes of the kind of loving, caring persons who had filled the ranks of the Christian fellowship. Clearly evangelism and social action were not divorced from each other. As the people of God preached the gospel, they also ministered to the practical needs of their members

(6:1–7) and reached out in generous, loving service to help and heal outsiders as well (e.g., the healing of the father of Publius by Paul, 28:7–10). It was said of the early Christians, "Behold how they love one another!" The seriousness with which the church treated the hypocrisy of Ananias and Sapphira is evidence of the reality of its caring and of its concern for integrity and credibility (5:1–11). Such an unselfish, caring fellowship was undeniably attractive to the pagan world, and it still is.

Conclusion

This study confirms the work of Copeland, who came to the following conclusions on the basis of his study of church growth in Acts.[10]

1. *In the Book of Acts, church growth involved not only numerical accessions and geographical extension but also growth in the ethical and spiritual dimensions.* Such qualities as faith, love, joy, honesty, and purity are expected in the fellowship created by the Word of God and the Holy Spirit. Missionaries took care not only to plant churches but also to nourish them in the faith. In other words quality must accompany quantity.

2. While there are examples of homogeneous grouping, *church growth in Acts seems to place a premium on heterogeneous membership.* The apostles and other witnesses sought to incorporate Jews and Gentiles, men and women, ordinary people and people of distinction in a given congregation. For example the Book of Acts knows of no "Gentile" church as such. There seem to have been "Jewish" Christian churches in Palestine but no "Gentile" churches beyond. These churches outside Palestine seem to have had a nucleus of members from the Jewish synagogue circle and a larger Gentile constituency. In a sense church growth in Acts may be viewed as a commentary on Paul's statement about inclusive unity in Christ in Galatians 3:28: "There is neither Jew nor Greek, there is neither slave nor free man, there is neither male nor female; for you are all one in Christ Jesus" (cf. Col. 3:11).

3. *The strategy of missions in Acts incorporates both human capacities and divine direction and empowerment.* The Spirit equips the whole church to witness; however, natural endowments, such as the eloquence of Apollos, are significant. "To the Jew first" was an important axiom but also an effective stratagem, for it utilized the synagogue circles of the Diaspora as bridges to the

Gentile world. And if good sense directed the choice of strategic centers, the Holy Spirit sometimes overruled human logic for purposes of His own strategy.

4. Of utmost importance to the author of Acts was the liberation of the gospel from anything that hindered or compromised its universal character. Therefore Luke viewed church growth, directed by the Holy Spirit, as the *deliberate overleaping of inhibiting barriers of religion, race, and other factors that divide person from person or people from people.*

5. *Church growth gives meaning to the interval between Christ's first and second advents.* "The kingdom manifested in Jesus Christ was the foundation of the church's mission. The consummation of the kingdom in his coming again was its goal. And so, between the times, the church served the kingdom—and its king; and her mission stretched to the ends of the earth and the end of the world."[11]

CHAPTER 5

The Holy Spirit's Intercessory Ministry

Curtis C. Mitchell

Of all the chapters in the Book of Romans, none has been more cherished by God's people than chapter 8. But of the many wonderful promises to be found in the chapter, perhaps none is less understood and appreciated than the promise of the Spirit's help in relation to believers' praying (Rom. 8:26–27).

No serious textual problems exist in the passage, but exegetical difficulties abound. The problems begin with the first word Ὡσαύτως ("likewise"). It is a rather common adverb of comparison used quite frequently by Paul when he desired to show a close connection with the context.

Three views are held on the relationship of these verses to the context. Most feel that Ὡσαύτως refers to the broad context in verses 19–25 (on "groaning").[1] Others tie Ὡσαύτως in with the broader context of the Spirit's ministry begun back in verse 14.[2] Some consider such attempts to tie the passage into the broad context as "rather fanciful."[3] They prefer to view the connection with the immediate context: As hope supports believers during suffering and enables them to wait patiently (v. 25), so (Ὡσαύτως) the Spirit helps them in their weakness.[4] Strange as it may seem, the contextual considerations have little or no bearing on the actual interpretation of the verses themselves.

The Need for the Spirit's Intercession

The obvious fact of the passage is the blessed assurance that "the Spirit helps our weakness." Indeed, the primary ministry of the Spirit in this present era is to be a "Helper" (παράχλητον) Paul uses συναντιλαμβάνεται, a rich word, to convey the idea of help. It pictures a man struggling with a heavy load beyond his ability to carry it alone.[5] Fortunately another person comes along and agrees to take hold of one end of the load. So instead of the man having to carry the burden himself it is now shared, and the two men carry the load that was too much for the one man alone. The Holy Spirit does not take over Christians' responsibilities and give them automatic deliverance without effort on their part. That would certainly not be envisioned in the word συναντιλαμβάνεται. Paul is not teaching a doctrine of passivity here. Clearly the Holy Spirit did not come to do His work and the believers' too; rather, He came to help them with theirs.[6] The personal involvement of the Holy Spirit in helping is seen not only by the use of the articulated noun τὸ πνεῦμα ("the Spirit"), but also by the middle voice of the verb συναντιλαμβάνεται ("helps"). The Holy Spirit is personally involved in helping the saints. The present tense of this same verb indicates that this blessed Holy Spirit is *always* ready to come to their aid and assistance.[7]

The Holy Spirit helps "our weakness" (τῇ ἀσθενίᾳ ἡμῶν). The word ἀσθενία ("weakness") occurs many times in the New Testament. The word is hardly ever used of purely physical weakness but is frequently used in a comprehensive sense of human frailty in general.[8] By far the vast majority understand ἀσθενία in this passage as man's fundamental ineptness as a result of the Fall.[9] Evidently the ἀσθενία has no moral connotations No rebuke is suggested toward saints who have ἀσθενία. Even Christ in His incarnate state was said to be "beset with weakness" (ἀσθενία). Most certainly the Lord God could well have been pleased to deliver saints completely from all effects of the Fall at the moment of regeneration, but obviously He has ordained otherwise.[10] Against such a backdrop He can evidently best display His power and bring greater glory to Himself.[11]

Paul then discussed a special manifestation of this ἀσθενία. The way it shows itself in saints most acutely and perhaps most frequently is in the realm of prayer. Paul wrote, "for we do not know how to pray as we should." The word γὰρ ("for") introduces an explanation and proof of the believers' great weakness, and in addition it states the reason for the Spirit's help. The nature of that weakness with regard to prayer is in the realm of knowledge. Clearly the main verb of the sentence is οἴδαμεν, preceded by the negative οὐχ: "we do not know."

As part of their human weakness, Christians are ignorant in the matter of prayer. Some say this ignorance refers only to special prayer emergencies of one sort or another.[12] Such a contention, however, cannot be sustained by the language. The expression is not, "we often do not know," but simply, "we do not know." In view of the continuing imperfection of even the best Christians, would it not be rather strange if it did not affect them in the matter of their knowledge with regard to prayer? Unless they are praying in exact concurrence with the clearly revealed will of God as set forth in Scripture, they simply do not know. Even when praying in exact conformity to Scripture, it is because God has revealed the matter, not because of Christians' knowledge. All praying by all Christians *insofar as it is their praying* remains under the "not knowing," set forth in verse 26.[13]

Amazingly Paul included himself in this "not knowingness." The first person plural οἴδαμεν includes the great apostle. An editorial "we" is not indicated, because of the manner in which Paul consistently used the first person plural in the chapter. Was not Paul filled with the Spirit? Did not Paul have the mind of Christ? Was not Paul a spiritual man? Was not Paul mightily used of God in missionary endeavor? Was not Paul ardent in his love for souls? Yet Paul said "we" really do not know what to pray. Hendriksen has rightly observed, "with the exception of the prayers of Jesus Christ, is there anything in the line of prayer more thought-filled, fervent and sublime than the Apostle's prayer recorded in Ephesians 3:14–19?"[14] Yet Paul wrote, "We do not know how to pray as we ought."

But what precisely is the nature of this prayer ignorance? Paul spoke of this in the words, τὸ γὰρ τί προσευξώμεθα χαθὸ δεῖ. The article τί, makes the entire clause the object of οὐχ οἴδαμεν ("We do not know").[15] Some difference of opinion exists as to whether the aorist subjunctive followed by the indirect question τί προσευξώμεθα should be taken as "what to pray" or "what to pray for." Is Paul referring to the *content* of prayer or the *object* of prayer? Since the object (what to pray for) determines the content (what to pray), the meaning of both is much the same, and the question is moot. Christians have a general sense of need at times, but they are often not clear on what particular thing they need. So they do not know "what to pray for" nor "what to pray." Paul's ignorance regarding his "thorn" (2 Cor. 12:7) is a case in point. Yet the answer he received shows that God most certainly did know, and the answer God gave Paul on that occasion "shows for what he [Paul] should have prayed."[16]

But Paul continued by adding the words χαθὸ δεῖ ("as we should"). Most concur that χαθὸ δεῖ is to be taken with τί προσευξώμεθα ("what to pray"), rather than οὐχ οἴδαμεν ("we know not"). The latter construction is possible but somewhat forced.[17] The adverb χαθὸ δεῖ does not refer to manner of praying, but rather to the correspondence between the prayer and what is really needed.[18] Paul himself confessed that he did "not know which to choose" (Phil. 1:22). Broadly speaking, Christians often do know (or so they think) what they are to pray for (e.g., the perfecting of the saints, the glory of God), but they do *not* know what to pray according to the need of the moment. They may know these ultimate ends, which are common to all prayers, but they may be ignorant as to what is necessary at each crisis in order to attain that desired end.[19]

Augustine was a notoriously wicked man before his conversion. His mother Monica, a Christian, was heavily burdened for her wayward son. Hearing that he was leaving home and planning to live in Italy, she prayed earnestly that God would not allow Augustine to go there, because she feared he would fall into deeper sin. But though she prayed sincerely, she really did not know what to pray as she ought because, as it turned out, Augustine did indeed move to Italy, but was gloriously converted there.[20] Monica knew the ultimate end (the conversion of her son), but she was ignorant of what was necessary in the immediate crisis (her son's move to Italy) to attain that ultimate desired end.

Christians are imperfect, immature, and insufficient. Paul obviously felt that the removal of the thorn would make him a more powerful witness for Christ, but he simply did not know what to pray (for) as he ought! "But . . . even the most sincere, most heroic, most powerful prayers . . . do not but serve to make clear how little the man of prayer is able to escape from himself. . . ."[21]

The Nature of the Spirit's Intercession

The help the Spirit gives in coming to the believers' aid (συναντιλαμβάνεται) is now clarified. Though Christians pray ignorantly, the Spirit "intercedes" (ὑπερεντυγχάνει) for them. This Greek word, a double compound of the verb τυγχάνω, occurs only here in the New Testament. Robertson refers to it as "a picturesque word of rescue."[22] The root means "to happen along." The preposition ἐν accents the idea of "on"; thus ἐντυγχάνω means "to happen on." The preposition ὑπέρ emphasizes that the one who "happens on" believers also acts "on behalf of" them. As a true παράχλητος ("advocate"), the Spirit finds them in their weakness, takes their part, and speaks on their behalf.[23]

Thus believers have two intercessors: Christ, who intercedes in heaven at the right hand of the Father, and the Holy Spirit, who intercedes while resident within believers. Christ prays that the merits of His redemptive work may be fully applied to His own, while the Holy Spirit prays that their unrealized needs may be met.[24]

Some would argue that the Holy Spirit's intercession is involved only in "extreme situations of perplexity" such as is demonstrated by Jesus' cry, "What shall I say?" (John 12:27).[25] However, as already indicated, the sons of God are *ever* in a state of weakness, and thus they are *always*, consciously or unconsciously, ignorant of what to pray in a given situation. Perhaps at times they stumble on the right things to say in their prayers in spite of their ignorance. It may well be true that at such times their prayers do not need to be "counteracted by the Holy Spirit."[26] However, in the vast majority of instances, they "do not know how to pray" as they should, and at such times they have the assurance that the Holy Spirit intercedes for them.

But precisely how does the Holy Spirit intercede? Does He do so directly or indirectly? Does He cry out to the Father on behalf of believers, or does He intercede indirectly by "stirring up in our hearts those desires which we ought to entertain"?[27] In support of indirect intercession, it is argued that He pleads in believers' prayers and thus raises them to higher and holier desires. The "groanings too deep for words" (στεναγμοῖς ἀλαλήτοις) are attributed to saints, which the Spirit then uses in making His intercession for them.[28]

Various reasons are given in support of indirect intercession. Most recognize that a strictly literal rendering of the words indicates the Spirit's direct intercession, but it is argued on theological grounds that "God can't groan."[29] But in the words of Hendriksen, "exegetical accuracy is as important as doctrinal purity. Both are needed."[30] God is not devoid of emotion. If God loves, grieves, and rejoices, why is it inconceivable that He groans?

Appeal is made to Galatians 4:6, "and because you are sons, God has sent forth the Spirit of His Son into our hearts, crying Abba! Father!" Some argue that God cannot be the Father of the

Holy Spirit, and hence the crying is that of the saints through the
Holy Spirit, not the Spirit's crying. It is also argued that this same
indirect intercession is true in Romans 8:26–27.[31] However, a
distinct difference exists between Galatians 4:6 and Romans 8:26–
27.[32] In the Romans passage, Paul used the emphatic form αυτὸ τὸ
πνεῦμα ("the Spirit Himself"). Then in order to make the meaning
even less ambiguous, he continued in verse 27 by saying that "he
who searches the hearts knows what the mind of the Spirit is."
The mind of the Spirit (τοῦ πνεύματος), not the mind of believers,
is searched by God.

Also Paul had already discussed the groanings of the saints in
verse 23. It seems unlikely that he would return to this subject
again in verse 26. Finally, the same word ἐντυγχάνει that refers
to the Spirit's intercession in verse 27 is used in verse 34 of
Christ's intercession at the right hand of the Father. Does not
Christ intercede directly for believers? How then can one contend
that the word is used of indirect intercession in verse 27, but of
direct intercession in verse 34?[33] Therefore exegetically the natural
sense of the language indicates that the Spirit residing within
Christians is said to intercede directly for them. His praying is
complementary to their sincere but ignorant praying and is
necessary to its efficacy.[34]

But why not then permit the Holy Spirit to do all the praying?
Why pray at all? (The same type of objection is often voiced with
reference to divine sovereignty. If God is sovereign, why pray?)
Several facts may be pointed out in response: (a) A Christian
needs to pray as part of God's divinely ordained sanctifying
process. (b) The Holy Spirit prays only in the hearts of those who
pray. If the believer does not pray, the Spirit does not intercede.
(c) God has commanded His people to pray, and in His sovereignty
He has conditioned many of His actions on human asking.[35]

The Spirit's intercession is said to be with "groanings too deep
for words" (στεναγμοῖς ἀλαλήτοις). The use of the instrumental
case indicates that it is by this means that the Holy Spirit intercedes.
Are these groanings audible or inaudible? Are they related to the
γλῶσσα spoken of in Acts and in 1 Corinthians?

Many commentators do not discuss these questions. Obviously
those who equate these στεναγμοῖς with the γλῶσσα contend
that they are audible.[36] But others do not equate the two phenomena
and yet feel that they are audible sighs or groans. They contend
that because of the pain and anguish of soul, expressions not

formulated into words arise from the hearts of believers as an audible evidence of the believers' inadequacy. The Spirit then takes these expressions of grief enabling them to take the form of prayer that will be understood by God the Father.[37] However, as noted, the language indicates that believers in their fallen state are *ever* in the condition of weakness, and therefore *every* prayer needs the Spirit's intercessory groanings. Is it not self-evident that believers usually do not audibly groan while praying? Yet Paul said that intercessory groanings always accompany genuine Christian praying. This would seem to suggest that the groanings are inaudible. They are wrought by the Holy Spirit deep within the Christian's heart to be searched out by the one who knows the mind of the Spirit.[38]

The context is also suggestive in determining the nature of these groans. The intercessory "groanings" (στεναγμοῖς) of the Spirit (v. 26) are usually recognized as the consummation of a triad of groanings beginning with the groanings (συστενάζει) of creation (v. 22), and followed by the groanings (στενάζομεν) of Christians (v. 23). Schneider refers to this sequence of groanings as a "crescendo" and a "triple sighing."[39] Obviously in Paul's mind the three groanings are related. In each case Paul selected a variation of the verb στένω in describing the three groanings,[40] and each time he described the verbal action of these groanings with the present tense.[41]

The nature of the first two groanings (creation's and Christian's) may thus shed light on the nature of the third groaning (the Spirit's). Are the groanings of fallen creation audible? Obviously not. At least such groaning is not audible to human ears. Likewise the groans of the redeemed human spirit are inaudible to human ears. Since the three groanings are related, as most contend, and since the first two are inaudible to human ears, does it not argue rather convincingly that the groanings of the Spirit are likewise inaudible to human ears? It seems that, barring strong exegetical evidence to the contrary, these groanings of the Spirit may be assumed to be inaudible.

Also Paul said the Spirit's groanings are "unutterable" (ἀλαλήτοις). And this has led to a continuing dispute as to whether ἀλαλήτοις should be translated "unuttered" or "unutterable." Most contend that the word should be translated unutterable." It is usually argued that these groanings are so deep, so profound, so moving, that they defy expression.[42] Cranfield is of the opinion that while the word itself could be translated either way, verse 27 suggests that "unuttered" is more likely since "the Spirit's groanings are not spoken, because they do not need to be since God knows the Spirit's intention without being expressed."[43] Actually, if these groans are inaudible to human ears and are clearly understood by the Father (v. 27), it would seem to make little difference whether they were "unuttered" or "unutterable." Humans would not hear them in either case!

Käsemann, however, insists that Paul was not dealing with the problem of prayer in general, but was speaking with reference to certain practices in congregational life which are open to misunderstanding. . . . What is at issue is the praying in tongues of 1 Corinthians 14:15."[44] Therefore Käsemann and others from as early as Chrysostom and Origen insist that the στεναγμοῖς ἀλαλήτοις refers to the προσεύχωμαι γλώσσῃ of 1 Corinthians 14:14–15. However, as Cranfield has pointed out, neither Käsemann nor others who have tried to equate the unutterable groanings with ecstatic utterances of glossolalia have presented exegetical evidence in support of their view.[45]

Several factors make it clear that the unutterable (or unuttered) groanings of verse 26 cannot be equated with praying in tongues. To begin with, as already demonstrated, these groanings are inaudible to human ears; and yet that certainly was not true of praying in tongues. Next, Paul emphasized that it is the Spirit *Himself* who intercedes with groanings, whereas he also stated that when a person prayed in tongues it was the believer's own *human spirit* praying (τὸ πνεῦμα μου προσεύχεται). The difference between the two phenomena seems obvious.

The Efficacy of the Spirit's Intercession

The Spirit's groanings may be inaudible and perhaps even unuttered; and yet they are clearly known and understood by God the Father. The Father is identified as "He who searches the hearts" (ὁ δὲ ἐραυνῶν τὰς χαρδίας).[46] This title demonstrates the Father's complete competence to comprehend the Spirit's groanings. Obviously, if He can search the inscrutable human heart, He is perfectly capable of comprehending the intercessory groanings of His own divine Spirit.[47] The important concept is that the Father, who is fully qualified, perceives completely "what the mind of the Spirit is" (τί τὸ φρόνημα τοῦ πνεὺματος). Here φρόνημα, used only in Romans 8, carries the idea of "aim, aspiration or striving."[48] In short, God perceives the intent of the Spirit's intercession that is hidden in those unuttered groans.

What God fully understands about the mind of the Spirit is next specified: "that He intercedes according to God" (ὅτι χατὰ θεὸν ἐντυγχάει). Most English translations render ὅτι in the casual sense of "because."[49] In fact, Käsemann labels this "the accepted view."[50] Taking ὅτι in this way makes the Spirit's interceding in accord with divine will, the *reason* God the Father knows the Spirit's mind. But such is not necessarily the situation. The Father knows all things, hence no reason for knowing the Spirit's mind need be given.[51]

The ὅτι in this context is better taken in the explicative sense, and translated "that."[52] Paul was explaining several wonderful facts concerning the Spirit's mind (aim or intention) in His intercessory groanings. First, God knows that the Spirit's groanings are in the nature of intercessions (ἐντυγχάνει). The object of the Holy Spirit's groanings is to lay bare all the deep hidden needs of the saints before the Father. Second, the Father knows they are intercessions for people who are special to Him. He knows that the Spirit intercedes ὑπὲρ ἁγιών ("for the benefit of saints"). Saints are those who have been set apart from the rest of humanity by God's sovereign choice (Eph. 1:3). For this reason the Holy Spirit's intercession for them is of special interest to the Father. Third, He, by knowing the mind of the Spirit, realizes fully that His intercessions are ever "according to God" (χατὰ θεὸν). These words are emphatic by position and indicate the most significant information in the entire explanatory phrase introduced by ὅτι.[53] The words χατὰ θεοὶ are almost universally recognized as meaning "according to God's will."[54] This means that the Spirit's intercessory groans always coincide completely with the Father's will.

The fact that the Spirit's intercessory groanings are in complete accord with the Father's will is especially significant to Christians. Since the Spirit in His intercession is helping them in their inadequate praying, then their praying (complemented by the Spirit's praying) is inevitably in harmony with the will of God. All prayer in harmony with God's will will be answered (1 John 5:14–15). Barth accurately observes that God "makes Himself our advocate with Himself that He utters for us that ineffable groaning, so that He will surely hear what we ourselves could not have told Him, so that He will accept what He Himself has to offer."[55]

Conclusion

Christians are inadequate when it comes to knowing what to pray. However, they are assured that they never pray alone! The indwelling Spirit helps them in a positive way with their problem of prayer-ignorance, by praying along with them. By supplementing their pitiful prayers, He brings them into complete harmony with the will of God. This takes place every time a Christian prays, even if He is unaware of the Spirit's intercession.

However, much of what is commonly labeled prayer is not prayer at all. Simply getting out a prayer list and mechanically mouthing pious-sounding generalities devoid of earnestness or urgency is not prayer, according to the Bible. Simply reciting the Lord's Prayer in a church service without mental or emotional involvement comes closer to being labeled vain repetitions than true prayer.[56] Such so-called prayer does not have the cooperative intercessory help of the Holy Spirit for the simple reason that it is not really Christian praying.

Hendriksen cites an example of the prayer phenomenon depicted in these verses. A pastor had become seriously ill, and his congregation held almost nightly prayer vigils for his recovery. But he continued to worsen and finally died. At the funeral his friend said, "Perhaps some of you are in danger of arriving at the conclusion that the heavenly Father does not hear prayer. He does indeed hear prayer, however. But in this particular case, two prayers were probably opposing each other. You were praying, 'Oh God, spare his life, for we need him so badly.' The Spirit's unspoken prayer was, 'Take him away, for the congregation is leaning altogether too heavily upon him and not upon thee,' and the Father heard that prayer."[57]

Prayer need not always be correctly formulated to be effective. Indeed, the most inarticulate desires that spring from the right motive have shape and value beyond anything that is present and definable to the believer's consciousness.[58] All too often the intercessory activity of the Holy Spirit is never taken into account.[59]

The significance of praying is not so much the fact of Christians' praying, but the assurance that it triggers the Holy Spirit's intercessory praying. The value of prayer ultimately lies in His intercessory groanings, not the believer's ignorant praying.

CHAPTER 6

Romans 8:28-29 and the Assurance of the Believer

D. Edmond Hiebert

And we know that God causes all things to work together for good to those who love God, to those who are called according to His purpose. For whom He foreknew, He also predestined to become conformed to the image of His Son, that He might be the first-born among many brethren."

Paul's words in Romans 8:28-29 express a ringing Christian assurance to the believing heart; they have brought comfort and encouragement to many troubled and afflicted believers down through the centuries. The opening words, "And we know," introduce a crucial assertion for victorious Christian living that is apprehended by faith. The verb "we know" (οἴδαμεν) denotes "the knowledge of faith and not mere intellectual investigation."[1] As Watson remarks, "As axioms and aphorisms are evident to reason, so the truths of religion are evident to faith."[2] The assurance expressed in Romans 8:28-29 is not a logical deduction of cold reason but rather an inner conviction of the believing heart wrought by the Holy Spirit on the basis of Scripture and verified in personal experience. In setting forth the great truths of the gospel in the first eight chapters of Romans, Paul used the verb οἴδαμεν six times (2:2; 3:19; 7:14; 8:22, 26, 28). Romans 8:28 states the crowning certainty of the Christian life.

Many Christians indeed have found the sweeping assertion, "all things work together for good" (Rom. 8:28, KJV), difficult to believe. Faced with the sufferings and catastrophic experiences of life, many believers and even Christian leaders have found it difficult to accept this categorical assertion. During World War II a prominent preacher designated Romans 8:28 as "the hardest verse in the Bible to believe." While willing to admit that the countless ravages that have befallen the human race are the logical consequences of human sin and rebellion against God, many devout believers, when some shattering experience has befallen them, have cried out in bewilderment, "Why does God allow this to happen to me?" How can this kind of experience be reconciled with Romans 8:28? When Jacob's sons, who had gone to Egypt to buy needed food, came back without their brother Simeon, and reported to their father that the next time Benjamin must also go to Egypt, the patriarch cried out in despair, "All these things are against me" (Gen. 42:36).

And today Christ-rejecting, secular humanists in their spiritual blindness may reject the assertion that "all things work together for good." Such individuals, unconscious of any beneficent activity of God in their lives, while observing a tumultuous world with weary eyes, may readily conclude that human life has no higher meaning. They may be prone to agree with the cynical poet who wrote:

> The world rolls round forever like a mill,
> It grinds out life and death, and good and ill,
> It has no purpose, heart, or mind, or will.

> Man might know this thing, were his sight less dim,
> Life whirleth not to suit his petty whim,
> For it is quite indifferent to him.

> Nay, doth it use him harshly, as he saith?
> It grinds for him slow years of bitter breath,
> Then grinds him back into eternal death.[3]

How utterly contrary such a cynical evaluation of life is to Paul's declaration in Romans 8:28–29! No one can truly accept the Gospel of Jesus Christ and accept such a cynical, godless interpretation of human existence. Instead the ringing assurance declared by Paul offers a message of inner certainty and reality that imparts meaning, power, and encouragement to the believing heart. The assurance that "God causes all things to work together for good to those who love God" is a message that the indwelling Holy Spirit vitalizes in the believing heart. It is a reality that "Christians know intuitively, though they may not always fully understand and sense it experientially."[4] The importance of the truth declared in Romans 8:28–29, as well as the questions, perplexities, and unwarranted assumptions that have been made, make clear the need for a careful study and interpretation of these verses in the light of the context.

The Contextual Setting

The particle δέ in verse 28 clearly marks a close connection with the preceding verses. Verses 28–30 form a kind of climax to the teaching in verses 18–27, while verses 31–39 form a concluding paean of praise celebrating the redemption in Christ, delineated in the first eight chapters of Romans, as establishing a bond of love that can never be broken.

The force of the connecting δέ has been understood in two ways. The rendering "but" in some English versions[5] indicates that its force is understood as adversative. Thus Godet suggests that δέ marks the contrast between the present groaning of creation, the source of suffering in the present age, and "the full certainty already possessed by believers of the *glorious goal* marked out beforehand by the plan of God."[6] But Meyer feels that if such a contrast was intended "it must have been marked in some way or other (at least by the stronger adversative ἀλλά)."[7] Nor does the admission in verse 26 that "we do not know how to pray as we should" offer a basis for an assumed contrast. It is more natural to hold that δέ here has the force of "and"[8] or "further,"[9] adding ground for encouragement amid the sufferings of this present life. This accords with the contents of verses 18–27.

In verse 18 Paul asserted his evaluation of the believers' present sufferings as "not worthy to be compared with the glory that is to be revealed to us." In verses 19–25 he supported his evaluation from creation's yearning for deliverance from corruption by pointing to the believers' present yearning for full redemption; in verses 26–27 he pointed to the present intercession of the Holy Spirit. Thus Lenski notes that to this intercession, "which aids us in our weakness in this distressing world, δέ adds another mighty comfort."[10] That truth is "that God causes all things to work together for good to those who love God, to those who are called according to His purpose." "We know" indicates that this asserted knowledge is accepted by believers as a truth not to be gainsaid. It is an inner assurance vitalized and strengthened by the indwelling Holy Spirit. Hendriksen suggests that this knowledge is probably based on "two additional grounds: (a) *Experience;* that is, the effect on him of knowing how God had dealt with him and with others in the past. . . . And (b) Acquaintance with *specific biblical passages* which teach that in God's providence all things result in blessing for God's children, evil being overruled for good (Gen. 45:5, 7, 8; 50:20)."[11]

The Central Assertion

The central assertion of verse 28 (NIV) is the truth that "in all things God works for the good" (πάντα συνεργεῖ εἰς ἀγαθόν). Taken alone, these four words may equally well be rendered as in the King James Version, "all things work together for good." The neuter plural πάντα, "all things, everything," has no indicated restrictions. In itself the term naturally includes all the experiences, whether sad or glad, that come into the lives of God's people. Yet in the light of the context (vv. 18–27) the primary reference of πάντα is to "every kind of painful experience in Christian lives, all those that press groans from our lips and make us groan inwardly in unuttered and unutterable distress. Some of the things that Paul has in mind he states in vv. 38, 39."[12]

According to a peculiar law of Greek grammar a singular verb may have a neuter plural subject.[13] Therefore the neuter plural παύτα, standing before the singular verb συνεργεῖ, naturally may be accepted as its subject. The present tense verb, "work together," denotes a continuing or protracted activity of unspecified duration, with the result that all things work "unto good" (εἰς ἀγαθόν) in the experience of the recipients. Paul's terse assertion does not further define the nature or scope of this "good," except to declare a beneficial impact.

Dunn notes that "the pious hope that everything will work out for the best for the godly is 'a common axiom of antiquity' (Käsemann)."[14] Thus Paul's words would not strike his readers as a new and strange assertion. It is an assertion that believers in all walks of life have found an assuring and comforting truth. But the axiomatic nature of Paul's assertion makes it necessary to guard against unwarranted interpretations.

Paul's assertion must not be taken to mean that all things automatically work for the good of all people. That would be a fatalism for good, a view denied by Scripture and human experience. This statement does not sanction the view of enthusiasts, whether religious or secular, who blithely exult, "Hip, hip, hurray, let come what may, all things will be OK!"

Nor did Paul mean that all things that come into believers' lives are in themselves "good." Paul was not blurring moral distinctions between the various things and experiences of this life. The fiery persecutions, or the slanderous accusations to which Paul's readers were subjected by a Christ-rejecting world, were not in themselves good. Even the unjust assertions or unkind deeds of fellow believers, motivated by misunderstanding or ill will, cannot be declared to be good, or for one's good, in themselves. Even some of the things experienced as the result of one's own deeds or choices are not always in themselves good. Nor did Paul mean that everything believers experience is God's will for them. Paul did not necessarily mean that those undesirable things that cannot be averted are God's will. Paul was not telling believers that when a thief stole a Christian's goods and escaped, the believers must piously say, "God willed it." God never condones sin in deed or attitude.

Paul's assertion that "all things work together for good" (KJV) must be understood in the light of the context. It is also desirable to look more closely at the original statement, πάντα συνεργεῖ εἰς ἀγαθόν. The common view is to take πάντα as the subject. However, the entire statement in verse 28, as well as a significant textual variant, indicate that πάντα may be taken as the emphatic object of the verb, with the singular subject of the verb ("He") being the true subject of the sentence. So understood, the sentence may be rendered, "And we know that to those loving God all things He works together unto good, to those according to purpose called ones being." That various early scribes and interpreters so read the verse is clear from the fact that the words ὁ θεός ("God") were added as the expressed subject of the verb in Papyrus 46 (dated about A.D. 200), uncials A (fifth century) and B (fourth century), cursive 81 (ca. 1044), and the Sahidic Coptic version, and is used in two of five known quotations of Romans 8:28 in the writings of Origen.[15] Though this textual evidence is too weak to accept ὁ θεός as the original reading, its presence indicates that "God" rather than "all things" was understood as the subject of the sentence. Since in the original Paul had already used the noun "God" (τόν θεὸν), to have written ὁ θεὸ as the expressed subject of the verb συνεργεῖ would have resulted in making Paul "a rather clumsy stylist."[16] But the textual variant establishes that Paul, having just mentioned God, would expect the reader to understand that "God" (ὁ θεός) was the intended subject of the singular verb. This interpretation is expressly indicated in the NIV rendering and various other English versions.[17]

Another identification of the intended subject has been suggested. This view asserts that the true subject of the verb in verse 28 is "the Spirit," named in verse 26. That the Holy Spirit is accepted as the subject of the verb here is evident from the rendering of verses 26–28 in the New English Bible. In his interpretive rendering Barclay names the Holy Spirit as the subject: "We know that through the work of the Spirit all the different events of life are being made to work for good, for those who keep on loving God, those whom his purpose has called."[18] But the view that the Spirit is the intended subject of the verb "work together" runs into difficulty in verse 29, for that verse would then read, "For whom He [the Spirit] foreknew, He also predestined to become conformed to the image of His [the Spirit's] Son." "This," Hendriksen notes, "is impossible, for nowhere in Scripture is Jesus Christ called the Son of the Holy Spirit."[19]

Most probable is the view that God is the intended subject of the verb συνεργεῖ: "He works together with all things unto good." Clearly Paul's thought is not that "all things" as impersonal realities by themselves work together constructively; rather it is God's providential working in and through these various things that assures that all things work together for good. This is expressly asserted when ὁ θεός is placed into the text. "This certainty," Grundmann remarks, "which is proper to all Jewish piety and derives from its consciousness of God, acquires here its fullness from the action of God."[20] This reading of Romans 8:28 is strongly supported by Paul's assertion in Philippians 1:6.

The present tense verb συνεργεῖ declares God's continuing activity in working all things "unto good" in the lives of His people. "For good" (εἰς ἀγαθόν) denotes the goal of the divine working, but the verb does not indicate when or how soon that goal is attained. The verb may mean that God "cooperates with" all these things to attain His goal for His own, but the expression εἰς ἀγαθόν suggests that in the providence of God all things "work together with or cooperate in" the achievement of the intended "good." Watson suggested a medical analogy: "Several poisonous ingredients put together, being tempered by the skill of the apothecary, make a sovereign medicine, and work together for the good of the patient. So all God's providences, being divinely tempered and sanctified, work together for the best to the saints."[21]

The "good" that God works to bring about in the lives of His people is not just a physical good, such as food, comfort, health, or pleasures of one kind or another experienced in this life. God works to fulfill His "purpose" for His own as outlined in verse 29. Thus Dunn remarks, "In the context here, where Paul has in view the eschatological climax which God has purposed for 'all things,' the ἀγαθόν will have an eschatological reference (cf. 14:16)."[22]

Yet Scripture and Christian experience confirm that even in this life God in His infinite way works "all things for good" for His own. Lenski refers to two biblical stories in support of this fact.

> The Old Testament story of Joseph is a striking example of the mysterious and the wonderful way in which God makes the evil done to us eventuate for our good. Another instance is the story of the persecution precipitated by Saul. It scattered the great congregation at Jerusalem to distant parts, it seemed to be a calamity but served only for the good of the church by planting it in a hundred new places to flourish more than ever.[23]

On a small scale Christians through the ages have testified to this reality in their own lives. After completing seminary training it was my joy to be invited to join the Christian training department in a midwestern Christian college. In the middle of the second year of a delightful ministry there, a sudden and severe illness brought me to the brink of death; the hospital stay stretched into 110 days. Recovery was slow and often discouraging. Before long the threat of physical deafness was evident and two years later deafness became total. Before that time some calls to administrative service came for which I did not feel adequate. With total deafness such calls were effectively terminated, leaving me free for concentrated study of the Scriptures and their systematic exposition in the college and seminary classroom and in a written ministry. In looking back over the years I can gladly testify that I could not have chosen a more delightful ministry.

The Careful Limitation

Paul carefully limited his confident assertion that "God causes all things to work together for good" to a distinct class of people. Paul added two limiting clauses, one placed before and the other following his central assertion, as seen in the rendering of Rotherham: "We know further that unto them who love God God causeth all things to work together for good—unto them who according to purpose are such as He hath called." The first marks a clear limitation from the human side, the second states a limitation from God's side.

THOSE WHO LOVE GOD

Those for whom God works all things for good are emphatically identified as "those who love Him" (τοῖς ἀγαπῶσιν τὸν θεὸν, "to those loving God"). The present tense articular participle characterizes these people by their abiding love for God, while the article with God ("the God") designates the true God whom Christians now love and serve. "Despisers and haters of God," Watson reminds, "have no lot or part in this privilege."[24] This abiding love for God is the difference between the regenerated individual and the unsaved.

This is the only place in Romans where Paul wrote of the believers' love for God; elsewhere the reference is to God's love for them. The verb for "love" (ἀγαπάω), here used to identify true believers, "is the word for the highest type of love, that of comprehension coupled with corresponding purpose."[25] Hogg and Vine call it "the characteristic word of Christianity."[26] It is not merely a love of emotion but a purposeful love that actively desires the welfare of others and sacrificially works toward that end. It reflects the love of God Himself toward needy sinners. Those who "love God" thus reveal an attitude and activity in accord with the very nature of God Himself. God is at the center of such a love-dominated life.

Such love in the hearts of believers is not meritorious; their love for Him does not prompt God to begin working all things for their good. Such a love is not native to the human heart; it can only be known as the result of God's love being poured out in the believers' hearts through the Holy Spirit (Rom. 5:5). As John wrote, "We love, because He first loved us" (1 John 4:19). It is this infusion of divine love that created the fundamental distinction between the saved and the unsaved. Thus Paul placed this factor forward. This criterion of "love to God is both the most elementary and the highest mark of being in the favor of God."[27] The believers' love "is nothing but the direct flowing back of the heavenly love which has been poured out upon" those whom God has called and saved.[28] Those who are lovers of God experience the reality that everything which may happen to them is being divinely used to further their highest good.

THOSE WHO ARE CALLED ACCORDING TO GOD'S
   PURPOSE

Paul's second limitation, placed after his basic assertion, passes from the human experience to the divine purpose and reaches into eternity past. Again the articular participle construction (τοῖς κατὰ πρόθεσιν κλητοῖς οὖσιν, literally, "to those according to purpose called ones being") again indicates the character of the distinct group in view. They are now defined exclusively in terms of God's purpose (κατὰ πρόθεσιν). The noun πρόθεσιν (literally, "an act of setting forth") here denotes God's pretemporal purpose, which is now working in and through history and moving toward the accomplishment of His intended goal. God, not men, determines the nature and progressive development of that purpose. He has taken the initiative in the lives of these individuals, not only inviting them but also effectively calling them in accord with His purpose for them. As a result they now are the subjects of the outworking of His purpose, and as such are the "called" (κλῆτοις). As Lenski notes, "The verbal is passive and involves God as the agent who called and the gospel as the divine means and the power by which he called."[29] Those in whose lives God is now working in accord with His redemptive purpose are assured that the outcome will be for their ultimate good, since His purpose is filled with His love.

A Christian's assurance concerning the beneficent result of the outworking of God's purpose is grounded not in fluctuating love for Him nor steadfast obedience to His call, but in His unchanging love for believers as His "called ones." This realization gives purpose and encouragement for daily life. But one must remember that what God is now doing is the outworking of His eternal purpose, not the believers' limited and fallible plans and aspirations. This brings present assurance and peace when believers cannot comprehend His dealings with them. At such times they can rest in the assurance Jesus expressed in John 13:7, "What I do you do not realize now, but you shall understand hereafter." Often God gives His own a clear or growing understanding of His purposes for them in this present life; but when they cannot understand His purposes in permitting frustrations, sufferings, and persecutions to assail them in this life, by faith they can accept that fact that He is working out His eternal purposes. But if one stops with verse 28, and fails to go on to verse 29, he generally fails to realize what God's ultimate purpose is.

The Clarifying Goal

In verse 29 Paul delineated God's comprehensive activities and ultimate purpose for those who are the subjects of His redemptive plan. The opening "for" (ὅτι) introduces the reason why all things work together for good to those who love God and have been called according to His purpose. The words "called according to His purpose" already contain the assured outcome, but Paul now "draws it out and details it in full because every part of it is so convincing and thus so comforting in the face of ills."[30]

THE COMPREHENSIVE ACTION

In verse 29 the purpose of God is unfolded in terms of His foreknowledge and foreordination of the redeemed. "For whom He foreknew, He also predestined to become conformed to the image of His Son." The use of the personal relative pronoun "whom" (οὕς), as well as the triple use of the demonstrative pronoun "these" (τούτους) in verse 30, underlines the truth that God's plan relates to individuals, not merely to the experiences they undergo. The two verbs rendered "foreknew" and "predestined" indicate that God's plan for the redeemed began in eternity past and reaches into eternity future.

"Whom He foreknew" (οὓς προέγνω) means more than that He knew about believers before they came into being. As Kelly remarks, "His foreknowledge is of persons, not of their state or conduct; it is not what, but whom He foreknew."[31] The Greek verb "foreknew" (προέγνω) means "to know in advance, to foreknow." The preposition προ does not change the meaning of the verb (γινώσκω); it only dates the knowledge. God's knowledge of those He chose goes back to eternity past (1 Peter 1:2, 20). In His omniscience God knew, knows, and foreknew all men. But, unlike οἶδα, this verb does not imply mere intellectual apprehension; it also indicates an active and affectionate desire to bless. "That this character, in which they were foreknown to God, presupposes the subjection to faith (the ὑπακοὴ πίστεως, i. 5), was self-evident to the Christian reader."[32] Paul's focus in Romans 8:29 is on the terminus, not on the intermediate stages (cf. v. 30).

The second verb, "He also predestined" (καὶ προώρισεν), likewise records God's activity on behalf of Christians; the action also relates to the eternal past but looks forward to what He wants to achieve with them. The simple verb ὁρίζω means "to mark out or determine the boundaries" (cf. the English "horizon"), hence "to determine or appoint." Used of persons it means to set out or determine the goal or destiny of those foreknown; the preposition προ again marks this divine action as taking place in eternity past. The indicated action cannot be restricted to one point but covers all that is involved until the consummation of the goal. Again the indicated action relates to individual persons, not necessarily what happens to them. This predetermined goal cannot be separated from the fact of God's self-motivated love for them. As Behm notes, this is "the New Testament faith in providence in its most individual form."[33]

THE CHRIST-CENTERED GOAL

The indicated goal, "to become conformed to the image of His Son" exhibits "not only the dignity of the ordination but also the greatness of the love from which the appointment flows."[34] Dunn declares, "It is the sureness of the end as determined from the beginning which Paul wishes to emphasize."[35]

God's purpose for His children is their conformity "to the image of His Son" (τῆς εἰκόνος τοῦ υἱοῦ αὐτοῦ). "His Son" (cf. "His own Son," 8:3) denotes Christ's unique and eternal Sonship. Motivated by His love for lost humanity, God sent forth His Son "in the likeness of sinful flesh and as an offering for sin" (8:3). In His sinless life, His vicarious atonement, and His triumphant resurrection, the incarnate Son perfectly realized the divinely intended destiny of the chosen sons of God. On the basis of Christ's perfection as the incarnate Son it is now God's purpose to form a great family of sons, all of them patterned after the "image" of the incarnate Son of God. The word "image" (εἰκών) denotes a derived likeness in believers. In the saints this image "is not accidental but derived as the likeness of the child is derived from its parents. Through the new birth we become children of Jesus Christ (Heb. 2:13) and thus inherit His image."[36] Thus the goal of God for His chosen sons is that they shall be conformed to and manifest something not merely like Christ but "what He is in Himself, both in His spiritual body and in His moral character."[37]

Interpreters differ on whether Paul had in mind "(a) *only* the *final* conformation; that is, only that part of transformation into Christ's image that will take place at his Return; or . . . to (b) the entire process of transformation, beginning already when the sinner is brought out of the darkness into the light."[38] If the reference is merely to the great eschatological change that will occur at the resurrection, then the first view is to be preferred. Thus Lenski holds that "Paul is pointing his readers from their sufferings to their comfort amid trials and to their assured hope, and this means their coming glory."[39] But in view of Paul's reference to Christ as "His Son" and His asserted uniqueness in that day, the moral element in the conformity cannot be overlooked. More than bodily conformity to Christ's image is involved. Dunn holds that "the implication of Paul's language here and elsewhere is of an image to be formed in Christians by process of transformation."[40] Since their conformity "to the likeness of His Son" was the goal of their predestination from eternity past, it is logical that this conformity involves not only their bodily transformation but also the moral transformation during the period before His return.

Clearly the bodily transformation of believers into the image of the risen Christ will be the glorious climax of their being "conformed to the image of His Son," but if only this is in view here then Paul passes over a fundamental aspect of redemption in Christ. In 2 Corinthians 3:18 Paul spoke of a present spiritual transformation of believers into the image of Christ through the work of the Spirit. This present transformation into the image of Christ is based on having the mind of Christ (Phil. 2:5–8) and is experienced in sharing the suffering of Christ in this life (3:10). Clearly both aspects of the believer's transformation into the image of Christ are included in the eschatological likeness to Christ portrayed in 1 John 3:2–3.

This blessed hope—that believers will be conformed to the image of His own Son—explains God's dealings with them as His chosen sons in this present age. He is ever at work to reproduce the moral image of Christ in them. All that now comes into their lives He uses for their good to further that glorious goal. His aim for them now is not to make them happy, materially prosperous, or famous, but to make them Christlike. He now uses "all things," the sad as well as the glad, the painful as well as the pleasant, the things that perplex and disappoint as well as the things they eagerly strive and pray for, to further His eternal purpose for them. In His infinite wisdom He knows what is needed to bring about that transformation. For some of His own He may need to use hotter fire and strike with harder blows than in His dealings with others to effect the formation of Christ's image in them. This may be because some believers may be more resistant to His molding activities or are more prone to insist on their own efforts.

When believers understand and accept the Father's loving purpose of developing Christlikeness in them as His beloved children, thus preparing them for that future day when the blessed

Savior will come again to take them home, then they can rejoice and thank Him for all He is doing in them. Christians may not now understand how all that comes into their lives works together for their good. Yet they can trust God's love and unreservedly entrust themselves to Him. As they increasingly experience the reality of this profound Christian assertion from the pen of Paul, they can gladly join in proclaiming its reality to others.

The closing statement in verse 29 adds the glorious truth that the ultimate aim in God's redemptive program is the preeminence of Jesus Christ as "the first-born among many brethren." The expression involves both His distinctiveness from and identity with the vast redeemed family of God.

In that coming day the presence of God's Son surrounded by "many brethren" conformed to His likeness declares their union with Him. He is the pattern for the entire family of sons, each conformed to His nature. The bodies of their humiliation will have been conformed to the body of His glory; all will manifestly be sons of the resurrection, either raised from the dead or instantly transformed into His likeness at His coming (1 Cor. 15:42–55). Spiritually made like Him, these "many brethren" will demonstrate God's redemptive purpose "to have a family of sons, beloved even as Christ is; and like Him in body, in spirit, in glory, in inheritance; dwelling as the Royal Family in the mansions Christ has gone before to prepare."[41]

But the reference to Christ as "the first-born" declares His abiding distinctness from all the other sons. They are conformed to His image; He is and remains distinct and unique as the Father's "first-born" (πρωτότοκον). This distinctive designation of Jesus Christ expresses His position of priority to and preeminence over all the other members of the family. In the Old Testament the term was used of the oldest son of his father; he was the object of special parental affection and inherited special rights; he was expected to further the welfare and concerns of the entire family. In the New Testament the term is five times applied to Christ in a spiritual sense to set forth His uniqueness as the eternal Son of God. Vine points out the chronological sequence of these references as follows:

> (a) Col. 1:15, where His eternal relationship with the Father is in view, and the clause means both that He was the Firstborn before all creation, and that He Himself produced creation . . . ; (b) Col. 1:18 and Rev. 1:5, in reference to His resurrection; (c) Rom. 8:29, His position in relationship to

the Church; (d) Heb. 1:6, R.V., His Second Advent (the R.V. "when He again bringeth in," puts "again" in the right place, the contrast to His First Advent, at His birth, being implied); cp. Ps. 89:27.[42]

In light of the marvelous statement of assurance in Romans 8:28–29, believers rejoice in knowing that all that God is now doing and will yet do in bringing many sons to glory will ever redound to the praise and honor of the blessed Lord and Savior Jesus Christ as the Firstborn of the Father. May this ringing message grip each believer's heart and mind, stimulate his devotion and service, and bring unceasing glory and honor to the matchless Savior and Lord!

CHAPTER 7

The End of the Law

Charles C. Ryrie

The discussion of the end of the Mosaic Law and the ramifications involved is one that usually bogs down in confusion. All interpreters of Scripture are faced with the clear teaching that the death of Christ brought an end to the Mosaic Law (Rom. 10:4) while at the same time recognizing that some of the commandments of that Law are restated clearly and without change in the New Testament epistles. To state the problem in the form of a question, How can the Law be ended if portions of it are repeated after it supposedly ended?

The Concept of the Law

Although the word "torah" was used quite widely in Judaism, it especially referred to the code that was given to Moses at Mount Sinai. The lives of outstanding rabbis were sometimes called "torah." The whole of the Old Testament was so designated, but particularly the Pentateuch was the Torah. This superiority of the Pentateuch was linked directly to the greatness of Moses (Num. 12:6–8; Deut. 34:10), though the rabbis were careful to point out that any difference was only in matters of detail not of principle.

The Law is generally divided into three parts—the moral, the ceremonial, and the judicial. The moral part is termed "the words of the covenant, the ten words" (Ex. 34:28), and from its Greek equivalent is derived the English "decalogue." The judgments begin at Exodus 21:2 and determine the rights between individuals with attendant judgments on offenders. The ceremonial part, which commences at Exodus 25:1, regulated Israel's worship.

Although this threefold division of the Law is quite popularly accepted in Christian theology, the Jews either did not acknowledge it or at least did not insist on it. They first counted all the particular precepts; then divided them into families of commandments. By this method they counted 613 total laws and 12 groups of commandments.

The numeral letters of torah denote six hundred and eleven of them; and the other two, which, as they say, are the first words of the decalogue, were delivered by God himself to the people, and so come not within the compass of the word Torah in that place: whence they take this important consideration, namely, Deut. xxxiii.4, "Moses commanded us the law," that is, of six hundred and eleven precepts; two being given by God himself, completes the number of six hundred and thirteen.[1]

These 613 individual laws were further divided into negative and positive commands, with 365 negative ones and 248 positive ones. This meant that there was one negative command for each day of the year, in order to keep individuals from temptation, and one command for each member of the human body to remind each person to obey God with his or her whole being.

In commenting on this, Schechter tries to minimize the actual numerical count in order to vitiate the Christian's use of this large number to emphasize the burden of the Law. He says that the numbers are relatively unimportant; this division into negative and positive commandments was largely homiletical—the need to beware of temptation and to obey God with one's entire body was what mattered, not the numbers.[2]

The 12 groupings of this Law corresponded to the number of the tribes of Israel. These were further subdivided into 12 families of affirmative commands and 12 negative commands. The affirmative families concerned (1) God and His worship, (2) the sanctuary and priesthood, (3) sacrifices, (4) cleanness and uncleanness, (5) alms and tithes, (6) things to be eaten, (7) Passover and other feasts, (8) rule and judgment, (9) truth and doctrines, (10) women and matrimony, (11) criminal judgments and punishments, and (12) judgments in civil causes. The negative families concerned (1) false worship, (2) separation from the heathen, (3) things sacred, (4) sacrifices and priests, (5) meats, (6) fields and harvests, (7) house of doctrines, (8) justice and judgment, (9) feasts, (10) chastity, affinity, and purity, (11) marriages, and (12) the kingdom. The total number of the commandments, which is far above the usual 10 the average person remembers when he thinks of the Law, and the intricate dividing of them, easily and effectively illuminates several New Testament passages that speak of the detail and burdens of the Law (cf. Heb. 9:1, 10; Acts 15:10; Eph. 2:15).

The fact that these specific laws were drawn from all parts of the Pentateuch emphasizes another important fact that must not be obscured by the dividing of the Law as did the Jews—and that fact is that the Law was also considered as a unit. Commandments from every part were equally important and binding on the lives of the Israelites.

This unified character of the Law is further seen by noticing the penalties that are attached to certain commands in each of the three categories of the Law—the commandments, judgments, and ordinances. One of the laws in the first division of commandments required the keeping of the Sabbath day. When a certain Israelite transgressed this command by gathering sticks on that day, the penalty was death by stoning (Num. 15:32–36). One of the precepts in the category of judgments concerned letting the land have its sabbatical year of rest. For 490 years Israel ignored that command, and God settled the account due His land by sending the people into Babylonian captivity, where many of them died (Jer. 25:11). In the third category one of the regulations concerned the proper way to worship. This was transgressed by Nadab and Abihu, who were punished with immediate death when they offered strange fire before the Lord (Lev. 10:1–7). In each of these three examples the punishment for disobedience involved death, even though the violation was of a different part of the Law. The commandments concerning the land or worship were no less binding, nor was the punishment less severe than the commandment to keep the Sabbath, which was one of the first 10. The Law was given as a unit.

James's use of the Law is based on this same concept of its unitary nature. When discussing partiality in the synagogues, James decried it on the basis that it contradicts the command to love one's neighbor as oneself (Lev. 19:18; James 2:8). The single violation, he wrote, makes them guilty of the whole Law (2:10). He could not make such a drastic statement if the Law were not considered as a unit. All this, of course, has a very important bearing on the doing away of the Law; for it seems to point to the fact that, unless the New Testament expressly says so, part of the Law cannot be ended without doing away with all of it.

Spiritual Evidence

The earliest specific declaration in New Testament times that the Law was ended came in the discussions of the Jerusalem Council. The question before the council was whether circumcision was necessary to salvation. After hearing the evidence from Peter and Paul that God was saving Gentiles apart from their keeping the Law and its ordinances, James declared emphatically that circumcision was not required for Gentiles to be saved (Acts 15:19). In testifying concerning the problem, Peter described the Law as "a yoke upon the neck of the disciples, which neither our fathers nor we were able to bear" (v. 10). The necessity of circumcision was not the only matter with which the Judaizers were troubling the Gentile coverts, for they were also trying to require them to keep the whole Law (v. 24). In the letters the council authorized to be sent to the churches, James stated that this was not obligatory for the Gentile converts (v. 24). He asked them to curb the exercise of their liberty in certain practices, but not on the basis that they were under the Law. Instead the basis was their love for their Jewish brethren and for the sake of the unity of the church. If there was ever a good opportunity to say that the Gentiles were under the Law, this was it, for that would have settled the matter simply and quickly. But the apostles, who were Jews themselves, recognized that the Law had no force any longer and so they did not try to impose it.

The council recognized what Paul stated later in his great doctrinal Epistle to the Romans, namely, that "Christ is the end of the law for righteousness to every one that believeth" (Rom. 10:4). This is the same theme Paul had preached earlier in the synagogue at Antioch in Pisidia on his first missionary journey, when he summarized his sermon by stating, "And by him all that believe are justified from all things, from which ye could not be justified by the law of Moses" (Acts 13:39). In these passages, as in others in the writings of Paul (Gal. 5:1; Rom. 3:21–22; 7:6), it is made clear that whatever the Law could or could not do came to an end with the work of Christ on the cross. Commenting on the specific phase, "the end of the law," Chafer concluded,

> Some see only that He, by His suffering and death, paid the penalty the law imposed and thus discharged the indictment against the sinner, which is comprehended in forgiveness. Others see that Christ fulfills the law by supplying the merit which the holy Creator demands, which is comprehended in justification. Doubtless both of these conceptions inhere in this passage; but it will be observed that whatever is done is done for those who believe—with no other requirement added—and that belief results in the bestowment of the righteousness of God.[3]

A passage in the writings of Paul is even more emphatic concerning the ending of the Law. In 2 Corinthians 3:7–11 Paul compared what is ministered through Moses with what is ministered through Christ. What Moses ministered is called a ministration of death and it is specifically said to have been written and engraved in stones. The only part of the Mosaic Law that was written in stones was the Ten Commandments—that category which some designate as the moral part of the Law. Thus this passage says that the Ten Commandments are a ministration of death; and furthermore the same passage declares in no uncertain terms that they are done away (v. 11). Language could not be clearer, and yet there are fewer truths of which it is harder to convince people. All kinds of exegetical maneuvering goes on in the attempt to make this passage say something else.

The writer to the Hebrews clearly stated that the Law has been superseded (Heb. 7:11–12). He affirmed that the priesthood of Melchizedek is greater than that of Aaron, and the proof he cited relates to tithing. Abraham gave a tithe of the spoils to Melchizedek, and since Levi—Abraham's great-grandson, out of whom came the Levitical priesthood—also paid tithes on that occasion in Abraham, the whole Levitical priesthood is seen as subordinate to Melchizedek. Then the writer concluded that if the Levitical priesthood could have brought perfection to the people, there would have been no need for the priesthood of Melchizedek. "For the priesthood being changed, there is made of necessity a change also of the law" (Heb. 7:12). Since Christ is the believers' High Priest, there has to have been a change in the Law, since He could not qualify as a priest under the Levitical priesthood. Therefore, since Christ is the believers' High Priest, they cannot be under the Law. Every prayer offered in the name of Christ is an affirmation of the end of the Law.

Thus the evidence of the New Testament leads to the conclusion that the Law—all of it, including the Ten Commandments—has been done away.

The Problem

However, the New Testament also includes in its ethic many of the specific commandments that were originally a part of the Mosaic Law. Since the Law has been done away in Christ, then why and on what basis are these Mosaic injunctions more binding on Christians? Are Christians under the Law (or at least certain of its commandments) or has it really been ended?

If the New Testament simply quoted the Ten Commandments, then the solution of the problem would be easy. One could conclude that the passages that teach that the Law has been done away with refer to all parts except the moral law. But the New Testament reiterates only nine of the ten commandments and it also quotes commands that are outside the moral part of the Law (Rom. 13:9; James 2:8). Thus the New Testament establishes no pattern whereby one may conclude that only the judicial and ceremonial parts of the Law were ended; and the problem remains. How can the entire Law be done away and parts of it be repeated in the New Testament epistles?

Some Solutions

One solution to the problem is simply to ignore it. The article on law in *Baker's Dictionary of Theology* does this. The writer states that Christians are reminded of "their duty in terms of the law. . . . The Christian is under the evangelical obligation of love and the written law becomes his guide, a rule of gratitude."[4] The writer says that the only aspect of the Law that ended was its condemning power. Second Corinthians 3:7–11 and Hebrews 7:11–12 are ignored in the discussion.

A more usual solution is that of Calvin, which is followed by many in the Reformed tradition. Calvin taught that the abrogation of the Law had reference to liberating the conscience from fear and to discontinuing the ancient Jewish ceremonies. He then distinguished between the moral law, which he said was abrogated only in its effect of condemning men, and the ceremonial law, which was abrogated both in effect and in its use. In discussing 2 Corinthians 3 he only distinguished the general differences of death and life in the old and new covenants.[5] He presented a fine exposition of the Ten Commandments, and it is interesting to note that in his discussion of the fourth commandment he did not consider Sunday as a continuation of the Jewish Sabbath (as the Westminster Confession did later).[6] Thus Calvin, as many who have followed him, considered part but not all of the Law as ended and the Ten Commandments as binding on the church today (although the fourth commandment concerning the Sabbath had to be interpreted nonliterally). This still does not solve the dilemma or relieve the tension between the Law as a unit being abolished and some commandments being retained.

The solution proposed in this chapter is basically one that distinguishes between a code and the commandments contained therein. The Mosaic Law was one of several codes of ethics God has given throughout history. That particular code contained, as noted, 613 specific commandments. But there have been other God-given codes. The laws under which Adam's life was governed combine to form what might be called a code for the Garden of Eden. There were at least two commandments in that code—dress the Garden and avoid eating the fruit of one tree. After the Flood, Noah was given commandments that included the permission to eat meat (Gen. 9:3). God revealed many commandments, statutes, and laws to Abraham that guided his life; together these may be called the Abrahamic code of conduct. The laws through Moses were codified formally and fearfully by being handed down from Mount Sinai. The New Testament speaks of the "law of Christ" (Gal. 6:2) and the "law of the Spirit of life" (Rom. 8:2). In the law of Christ are the hundreds of commandments of the New Testament epistles, and together these form a new and distinct code of ethics.

The Mosaic Law has been done away in its entirety as a code. God is no longer guiding the people's lives by this particular code. In its place He has introduced the law of Christ. Many of the individual commands within that law are new, but some are not. Some of the ones which are old were also found in the Mosaic Law and they are now incorporated into the law of Christ. As a part of the Mosaic Law they are completely and forever done away. As part of the law of Christ they are binding on believers today. There are also in the law of Christ commandments from pre-Mosaic codes, as, for instance, the permission to eat meat (1 Tim. 4:3). But the inclusion of this one, for example, does not mean that it is necessary to go through theological contortions in order to retain a part of the Mosaic code, so that that particular permission may be retained in this New Testament era. Likewise it is not necessary to resort to nonliteral exegesis of 2 Corinthians 3:7–11 or Hebrews 7:11–12 or the fourth commandment to understand that the code is ended and familiar commandments are included in the new code.

May this procedure not be likened to the various codes in a household with growing children? At different stages of maturity new codes are instituted, but some of the same commandments appear often. It is no contradiction to say that the former code is abolished but that a number of its commands are repeated in the New Testament. It is as natural as growing up. So it is with the Mosaic Law and the law of Christ.

CHAPTER 8

Presentation and Transformation: An Exposition of Romans 12:1–2

D. Edmond Hiebert

I urge you therefore, brethren, by the mercies of God, to present your bodies a living and holy sacrifice, acceptable to God, which is your spiritual service of worship. And do not be conformed to this world, but be transformed by the renewing of your mind, that you may prove what the will of God is, that which is good and acceptable and perfect" (Rom. 12:1–2).

These verses clearly mark the transition from the doctrinal to the practical emphasis in this matchless epistle. The first eleven chapters "fairly revel in the great mysteries of the plan of redemption. But when we come to chapter twelve the tide turns. Now it is the practical, the everyday."[1] It is a clear reminder that true Christianity involves both "believing" and "behaving" the gospel. The history of Christendom reveals the tragic results when the vital relationship between doctrine and conduct is lost. As Nygren well remarks, "A doctrine, a gospel, which has no significance for man's life and conduct is not a real gospel; and life and conduct which are not based on that which comes to us in the gospel are not Christian life and Christian conduct."[2] In a living Christianity, faith and conduct are inseparable.

This connection is indicated by the opening "Therefore" (οὖν[3]) in Romans 12:1. The doctrinal realities already unfolded form the foundation for the Christian life in all its aspects. Addressed to believers (1:6–7), Paul's order in this epistle clearly reveals the true relationship between doctrine and conduct (cf. Eph. 4:1; 1 Thess. 4:1). As Wuest asserts, "Doctrine must always precede exhortation since in doctrine the saint is shown his exalted position which makes the exhortation to a holy life, a reasonable one, and in doctrine, the saint is informed as to the resources of grace he possesses with which to obey the exhortations."[4]

The intended scope of the backward look conveyed by the word "therefore" has been understood differently. Knox asserts that "the passage begins without any connection with what precedes," and he views οὖν as "serving only to mark the transition, and not pointing back to any specific basis of the appeal in the earlier part of the letter."⁵ This particle may carry a transitional rather than an inferential force, but in view of the similar usage in Ephesians 4:1 and 1 Thessalonians 4:1 it is commonly accepted that οὖν here does have an inferential force, looking back to what has gone before. This seems clearly to be its meaning when used with the verb παρακαλέω ("to beseech, urge"; cf. 1 Cor. 4:16; Eph. 4:1; 1 Tim. 2:1).

Interpreters are not agreed, however, as to how far back this "therefore" reaches. Lange holds that the inference relates back directly to Romans 11:35–36, which "constitutes the organic apex of the entire doctrinal division."⁶ Cranfield recognizes that the terminology employed may suggest "that Paul is thinking only, or, at any rate, specially of chapters 9 to 11."⁷ He argues, however, that "it would seem intrinsically more probable that Paul thought of his exhortation as being based upon the whole of what he had so far written to the Roman Church," and he concludes that "the reference of οὖν is to the whole course of the epistle's argument up to this point."⁸ This inclusive scope of the inference seems most probable and is generally accepted. Paul's "therefore" reflects an inseparable connection between doctrine and conduct. "Doctrine is that which gives enforcement to duty; it is that which furnishes motive for service."⁹

The verb here rendered "I urge" (παρακαλῶ) is a favorite term with Paul (used about fifty times) and has been characterized as "one of the tenderest expressions in all the Bible."¹⁰ The compound verb, which basically means "to call alongside of," pictures someone calling another to his side and lovingly presenting his message to him. Depending on the content and purpose of the message, the verb may be rendered "appeal to, urge, exhort, entreat, or beseech." Thus instead of simply asserting his apostolic authority, Paul preferred to appeal to the inner consciousness of his readers. In writing to Philemon, Paul told him, "Therefore, though I have enough confidence in Christ to order you to do that which is proper, yet for love's sake I rather appeal to you" (Philem. 8–9). In thus presenting his message to his readers Paul avoided using external compulsion of an objective command and instead relied on their inner realization of the rightness of the appeal being made. Paul was well aware that "many are sooner wrought upon if they be accosted kindly, are more easily led than driven."[11] He knew that acceptable obedience to the appeals being made is always the grateful, voluntary response of the redeemed heart to the many mercies of God.

In saying, "I urge you" (παρακαλῶ   ὑμᾶς), Paul directly addressed the recipients of his appeal. In explicitly identifying them as "brothers" (ἀδελφοί) he gave expression to their inner identity as already members of the family of God. Because they were already believers and therefore members of God's family, Paul was prompted and encouraged to present this appeal to them. The appeal Paul made here is directly applicable only to those who by faith have personally received Jesus Christ as their Redeemer.

In Romans 12–15 Paul presented a number of spiritual directives involving varied aspects of his readers' lives as believers; but in 12:1–2 the appeal is personal and depicted the true foundation for the effectual attainment of the other duties that follow. These two verses, structurally forming one compound sentence, present a twofold plea. The first verse calls for an explicit act; the second commands a resultant lifelong process. These verses are a call for an act of presentation and the resultant duty of transformation.

The Appeal for Presentation

In verse 1 Paul mentioned the true motivating basis for the presentation, described the essential nature of such a presentation, and added a summary evaluation of the presentation.

THE MOTIVATION FOR THE PRESENTATION

Before stating his appeal, Paul held before his readers the fact of the many mercies of God that should prompt them to make the presentation he desired of them. The words "by the mercies of God" (διὰ τῶν οἰκτιρμῶν τοῦ θεοῦ) look back to the varied divine mercies Paul set forth in the first 11 chapters. The word οἰκτιρμός ("mercy"), always in the plural in the New Testament except in Colossians 3:12, basically denotes the reaction of pity or compassion for the ills of another. God's pity and compassion have found concrete expression in His redemptive actions. The articular designation τοῦ θεοῦ ("of God") stresses that the mercies in view are those of the very God Paul's readers had come to know through the gospel declared to them by God's messengers. McBeth identifies these mercies as those "expressed in the revelation of sin, the mercy of the atonement, justification, sonship, sanctification, union with Christ, life in the Spirit, the hope of Israel, and glorification."[12] When these redemptive mercies of God are known and personally accepted by the sinner through saving faith, they form a mighty motivating force, prompting the believer willingly to do what is being asked. This flood of mercies has its source in the tender heart of God and was not due to any merit on the part of the believers addressed. As Harrison remarks, "Whereas the heathen are prone to sacrifice in order to obtain mercy, biblical faith teaches that the divine mercy provides the basis for sacrifice as the fitting response."[13]

The divine mercies were given supreme expression in the life, death, and resurrection of Jesus Christ, the incarnate Son of God. In Him is embodied the abiding challenge to believers to present themselves unreservedly to Him.

One day a young Austrian nobleman strolled into a small church in a European village. As he loitered along the aisle, his attention was arrested by a painting of the crucified Christ hanging on the wall. The soul of the artist who painted the picture had been flooded with love for his Savior because He had redeemed him from a life of sin and folly. Underneath the picture of the Sufferer the artist had written the lines, "All this I did for *thee,* What hast thou done for *Me?*"

The young nobleman saw the love depicted in every feature of that divine face and was drawn to Jesus' bleeding brow and pierced hands. Having slowly viewed the varied aspects of the picture, his gaze rested on the couplet under the picture. A new revelation of the claim of Jesus Christ gripped his heart. Hours passed as the young nobleman gazed on the face of his suffering Savior. The lingering rays of the afternoon sun fell on the bowed form of Nicolaus Zinzendorf, weeping and sobbing out his devotion to the Christ whose love had not only saved his soul but also conquered his heart.

From that little church Zinzendorf went forth to become the leader of the mighty missionary activities of the Moravian church that have reached to the ends of the earth.[14] Theirs was the response that Paul's heart yearned for on the part of every believer, motivated by a gripping realization of the mercies of God.

THE CHARACTER OF THE PRESENTATION

With penetrating terseness Paul set forth the character of the presentation desired: "to present your bodies a living and holy sacrifice, acceptable to God." Young more literally renders the Greek, "to present your bodies a sacrifice—living, sanctified, acceptable to God."[15]

The compound infinitive παραστῆσαι ("to offer") basically means "to place or stand alongside of," hence to place at someone's disposal. While this verb was not used in the Septuagint in connection with offering sacrifices, in contemporary Greek the term was so used. Its use as a religious term denoting "to offer" would be readily understood by Paul's readers; hence the omission of "to God" is understandable as necessarily implied.

The aorist tense of the infinitive παραστῆσαι makes clear that Paul was thinking of a definite action on the part of the believer, an act directed by his will. With this sacrificial implication the aorist active infinitive denotes a deliberate action involving the thought of finality. A sacrifice laid on the altar could not later be retrieved; so the presentation here urged was to be made for life, not to be retracted later.

Paul explicitly identified the offering as τὰ σώματα ὑμῶν ("your bodies"). This expression seems most naturally to denote the readers' physical bodies as the agent through which their new life in Christ is to express itself. But various commentators prefer to interpret the words "your bodies" as equivalent to "yourselves." Thus Barnes argues that since a sacrifice was made in its entirety, "Paul evidently meant here the same as to say, present yourselves, your entire person."[16] After citing different instances of Paul's use of the word "body," Cranfield concludes that the term here does not have a limited connotation but means "yourselves." He quotes Calvin in support: "By bodies he means not only our skin and bones, but the totality of which we are composed."[17] Thus in his translation of the letters of Paul, Way gave the rendering, "bring your lives, and set them by the altar, as a sacrifice."[18]

However, in view of verse 2 such an inclusive meaning for "bodies" here seems questionable. Liddon appropriately notes, "That σώματα ὑμῶν means not 'yourselves,' but 'your *bodies*,' is clear from the antithesis of νοῦς ['mind'] in ver. 2."[19] After pleading for the presentation of the physical body in verse 1, Paul dealt in verse 2 with the transformation of the inner life. It seems that Paul's usage here is best understood in the light of what was said in 6:12–13: "Therefore do not let sin reign in your mortal body that you should obey its lusts, and do not go on presenting the members of your body to sin as instruments of unrighteousness; but present yourselves to God as those alive from the dead, and your members as instruments of righteousness to God." Christianity recognizes that the human body shared fully in the tragic impact that sin has brought on fallen humanity. But true Christianity does not therefore belittle the flesh and treat it with contempt and abuse. Rather, as the product of the creative activity of God, it is included in the redemptive program of God. Thus as Alford notes, Paul's appeal that their bodies be presented to God is "an indication that the sanctification of Christian life is to extend to that part of man's nature which is most completely under the bondage of sin."[20] In making his appeal Paul was concerned that "the same body through which sin once found its concrete expression now must be presented to God as the vehicle of righteousness (Rom. 6:19)."[21]

A body fully yielded to God is essential if believers are to make a spiritual impact on the world. Through their bodies they gain consciousness of the world around them and can communicate with it. Since the body is the vehicle that implements the desires and choices of the soul, the voluntary yielding of the body to God's control is essential for effective Christian living. Through sanctified bodies believers can render God-pleasing service.

Paul's appeal is that believers present their bodies as "a living and holy sacrifice, acceptable to God" (θυσίαν ζῶσαν εὐάρεστον ἁγίαν τῷ θεῷ). The New International Version renders the singular θυσίαν ("sacrifice") as plural to correspond to the plural "your bodies," but Paul's singular individualizes that thought, thereby stressing that each believer must personally acknowledge God's claim on his own body to be presented to Him as his own "sacrifice." The ritual terminology conveys the appeal "to devote themselves to God, as if they had no longer any claim on themselves; to be disposed of by him; to suffer and bear all that he might appoint; and to promote his honor in any way which he might command."[22] While believers may be prone to speak about "making sacrifices for the Lord"—an expression not found in the Bible—Paul's appeal goes vastly beyond such a view of Christian responsibility.

Paul added three adjectives to characterize the sacrifice in view; all three stand after the noun. English versions, by placing the first adjective before the noun, "a living sacrifice," tend to suggest to the reader that special emphasis is being placed on the sacrifice as "living," while the other two are added as an afterthought. But the original order suggests that all three aspects of this sacrifice should be kept together.

The first adjective, "living," used in connection with the familiar Old Testament term "sacrifice," recalls the story of those sacrifices. Yet it emphatically marks the contrast between the two kinds of sacrifices. All the animal sacrifices offered to God under the Law were dead sacrifices; the victims were all slain before they were placed on the altar to be offered to God. But now God desires "living" sacrifices. As Brown remarks, "The death of the one 'Lamb of God, taking away the sin of the world,' has swept all dead victims off the altar of God, to make room for the redeemed themselves as 'living sacrifices' to Him who 'made Him to be sin for us.' "[23] But the "living" in view here does not simply mean that believers are now to live for God as long as they remain alive in their old sin-stained body here on earth. Rather, their lives are to be lived under the impact of that "newness of life" (Rom. 6:4) which the Holy Spirit imparted to them in regeneration. Because of that new life, their bodies, yielded to Christ, are now living sacrifices and are destined to share in the blessed eternal life in the first resurrection (Phil. 3:20–21).

Having been offered to God as a living sacrifice, the believer's body is consequently to be characterized as "holy" (ἁγίαν). This adjective basically means "separated from" or "set apart." The Greeks used it of something separated from common usage and devoted to the service of their gods. In the New Testament the term carries a moral and spiritual significance, separated from the sphere of sin and devoted to God and His service. The believer must persistently recognize that he or she is no longer at liberty to use his or her body in sinful and unholy ways. The term stresses the ethical character of the believer's services and practices. "Since God is the sort of God He has revealed Himself to be, to belong to Him involves the obligation to strive to do and be what is in accordance with His character."[24] This call for holiness, which relates to the believer's body as well as his spirit, shows that this ethical character of the body and its functions must not be ignored. By way of application one can readily see that sexual vice in all its forms, so prevalent in Paul's day and the present, contradicts the criterion set forth here.

The third adjective declares God's assured response to the believer's offering his body to God: it is "acceptable to God" (εὐάρεστον τῷ θεῷ). This is the evaluation by God, whom believers have come to know through the gospel; this assurance is essential since no offering could have meaning or value that was not "pleasing" to Him. The compound adjective, made up of ἀρεστός ("acceptable, approved, satisfactory") and εὐ ("good, well"), "speaks of something which is well approved, eminently satisfactory, or extraordinarily pleasing."[25] God's assurance that the offering of the body would be highly pleasing to Him should be a further motive prompting believers to make the sacrifice. "That any creature should be able to offer what could 'please' the infinite Creator, is wonderful; but that such wretched, fallen ones as the sons of men should do so, is a marvel of which only the gracious God Himself knows the depth!"[26] Believers who may be able to offer to God only a body that has been deformed, mutilated, or limited, and/or heavily sin-stained, are yet assured that their presentation of their bodies will be "well-pleasing" to Him. But more than the physical condition of the body is involved. The Scriptures make it clear that no sacrifice was acceptable to God unless the motives and character of the sacrificer were also acceptable to God. The believer's presentation to God of his body "is acceptable to Him as the expression of giving God His true place, and of man, the believer, taking his."[27]

THE EVALUATION OF THE PRESENTATION

The added words, "which is your spiritual service of worship" (τὴν λογικὴν λατρείαν ὑμῶν), standing in apposition to the whole preceding clause, set forth the divine response to the believer's act of presentation. They indicate what makes this sacrifice well-pleasing to God. The pronoun "your" makes clear that God's evaluation relates not merely to their physical bodies but includes the whole person. He takes note of the inner volitional response made to the appeal for the surrender of their bodies to Him.

The exact force of these words is difficult to convey and English translations offer varied renderings.[28] The rendering "spiritual worship" suggests that the believer's conscious presentation of his body to God is accepted by Him as "spiritual" worship, in contrast to the ritual offerings of the dead bodies of irrational animals under the Mosaic Law. Thus Reapsome comments that a believer's action is "spiritual" "in the sense that it is the offering of his spirit, his will, his ego, the inner self where a person's real desires and motivations lie hidden from view."[29] The inner spiritual motive of the believer in presenting his body to God and His service imparts its own character to the offering made.

However, the word rendered "spiritual" is not the term usually rendered by the word "spiritual." The adjective λογικὴν occurs elsewhere in the New Testament only in 1 Peter 2:2, and does not occur in the Septuagint. It is the term from which the English word "logical" is derived. Accepting this import of the adjective, the meaning here is that the action in view is the rational and logical response to what God has already done in Christ. This is represented in the King James Version by the words "your reasonable service." Vine comments that "the presentation is to be in accordance with the spiritual intelligence of those who are new creatures in Christ and are mindful of 'the mercies of God.'"[30] McBeth points out that the definite article with the words here used "marks the sacrifice as the only logical service and as the only Christian service. Thus to present the bodies is logical and reasonable."[31] Such an action is consistent with a proper understanding of the matchless, love-prompted revelation in Jesus Christ. It is fully in accord with the spiritual intelligence of those who have become new creatures in Christ.

The noun λατρείαν ("worship") is associated with the sacrificial ministries of Israel under the Old Covenant as denoting its "temple worship" (Rom. 9:4; Heb. 9:1), the ritualistic services which the people attended. With their personal acceptance of the perfect sacrifice of Christ on Calvary, the believer's offering of his body to Christ is worship, an inner spiritual service rendered to God. Such a definite yielding of the body to God is a God-pleasing "religious service" enabling the believer to lead a life of acceptable service to God. A life of service through a consecrated body is the true sequel to its presentation to God as an act of worship. This offering of the believer's body as an act of spiritual worship does not preclude further participation in "worship services," but that participation should be continuous with the commitment that has been made.

The Duty of Transformation

Romans 12:2 begins with καὶ ("and"), not represented in the New International Version. This conjunction makes a logical sequence to the appeal made in verse 1. The call for presentation in verse 1 is foundational to this resultant duty of inner transformation. In setting forth this duty Paul stressed the hindrance to transformation, indicated the means of this transformation, and elaborated on the results of such a transformation. Verse 2 contains two significant grammatical changes from the forms used in verse 1. Instead of an infinitive ("to offer," v. 1), verse 2 has two finite verbs in the imperative. While some Greek manuscripts and early versions used infinitives to make verse 2 conform to verse 1,[32] it is now generally accepted that the textual evidence favors the imperatives.[33] Also of note is the change from the aorist tense "to offer" to the present tense in the two imperatives.

THE HINDRANCE TO THE TRANSFORMATION

In developing the duty of Christian transformation Paul first demanded that believers must recognize the powerful hindrance to transformation and must counter its force in their lives. It is emphatically stated as a negative command: "Do not conform any longer to the pattern of this world." As Murray remarks, "The Pauline ethic is negative because it is realistic; it takes account of the presence of sin."[34]

The negative (μὴ) with the present imperative (συσχηματίζεσθε) forbids the practice: "Don't be doing it." A believer's continued practice of world conformity is inconsistent with having given his body to the Lord and His service. Indeed, such a practice is forbidden because it negates and seriously mars the presentation the believer has made. In the New International Version the added words "any longer," not expressed in the original, make clear that their former world conformity must now cease.

The verb rendered "conform" (συσχηματίζω), which occurs elsewhere in the New Testament only in 1 Peter 1:14, as a compound verb seems to denote a conformity that is external and does not truly represent the believer's inner life. The noun σχῆμα, from which is derived the Greek verb and also the English word "scheme," denotes a pattern of life that does not come from within but is imposed from without. The verb conveys the thought of following a manner of life that is unstable and changing rather than enduring. Paul's prohibition is directed against a manner of life that does not come from nor is representative of what believers are in their inner being as the regenerated children of God. But Paul knew that adopting such a pattern of life inevitably mars the inner life.

The form of the verb may be either middle or passive. The passive is suggested in the King James Version, "be not conformed." This suggests that this form of life is being imposed from without. But the preposition σύν ("together with") in the compound form suggests personal involvement in the acceptance of the form. Clearly the world exerts strong pressure on believers to conform to it, but they are called on to resist that pressure. Phillips's well-known paraphrase is, "Don't let the world around you squeeze you into its own mold."[35] The present tense of the verb places on the readers the duty to resist this conformity all their lives.

The character of this persistent force is identified as "the pattern of this world" (τῷ αἰῶνι τούτῳ, literally, "to this age"). While the word "age" (αἰῶν) basically denotes a time period, in this verse "this age" clearly involves much that is associated with the term "world" (κόσμος), which most English versions use here.[36] Liddon well notes, "The Apostolic Christians spoke of the non-Christian world as αἰῶν οὗτος; the αἰῶν μέλλων ['the coming world'] being that which had become partaker in the Messianic Redemption. Thus the phrase lost its chronological significance, and acquired a purely moral or religious one."[37] It is the world of fallen humanity, characterized by sin, suffering, and estrangement from God. It is marked by self-will and self-seeking and is characterized by its disregard for or open rebellion against God's will. Its ruler is the devil (2 Cor. 4:4) and thus it is characterized by its antagonism to all that is distinctly Christian. Conformity to this world inevitably hinders and perverts the spiritual transformation which is the true goal of the Christian life.

THE NATURE OF THE TRANSFORMATION

In contrast to the negative duty not to conform to the world, the strong adversative particle ἀλλά ("but, on the contrary") marks the positive duty of Christian transformation: "but be transformed by the renewing of your mind."

The verb "transformed" (μεταμορφοῦσθε) denotes a change more inward and complete than the preceding verb. In the Gospels this verb is used of the transfigured body of Christ (Matt. 17:2; Mark 9:2). In Romans 12:2 and in 2 Corinthians 3:18 the verb is used of believers to denote their inner spiritual transformation. The Greek term is embodied in the English word "metamorphosis," which denotes, for example, the amazing change of a lowly worm into a beautiful butterfly. So the change in view here is not a superficial fluctuation of fashion or conduct but a vital change revealing a new life.

The present passive verb notes that this transformation is not a change produced by one's own efforts; it is the work of the indwelling Holy Spirit, as Paul noted in 2 Corinthians 3:18. And the present tense emphasizes that this transformation is progressively realized, not a single crisis experience. Further, the second person plural imperative "be transformed" indicates that believers have the volitional responsibility to maintain the conditions under which God brings about the transformation. Believers are not powerless puppets in their experience of God's work of sanctification; they eagerly desire and aim to promote it in complying with God's directives for Christian living.

The phrase "by the renewing of your mind" (τῇ ἀνακαινώσει τοῦ νοός) reveals that the believers' renewal works at the center of consciousness, a renewal that eventually makes the whole life new. The word "mind" "denotes, generally speaking, the seat of reflective consciousness, comprising the faculties of perception and understanding, and those of feeling, judging and determining."[38] The Holy Spirit works to transform the evil impact that sin has left on varied aspects of the human mind. The transformation being wrought on the inner life, the soul of the individual, will reveal itself through the body as the instrument of the soul. As Barnes observes, "Christianity seeks to reign in the soul; and having its seat there, the external conduct and habits will be regulated accordingly."[39] This inward transformation of the believer's life is the only effective preservative against outward conformity to this present age.

As a believer consciously recognizes his need for inner cleansing and the resultant renewal in daily conduct and as he yields to the promptings of the Spirit, he rejoices in the reality of God's inner work, producing the fruit of holiness in life. This inner transformation will increasingly express itself through his body in what he says and does, and approves or rejects.

THE RESULT OF THE TRANSFORMATION

Paul then wrote, "that you may prove what the will of God is." This statement points to the glorious result of the believer's inner transformation. The New International Version begins a new sentence here, but the Greek continues the sentence with εἰς and an articular infinitive (εἰς τὸ δοκιμάζειν ὑμᾶς τί τὸ θέλημα τοῦ θεοῦ). In this construction, as Harris notes, "Paul's point is not that the aim of the transformation of character is the discernment of God's will, but rather that the Christian's ability to ascertain God's will naturally results from the renewal of the mind."[40] The personal pronoun "you" (ὑμᾶς) naturally limits this ability to believers; unsaved individuals do not have this ability. The transformed believer is "to test and approve what God's will is." The verb "to test" (δοκιμάζειν) means "to put to the test for the purpose of approving, and finding that the thing tested meets the specifications laid down, to put one's approval upon it."[41] The New International Version indicates this anticipated result of the testing by the words "test and approve." The thought of approving that which is tested is indicated in the indirect question (τί τὸ θέλημα τοῦ θεοῦ, "what [is] the will of God." The present tense infinitive makes clear that this testing of what God's will is in any given situation or question must be an ongoing practice.

In every new situation a believer faces he or she must ask what God's will is. Each believer stands personally before God; he cannot leave to others the decision of what is God's will for him. With his fellow believers he confidently affirms that God's will is revealed to His followers through His inspired Word. But it may be quite another matter to discover what precisely is God's will for his own life in any specific situation. Yet the outworking of God's will for him in submitting himself to the leading of God will be in accord with what God has revealed as His will for His children. As a committed believer faithfully follows the leading of the Holy Spirit in the outworking of God's will for him individually, he comes to the devout realization that the unfolding of the divine will in relation to his life and to his ministry for the Lord is indeed "good, pleasing, and perfect."

In Paul's statement, τί τὸ θέλημα τοῦ θεοῦ, τὸ ἀγαθὸν καὶ εὐάρεστον καὶ τέλειον (literally, "what the will of God is, [what is] good, pleasing, and perfect"), the intended grammatical relationship of the three adjectives to the preceding word θέλημα has been understood in two ways. One view, reflected in the New International Version rendering—"what God's will is—his good, pleasing and perfect will"—accepts the three terms as adjectives further describing God's will. Similarly the King James Version rendering is, "what is that good, and acceptable, and perfect will of God."

Others, like Bengel, hold that "these adjectives are not epithets of the will of God, but abstract neuters."[42] Lenski says that "these adjectives are substantivized, are treated as a unit (one article), and form an apposition."[43] Then these three terms describe the nature of the things the believer encounters as he follows God's will. This view is reflected in the marginal rendering in the American Standard Version: "the will of God, even the thing which is good and acceptable and perfect." *The Twentieth Century New Testament* translates the clause, "discern what God's will is—all that is good, acceptable, and perfect." The Amplified Bible characteristically combines both: "so that you may prove [for yourselves] what is the good and acceptable and perfect will of God, even the thing which is good and acceptable and perfect [in His sight for you]."

While it is possible to interpret Paul's words either way, the former rendering seems the more probable. The center of thought here is the will of God. As Ziesler explains, "the Greek syntax is better understood as conveying that the believer comes to discern what the will of God is, namely, that it is good and acceptable and perfect."[44] Fully in accord with God's will as revealed in His Word, the "will of God" here clearly denotes His active will for each of His redeemed children. His will relates to all phases of a believer's life.

The adjective "the good" (τὸ ἀγαθὸν) indicates that the will of God for the individual believer is morally good and beneficial in its nature and its impact on his life. What God wills for His saints is intrinsically consistent with His own nature (Mark 10:18; Luke 18:19).

The second adjective, used previously to describe the believer's sacrifices, now characterizes God's will for His saints as "pleasing" (εὐάρεστον, "well-pleasing, acceptable"). Haldane well remarks,

> That which the Lord enjoins is acceptable to Him, and surely this is the strongest motive to practice it. Nothing else is acceptable to Him, however er specious it may appear to human wisdom. All injunctions that proceed merely from men in Divine things are unacceptable to God. He approves of nothing but obedience to His own commandments.[45]

What is acceptable and pleasing to God the transformed mind of the believer also finds acceptable and pleasing. "Dedication leads to discernment and discernment to delight in God's will."[46] To the unsaved mind the assertion that God's will is "well pleasing" appears to be an arbitrary, unfounded fancy.

The third adjective affirms that God's will for the believer is "perfect" (τέλειον) or complete, lacking nothing. It does not overlook or ignore any matter or area in the believer's life that might plunge him into sin and destruction. The will of God, the transcription of His own perfection, now is concerned with all the experiences of the believer (Rom. 8:28–29) and will attain its full realization for him when he will ultimately be transformed into the image of Christ (1 Thess. 5:23; 1 John 3:2). Then His perfect will for His saints will have attained its ultimate perfection. "This is a miracle of transformation, a readjustment to both temporal and eternal realities."[47]

This twofold challenge to believers in Christ is foundational to all Christian living. Their voluntary, love-prompted acceptance of the divine call to presentation and transformation results in the progressive renewal of their minds, enabling them to discern what is God's will for them and to commit themselves to personal obedience to God's good, pleasing, and perfect will, viewed in the light of God's blessed purpose for them in time and eternity.

CHAPTER 9

Should Women
Wear Headcoverings?

Kenneth T. Wilson

First Corinthians 11:2–16 is among the most challenging passages in the Bible. Key words and the thrust of the passage lend themselves to numerous, often conflicting opinions. Because of the controversial and difficult nature of this section, any interpretation must be held with a certain degree of caution.

The Structure of 1 Corinthians 11:2–16

This passage is composed of three major units. In the first (11:2–6) and third (11:13–15) units Paul presented reasons for proper decorum in public worship. In the second unit (11:7–12) he discussed male-female functional distinctives within the framework of essential equality as a part of God's created order. An opening statement (v. 2) and concluding exhortation (v. 16) round out the passage.

Paul clearly appealed to cultural issues in the first and third units, where the explicit statement is made that women should cover their heads. The issues are the shame associated with an uncovered head (vv. 4–6) and the teaching of "nature" (vv. 13–16). Yet in the middle section, where he appealed to noncultural issues (vv. 7–12), he avoided calling for women to cover their heads. Instead he asked that they have "authority" on their heads, though this breaks the parallel structure maintained in the other sections.

Comments on 1 Corinthians 11:2–16

In 7:1–11:1 Paul answered questions concerning the church's moral life, and then in 11:2–34 he addressed problems pertaining to the worship of the church. He then discussed spiritual gifts (chaps. 12–14) and the resurrection (chap. 15).

AN EXPRESSION OF GOODWILL (11:2)

Paul introduced a new section in verse 2 with the use of δέ ("now").¹ Does this section continue Paul's replies to the Corinthians' questions, which began in 7:1, or was Paul now dealing with things that had either been reported to him or that he felt were important?² Perhaps he was referring to their letter by means of a quotation in this section,³ and then he moved on to clarify their concern as he had done in 8:1. In any case, the discussion of worship and the Lord's Supper in chapter 10 would certainly have brought further issues of public worship to mind, and the discussion of practices at the Lord's Supper fits well in the flow of the argument at this point, providing a smooth transition to the use of spiritual gifts in worship services in chapters 12–14.

After Paul encouraged the Corinthians to be imitators of him (11:1), he praised their conduct because they remembered him (v. 2). This unexpected commendation of the Corinthians has raised questions about Paul's purpose here. This could be the typical Pauline pattern of beginning a difficult section with encouragement (cf. 1:1–9). Some have supposed that Paul was being sarcastic, as he was earlier in 4:8.⁴ Others feel that Paul may be quoting something the Corinthians wrote in their letter. It seems best to take this as a true commendation, in view of the literary device whereby Paul introduced a section with praise when possible and then gave a needed rebuke and correction.⁵

The nature of this commendation is twofold. First, the Corinthians' remembrance of Paul is commended (v. 2a). Second, their remembrance was evident in that they held "firmly to the traditions" (τὰς παραδόσεις κατέχετε). To "hold firmly" is to observe something faithfully.⁶ Παραδόσεις probably does not refer to mere "traditions" that have no authority in the church, since Paul mentioned them as ones he had conveyed. Some writers feel that the traditions were all the teachings Paul had given the Corinthians, either while he was at Corinth (Acts 18:1–17) or in the letter referred to in 1 Corinthians 5:9 that has not survived.⁷ Godet feels these traditions are only the ecclesiastical traditions of the church without reference to doctrine.⁸ Yet Paul used this word (παράδοσις) with reference to his oral teachings as well as his letters, which contained both practice and doctrine (cf. 2 Thess. 2:15). Παράδοσις is literally "a handing down"⁹ and this can mean either teachings handed down from an apostle or from

Christ. Whatever the case, these are authoritative teachings and Paul commended the Corinthians for obeying them. With the positive foundation set by this commendation Paul then rebuked the Corinthians for violations in their worship (11:2–14:40).

A REFLECTION OF GOD'S CREATIVE DESIGN MANDATED (11:3–16)

Some have suggested that the question of headcoverings in the church was not an important issue with Paul.[10] Yet his tone reveals otherwise. That the Corinthians needed strong exhortation in this area is seen in the asyndeton (lack of connectives) in verses 13–15. By the use of asyndeton "the point of the sentence . . . is heightened by the brevity of the components."[11] The importance of the issue is also shown by Paul's extended discussion and numerous reasons for maintaining proper practice in the use of headcoverings.

An argument from design and disgrace (11:3–6). This section begins with a contrastive δέ ("but" or "now"), which shows that this was something about which the apostle could not praise the Corinthians.[12] Paul wanted them to know the principle of headship. A hierarchical structure exists in the universe.[13] This structure begins with God and moves downward to Christ who is over man, who in turn is over woman (v. 3). This doctrine of headship is foundational to the entire passage. This is in keeping with Paul's practice of affirming a theological principle as the basis for Christian behavior. The rejection of this doctrine is what led the Corinthian women to throw off the customary symbol of this order.

The order in which the examples of hierarchical relationship appear—Christ-man; man-woman; God-Christ—places the relationship under discussion in the middle for emphasis. This may also have been an intentional ordering to avoid placing woman at the bottom of the list (as also in vv. 12–13).

The word "head" (κεφαλή) used to describe the relationship between the members of the structure, has posed numerous problems. The term can refer to the source of something, similar to the "headwaters" of a river. It may also refer to the authority of one person over another. Some see in the term a reference to both source and subordination to authority.[14]

Those who understand headship in this passage as a reference to source alone appeal to the discussion of man being the source

of woman in creation (v. 8). This is a strong argument.[15] The
grounds for taking it instead as a reference to subordination to
authority with no reference to origination or source center on the
fact that God is said to be the "head" (κεφαλή) of Christ (v. 3). A
case is then made for God being the authoritative Head of Christ
and not His Source. It is also pointed out that to say that Christ
originated in God is to be guilty of the heresy of Arianism.[16]

Two points should be made in defense of the view that κεφαλή
refers to source as well as authority. First, Paul seemingly picked
up both meanings of κεφαλή in the following verses. Verses 3–6
deal with subordination to authority and verses 7–12 deal with
source. Second, Paul used the term elsewhere to refer to both
subordination (Col. 2:10) and origination (2:19). In response to
the Arian charge, one should note that though Paul taught that
Christ is subordinate to the Father in His sonship (1 Cor. 3:23;
15:28), Paul was not teaching that Christ originated from God.
Nor did John teach this when he affirmed that Christ was "the
only begotten from the Father" (John 1:14).[17] Here Paul was
showing the order of God in relation to both origination and
subordination.[18]

Paul then made two claims that relate to the covering of men
and women. His first assertion deals with the men of the church.
Paul asserted that "every man who has something on his head
while praying or prophesying disgraces his head" (1 Cor. 11:4).
There is some ambiguity regarding what was on their heads. A
literal translation reads, "having down from the head" (κατὰ
κεφαλῆς ἔχων). What is down the head? This may be the man's
hair, which would mean that the man should not have long hair.
But this does not make sense in the context, which demands that
what is down the head is a covering. This meaning can be seen in
the context, for clearly this is parallel to the headcovering of the
woman (v. 5). Therefore this verse is claiming that a man is not to
have a covering on his head when he prays and prophecies.

The reason men were not to wear a headcovering is related to
the principle of headship Paul had just established—a man would
thereby disgrace his head (v. 4). The question is whether this is a
disgrace of the literal head or of the One who is head over the man
(i.e., Christ). Those who think this is a reference to a man's head
see the connection between "head" (κεφαλή) in the first part of this
verse and its use here.[19] Those who say this is a reference to the
hierarchical head, Christ, appeal to the use of κεφαλή in verse 3.[20]

It seems preferable to see here a reference to both the hierarchical and the literal head. "Head" is a key word in this passage and the difficulty in determining the meaning seems to be that Paul had both in mind. Therefore the man who prays with his head covered dishonors Christ and himself. The reference to the literal head names the part for the whole. If the head is dishonored, so is the entire person.

The custom for women in New Testament times was to cover their heads. Not to do so was to ignore the distinction between male and female. It would also seem that headcoverings (perhaps something like a modern-day shawl) showed submission to a visible authority.[21]

Paul next described what the women's practice of headcoverings ought to be in light of the principle of headship (vv. 5–6). The extent to which Paul emphasized women in this passage seems to indicate that his reference to men was simply to point out the contrast and that the women were in violation of his instruction.[22]

Though there is much dispute about the practice of headcoverings in Corinthians, two things are clear: (a) men did not wear them and women did, and (b) the headcovering was a sign of distinction between men and women.[23] Talbert concludes that "where the covering was worn, it appears to have been a social symbol attesting one's femaleness."[24] Lowery summarizes the issue well: "It cannot be unequivocally asserted, but the preponderance of evidence points toward the public covering of women as a universal custom in the first century in both Jewish culture and Greco-Roman."[25] This is also supported by Paul's appeal to nature.

These headcoverings were in the form of hoods pulled up from a shawl, rather than facial coverings.[26] It seems that the Corinthian women had abandoned headcoverings in worship because of misunderstanding the equality of all who are "in Christ."[27] Paul had taught elsewhere, and likely also at Corinth, that in Christ "there is neither male nor female" (Gal. 3:28). This may have caused the Corinthian women to conclude that, like the angels, they need not concern themselves with male-female distinctions. Paul countered this by showing women their need to wear headcoverings, thereby maintaining the sign of distinction between men and women. Their redemption did not override the creative order.[28]

Paul wrote that "every woman who has her head uncovered . . .

disgraces her head" (v. 5). If the woman does not have a headcovering,[29] she dishonors her "head" (κεφαλή). As in the case of the men (v. 4), the word "head" refers to both the literal and the hierarchical head. She dishonors her hierarchical head, for she is claiming to be equal to him rather than distinct from him.[30] "Head" (κεφαλή) is again being used as a part for the whole. Hence the woman was bringing dishonor to herself.

Verse 6 contains the first class condition of εἰ followed by the indicative mood (εἰ . . . αἰσκρὸν),[31] translated literally, "If it is a disgrace for a woman . . . and it is, then. . . ." The point is that it was indeed a disgrace for the woman to have her head uncovered. Examples of this disgrace ranged from temple prostitutes whose heads were uncovered to women who were found to be adulteresses.[32] In that culture not wearing a headcovering was an act of shame.

Paul then argued that if a woman abandoned her headcovering, she might as well "have her hair cut off" (καὶ κειράσθω, v. 6). Wallace identifies "cut off" as a permissive middle, which would mean if a woman willfully refused to wear a headcovering, then she should willingly submit to having her hair cut.[33] For her to do this, however, would be to place herself among the dishonored. Therefore since she would not be willing to be dishonored in that way, she should wear the headcovering and not act as if she were dishonored.

Who is the "woman" (γυνή) in verses 5–6? Some say she is a woman who is married to the man referred to in verse 4. Others see this as a reference to all women in their relationship to men in the meetings of the church.[34] The best alternative seems to be that this is a reference to all women because (a) marriage is not mentioned in this passage, (b) the principles seem to illustrate the fact that men in general are the head of women in general, and (c) the issue involves male-female distinctiveness.

Paul next dealt with the question of when this headcovering of women was to be done. The problem is in the use of the words "while praying or prophesying" (v. 5). If these words were applied only to the men mentioned in verse 4, then the occasion would be the meetings of the church. But Paul used the words in reference to women. If this was a reference to church meetings, Paul appears to have contradicted himself when he wrote in 14:34–35 that women should be silent in the church. This problem has been solved in a number of ways. (1) Some believe the meeting in 11:5

is not a meeting of the congregation. This is supported by the fact that the phrase "because you come together" does not appear until verse 17. (2) Another view is that 14:34–35 refers to "speaking in ecstatic language."[35] These writers refer to Paul's usage of the words in chapter 14. (3) Others think Paul was restricting actions that he would later forbid.[36] (4) Another solution is that Paul forbade women to teach men, as stated in 1 Timothy 2:11–15. (5) Many believe that Paul was here giving a true exception to the general rule that was set forth later. That is to say, women are allowed to speak only (a) when their heads are covered and (b) when they are prompted by the Holy Spirit to speak.

Most likely Paul had in mind the meeting of the gathered church in light of the broader context in which worship and the Lord's Supper were discussed in chapter 10. The mention of the practices of the church in 11:16 is further support that this is the gathered church. How then can this be harmonized with Paul's call in 14:34–35 for the women to be silent? The solution seems to be that in 14:34–35 Paul was regulating the participation of the women in church in evaluating the prophets.[37] Women were not to participate in this evaluation as the men did, but were to ask questions of their husbands at home. Support for this is in the structure of 1 Corinthians 14:26–35. The context deals with the regulations surrounding the exercise of the two spiritual gifts being addressed in that passage, including tongues-speaking in verses 27–28 and prophecy in verses 29–35.[38]

According to this view, women could pray and prophesy in the church meetings so long as they were wearing their headcoverings. They were not to participate in any evaluation of other prophets. This view seems to fit perfectly with Paul's other instruction that women are not to exercise authority over men, because evaluation of their prophesying would certainly be an exercise of authority.

Christian women in Corinth were allowed to pray, but they were not allowed to teach or exercise authority over men (1 Tim. 2:12).[39] They could also prophesy (1 Cor. 11:5), but the meaning of this is debated. It may mean the delivering of revelation from God, which today would limit them to the public reading of Scripture. It may also refer to delivering a message given spontaneously in response to God's leading.[40] Whatever the meaning, they were permitted to do so, so long as it was not teaching or exercising authority over men and so long as their heads were covered.

An argument from creation (11:7–12). Paul began this section by stating, "For a man ought not to have his head covered" (v. 7a). The word "ought" (ὀφείλει) is used in the sense of an obligation. Some controversy surrounds the exact translation of οὐκ ὀφείλει. Did Paul mean a man "is not obligated,"[41] or was he saying the man "ought not"?[42] It is better to view this as a command, because as Paul did not leave women a choice, so it is not likely that he was giving men liberty to do as they pleased.

Why was the man obligated not to cover his head? The answer, as Paul said, is that man "is the image and glory of God" (v. 7b). What did Paul mean by these words? Genesis 1:26 states that man was created in the "image" and "likeness" of God. It should be noted that the Old Testament applies these terms to the woman as well as the man (Gen. 1:27), which means that the woman is also made in God's image. But Paul's point is found in the use of "glory" (δόξα), also used to describe the woman's relationship to man. "Image" in 1 Corinthians 11:7 indicates a reflection.[43] So for a man to cover the reflection of God in a service in which he is praying to Him or delivering a prophetic word from Him would be inconsistent. To cover the reflection of what one is worshiping is counterproductive.

When Paul used the word "glory," he was not alluding to a specific Old Testament verse as he had done in the case of "image." Rather he was summarizing what the Old Testament teaches. Paul used the participle "being" (ὑπάρχων) with reference to the man, rather than the verb "is" (ἐστιν) which he used to describe the relationship of the woman to the man. Though the reflections are similar, they are not identical. Some conclude that the terms "image" and "glory" are practically synonymous.[44] Since Paul used the term "glory" and not the synonym "likeness," he may be suggesting some other meaning for "glory." Hurley points to Paul's use of "glory" in 15:40–41 in which he refers to the honor of the celestial bodies.[45]

"In Greek thought an 'image' gives tangible, perceptive expression and substance to that which is invisible."[46] Thus man gives or reflects the glory of God.[47] In some manner this glory is resident or reflected from the head of the man and should not be covered.

Paul next showed that headcoverings must be worn because of the order of God's creation: "but the woman is the glory of man" (11:7c). What did this mean? The thought may be as Findlay notes, "But the woman (ought to have her head veiled, for she) is the glory of man."[48] Another option, presented by Fee, argues that the other side of the formula is intentionally left until verse 10, where Paul used the term "ought" in reference to women.[49] This latter understanding fits well and is displayed in the following layout by Fee.

A   Man   ought not to have his head covered,
  B   since he   is the image and   glory of God;
        on the other hand
  B' Woman is man's   glory
        for this reason
A'   She   ought to have authority on her head because
        of the angels.[50]

In parallel thought to verse 7b, Paul claimed that in some way "the woman is the glory of man" (v. 7c). The reason for this is given in verses 8–9.[51] These verses show that the sequence of creation demonstrates how woman brings glory to man—she comes from him and completes him. Paul's use of prepositions in verses 8–9 is crucial. He claimed that the woman is "out of" (ἐξ; NASB, "from") man and not vice versa. This is an obvious reference to the original creation of the first woman, in which she was formed from the rib of the man (Gen. 2:22–23). Therefore, as Paul wrote, woman brings man glory, for she was actually created "out of" his body.

A second reason the woman is the glory of the man is that she was created "for the man's sake" (διὰ τὸν ἄνδρα, v. 9). The translation of διὰ varies. Ellicott has "because of the man."[52] Others translate, "on account of the man."[53] Grosheide calls this the purpose for which Eve was created.[54] The reference is to Genesis 2:18, where God recognized that the man needed a companion who would complete him,[55] and so He created Eve. Thus since woman was created because of man's need for a companion, she brings him glory.

In 1 Corinthians 11:10 Paul gave an imperative for the woman. As the man was to have his head uncovered "therefore the woman ought to have . . . authority on her head, because of the angels." This statement has two closely related problems: (1) What is the meaning of "authority" (ἐξουσία)? (2) What is the meaning of "because of the angels" (διὰ τοὺς ἀγγέλους)?

Does the word "therefore" (διὰ τοῦτο) point backward toward

the discussion of the order of creation,[56] or does it point forward, simply giving another reason for the woman's headcovering?[57] The fact that Paul in the following verse clarified the order of creation and its significance suggests that he did not break his thought and then return to it. Instead, since the reference to the angels is closely related to the discussion of the order of creation, the word "therefore" points backward to the reason Paul expressed in the preceding verses and also forward[58] to the reason presented in the following verses.

"Authority" (ἐξουσία) was a key word for the Corinthians (8:9; cf. 9:4–6, 12, 18). There are several possible meanings for it: (a) freedom of choice, right to do as one wishes, (b) ability to do something, (c) authority to do something, or (d) power exercised by rulers. The question here is whether the "authority" is the woman's or the man's. Those who feel that ἐξουσία is a metonymy for the headcovering, or that this is a "sign of the authority" of the man over the woman, point to the meaning of the headcovering in the culture of that day.[59] Yet that does not explain why Paul used "authority" instead of "headcovering" or "sign of subjection." The fact that Paul did not refer specifically to the headcovering here indicates that the issue is not the exact use of the headcovering but the larger issue of the disregard of distinctions. This clearly shows that cultural conditioning is present in the passage.

Thus it seems appropriate to understand "authority" here to refer to the woman's freedom or authority and not the man's. Specifically it is her authority to participate in the worship of the church. In the synagogue women were not allowed to speak, but now in Christ they have freedom or authority[60] to speak in worship.[61] Thus the woman should wear a sign of her authority in order to allow her to have the freedom and authority to pray and prophesy in the presence of the man who is "head" over her. "The sign of authority refers to the head covering which serves as a social symbol of the woman's femaleness. . . . Paul's point is that wearing the veil means acceptance of one's created sexuality."[62]

Placing the symbol of authority on the head was a cultural practice. The fact that the symbol was worn on the head also allowed Paul to pursue a word play on the word "head," as noted earlier. The use of "on the head" therefore does not demand that a symbol on the head be retained today, but only that the symbol in that day was to be on the head.

At least five options have been suggested for the meaning of "because of the angels" (διὰ τοὺς ἀγγέλους). (a) Because the ministers of the church may be tempted by the beauty of the women to lust, they should cover their heads.[63] (b) Because evil angels may lust after women, their heads should be covered.[64] (c) Good angels may be tempted to lust.[65] (d) Since angels are guardians of the created order, to violate that order explained in the preceding verse would offend the angels.[66] (e) Since the angels are present in worship, women should conduct themselves properly so as not to offend them.[67]

The first option (the temptation of ministers) should be rejected in light of the findings of Hurley concerning the type of headcoverings as well as the consistent use of ἀγγέλους in Corinthians to describe angelic beings, not earthly messengers. Hurley concludes that because a full facial veiling was not in practice, the headcovering would not prevent the ministers from lust.[68] The second and third options are also to be ruled out because evil angels would not be the normal meaning of ἀγγέλους with the article.[69] It is also unlikely that elect angels would lust after women, for nowhere else in Scripture are they pictured as doing this.

The last two explanations are the only likely options. Of these the first has a few problems. Waltke cites Moffatt as basing this interpretation on the midrash of Genesis 1:26–27.[70] However, Genesis 1:26–27 does not refer to the presence of angels in creation at all. Rather the midrash was a Jewish misunderstanding of the plural form used for God in the beginning chapters of Genesis. If this view is accepted on the basis of Paul's understanding of the midrash, then he was basing his argument on something that was not true. This is incompatible with a high view of Scripture. This leads to the conclusion that the last view best accords with the evidence. Angels are presented elsewhere as spectators of the affairs of humans (1 Cor. 4:9; Eph. 3:10; 1 Tim. 3:16). Thus the meaning is, "If a woman thinks lightly of shocking men, she must remember that she is also shocking the angels, who of course are present at public worship."[71] The angels would be shocked not because they are the guardians of creation, but simply because they have knowledge of the order of creation and what it involves (Job 38:7).

The reference to angels takes on new meaning in light of the Corinthians' apparent feeling that they had arrived at an angelic status.[72] Paul mentioned angels a number of times in 1 Corinthians (4:9; 6:3; 11:10; 13:1).

In 11:11–12 Paul paused to clarify the statement he had just made about the order of creation and its significance.[73] The idea of clarification is introduced in verse 11 by the adversative "However" (πλὴν). He had used the prepositions ἐκ and διά in dealing with the source of the woman in reference to original creation (vv. 8–9). In verses 11–12 he again used important prepositions in underscoring the equality of men and women in Christianity. In verse 11 Paul stated that men and women are not "independent" (χωρὶς) of each other, and in verse 12 he affirmed that man and woman each depend on the other. Woman "originates from [ἐκ] the man," a clear reference to verse 8 and to Genesis 2:21. Also the man is said to be "through [διά] the woman," a reference to his birth through her. As in Genesis 2, man and woman complete and need each other. They are equal in light of the fact that both depend on God, for they "originate from God" (v. 12b). The equality of believing men and women "in the Lord" (v. 11) is illustrated in the birth of the man through the woman and the creation of the woman out of the man.[74]

The dependence of both sexes on each other and their common dependence on God shows in the natural world what is true in the spiritual world—men and women are equal. This does not in any way discard the command for them to recognize male headship. Headship deals with *functional subordination*, not with equality. This is clear in light of the headship ascribed to God the Father in relation to the Son in verse 3. Paul's instruction, then, was to maintain the practice that recognizes that though male and female are dependent on each other, in God's plan they are distinct.

Paul supported his instruction by two lines of reasoning—the principle of headship and the order of creation. Both principles show that women should wear their headcoverings in public worship and that men should not have their heads covered. Returning in verses 13–15 to his main point, Paul discussed another reason why headcoverings should be worn by the women.

An argument from nature (11:13–15). In these verses Paul reached the climax of his argument. Grammatically it is noteworthy that the apostle here used a figure of speech called asyndeton. Bullinger describes asyndeton as "without any conjunctions."[75] This figure has an emphatic use. "The resolution of a sentence into unconnected components produces a more powerful effect than would a more periodic form proper. The point of the sentence moreover is heightened by the brevity of the components."[76] In verses 7–12 Paul used the "periodic form" by using numerous coordinating conjunctions (γάρ, δέ, πλήν, διὰ τοῦτο, and ὥσπερ). The shift in verses 13–15 is evident because connectives are few, and generally the ones used connect parts within the sentence rather than the sentences themselves.

Paul called on the Corinthians to "judge for yourselves" (v. 13), that is, to take note of what he was about to say. "For yourselves" (ἐν ὑμῖν) can mean either a decision reached by the church, without reference to outsiders, or it may refer to a decision reached within oneself.[77] Since Paul appealed to the teaching of "nature" (v. 14), it would seem that the appeal here is to individuals, not the church as a whole.

Paul raised questions the Corinthians should be able to answer without any help from him. The first deals with the matter at hand, that is, headcoverings. In light of the reason he put forth at this point, the Corinthians should decide that it was not proper for a woman to pray with her head uncovered (v. 13). The meaning of "proper" (πρέπον) is general, what is known to be right and appropriate.[78] From what they now knew, they should see that women worshiping without a headcovering was not appropriate. This appeal to a sense of propriety is another indication that at least some cultural conditioning is present in the passage.

As added support Paul wrote of the teaching of "nature" (v. 14), which would serve as a final catalyst in the Corinthian believers' decision. Two related questions—one pertaining to the length of men's hair, and the other to women's hair—call for a positive answer.[79] Findlay calls "nature" (φύσις) "a constitutional feeling,"[80] while Grosheide calls it "the general notion which all people have by virtue of their being human beings."[81] Godet on the other hand feels that "nature" refers to the physical organization of women,[82] a view that lacks evidence. The claim that men's hair does not grow as long as women's hair, even if true (and it is not), would not have been known by the Corinthians in the first century.

Grosheide's view of "nature" as that which all have as human beings is inadequate, since not all felt that long hair was a shame, even in the ancient world.[83] So, it is preferable to take the meaning of Bauer's first reading, that which is "inherited fr[om] one's ancestors."[84] Fee gives this sense when he writes, "By 'nature' Paul meant the natural feelings of their contemporary culture."[85] Their culture taught that as a general rule, men have short hair and women have long hair. This is seen in Paul's vow, which indicates that it was unusual for men to have long hair (Acts 18:18). Thus people at that time understood that "if a man has long hair, it is a dishonor to him" (v. 14). Robertson and Plummer attest that "at this period, civilized men, whether Jews, Greek, or Romans wore their hair short."[86] This again points to Paul's grounding in the culture of his day in making this special appeal about covering or not covering one's head.

The second question pertained to the length of women's hair (v. 15). The question here is how the hair of the woman is "glory" (δόξα) for her. Some interpret glory as meaning "pride."[87] This seems to be the sense of the passage so long as one does not suggest any negative connotations. Why is a woman's hair her glory? It has been given to her "for a covering" (ἀντὶ περιβολαίου) and thus distinguishes her from man, allowing her to function properly in her created role. The word "covering" (περιβολαίου) differs from the word for headcovering in the earlier verses. Some have missed this point altogether.[88] To suggest that the hair replaces the headcovering is to ignore the message Paul was communicating, namely, that women needed to wear headcoverings in congregational worship.[89] The argument that ἀντὶ should be translated "in place of" loses force when this fact is realized. Society informed women that their hair had been given as a covering and was thus their "glory." To apply this directly to the issue of headcoverings is to miss Paul's point. Long hair is the proper woman's covering in the *natural* realm.

The apostle's point is this: Since a woman has a covering in the physical realm, which is taught by nature, she should also have a covering in the spiritual realm, which is the headcovering.

The difference in words for the coverings raises the question of what kind of headcovering Paul was speaking about in this passage. Hurley is helpful here, even though he takes the position that the hair replaces the covering. He shows from many extrabiblical sources that the coverings used in Paul's day covered the head. As stated earlier, they were not full facial veils; they were often attached as hoods to the women's garments.[90]

A final word (11:16). Alford says that this verse "cuts off the subject already decided abundantly, with a settlement of any possible indifference by appeal to universal apostolic and ecclesiastical custom."[91] As indicated by the first class condition, Paul addressed a reality,[92] not a mere possible situation. "Contentious" (φιλόνεικος) describes the manner in which the man "thinks" (δοκεῖ). The word φιλόνεικος, used only here in the New Testament, means quarrelsome, or one who disputes.[93] The point is that if anyone, whether one in the church or one who comes and introduces himself as a teacher, is thinking in a contentious manner, he is here put down by the authority of the apostolic company.[94]

Such a person should succumb to Paul's instruction because "we have no other practice, nor have the churches of God" (v. 16b). This statement can mean either that there was no custom of being quarrelsome, or that there was no custom of women praying with their heads uncovered. The first option is that of early expositors cited by Ellicott.[95] It seems better, in light of the forcefulness with which Paul concluded, to say, as do the majority of the interpreters,[96] that the second view is preferable.

When Paul wrote "we" (ἡμεῖς), he meant either himself and the apostolic circle, or himself alone in an editorial sense. In light of the emphasis in the following phrase, it seems better to understand this as an editorial "we." He then moved on to enlarge the circle of support by mentioning the "churches of God," thus showing that he was not asking anything special of the Corinthians, for this was how all God's people conducted themselves.

Was Paul basing his "practice" (συνήθειαν) on a mere custom of the church, being disturbed because the Corinthians were violating an optional custom? This seems unlikely. Rather, Paul was dealing with practices important in the church.

Contemporary Applications

If this passage is perceived as addressing the question of what headcoverings women are to wear in church worship settings, then the conclusion is likely to be that headcoverings must be worn by women today. If the issue of the passage is the problem of throwing off the accepted symbol of male-female role distinctions, then the cultural factor becomes more significant and other appropriate symbols are more likely to be accepted. To state this differently, Paul was either telling the Corinthians to wear headcoverings as a sign of God-ordained male-female role distinctives or he was telling them to wear the proper cultural symbol of God-ordained male-female role distinctives. In this second option Paul was telling the Corinthians not to abandon the culturally accepted symbol of male-female role distinctives.

While these two possibilities may have led to the same

application for the Corinthians, their application today will vary. The first option demands that women today wear coverings in recognition of God's creative order. The second option demands that women not wear an expression of a false theology and thus signify a rejection of God's creative order.

The question before the interpreter is not whether this passage should be applied today. It should. The question is *what* should be applied. Should women wear headcoverings, or should they dress in such a way that they do not obliterate the God-ordained distinction between men and women? The common appeal that this is simply a symbol and that the attitude is what really counts is clearly to be rejected. Symbols have always been significant for God's people. The entire sacrificial system of the Old Testament was symbolic as well as the two ordinances observed by the church today, baptism and the Lord's Supper. The symbolic nature of headcoverings is no basis for rejection of the practice.

This chapter has concluded that Paul did indeed require the women believers in the Corinthian church to wear headcoverings when they attended worship services, and he required the men not to have their heads covered. Man's head is not to be covered, because he reflects God's glory, but the woman's head was to be covered as an indication of her role as a woman. Otherwise she would detract from her glorious role of completing the man.

In a broader sense Paul can be understood as asking for appropriate dress in the church—dress that reflects God's intent in the headship of Christ over man and the headship of men over women.

The headship established by God should not be disregarded. To overlook God's distinctive function for men and women is disgraceful. That is true in any culture. The expression of disregard in the Corinthian culture was the removal of women's headcoverings. Paul's response was to tell them to wear what was the normal cultural expression of male-female distinction. In the Greco-Roman culture that distinction was revealed by women wearing headcoverings.

However, to require women today to wear headcoverings in church is to ask them to do something abnormal rather than normal. This is exactly what Paul wanted to avoid. He wanted women to do what was normal in their culture in reflecting their womanhood and the creative order and distinction set forth in verse 3. To be obedient to this passage Christian women should not dress in a way that blurs the distinction between male and female. Fee's comments on this section support this understanding.

> Although various Christian groups have fostered the practice of some sort of headcovering for women in the assembled church, the difficulties with the practice are obvious. For Paul the issue was directly tied to a cultural shame that scarcely prevails in most cultures today. Furthermore, we simply do not know what the practices were which they were abusing. Thus, literal "obedience" to the text is often merely symbolic. Unfortunately, the symbol that tends to be reinforced is the subordination of women, which is hardly Paul's point. Furthermore, it would seem in cultures where women's heads are seldom covered, the enforcement of such in the church turns Paul's point on its head.[97]

If women are asked to wear headcoverings in church *today*, they are asked to do what is abnormal, though Paul was asking them to do what was normal.

In light of the fact that Paul based his instruction on the universal concepts of headship, the order of creation, and what the Corinthians knew to be true about proper headcoverings in the physical realm, as well as a universal practice, this writer concludes that the principles of this passage are indeed valid for today. It seems that Paul was asking the Corinthians to follow a normal cultural practice that in that day reflected an understanding that God has created men and women to function in different roles. As long as men and women today are not communicating by their dress that the creative order and distinctions are done away, they are being obedient to this passage. Whereas this passage does not require women to wear headcoverings today,[98] the application of the principle of the passage is still called for.

In addition to the exegetical considerations presented above, the following practical points should be observed. It is apparent that the present-day practice of women wearing headcoverings in church does not communicate immediately Paul's thought. Yet one must determine whether this is sufficient grounds for rejecting the practice as a whole. Almost all symbols require education for their meaning to become clear. This is true in the symbolic practices of baptism and the Lord's Supper, which do not immediately communicate the ideas of initiation and fellowship.

"In the culture of the early church, while headcoverings may not necessarily have been universally worn by women in public settings, their meaning was nonetheless clear."[99] Today, however, pastoral experience has revealed that the presence of headcoverings results in confusion for visitors and those unfamiliar with the meaning of the symbol. This violates the principle that the church should not do things seemingly strange to "some who do not understand or some unbelievers [who] come in" (14:23, NIV).

If the practice of women wearing headcoverings is maintained, the church must wrestle with the difficulties this presents in reaching and retaining newcomers. The strong communication of the principle of headship that Paul is addressing remains, but confusion cannot be avoided when headcoverings are worn.

If a symbol is to be maintained, a suitable alternative to the wearing of headcoverings could be the presence of a male leader in the services in which women participate.[100] Other alternatives include the wearing of a wedding ring or hair pins; yet consideration must be given to whether these communicate the intended meaning any more clearly than a headcovering without further teaching.

Faithfulness to the teaching of this passage can be maintained so long as the participants in worship services do not follow a practice that denies God's creative order reflected in male-female distinctions. This results in the conclusion that no symbol is actually called for in the passage. Instead, the passage is forbidding the presence of a symbol or practice that denies male-female distinctions and roles.

CHAPTER 10

Another Look at 1 Corinthians 15:29, "Baptized for the Dead"

John D. Reaume

First Corinthians 15:29 has puzzled many Bible students throughout church history. In this verse Paul wrote, "Otherwise, what will those do who are baptized for the dead? If the dead are not raised at all, why then are they baptized for them?" More than two hundred interpretive solutions have been proposed, but only a few remain as legitimate possibilities.[1]

A surface reading of the passage leads to the interpretation that believers were actually being baptized for the benefit of those who died without baptism. This practice is also known as vicarious baptism, that is, substitutionary baptism for the dead.[2] The interpretation of vicarious baptism is problematic for two reasons: first, there is no historical evidence of the practice of baptizing for the dead during New Testament times,[3] and second, it seems doubtful that Paul would have written of such a practice so contrary to his theology without condemning it.[4]

Despite these problems, a majority of modern scholars have adopted this interpretation while at the same time rejecting other possible interpretations that may in fact be more legitimate. A reexamination of this text and possible interpretations will highlight the deficiency of this majority view and suggest other more plausible explanations. A survey of the most common positions will be followed by an examination of the verse and the various exegetical problems encountered in it. Then a summary of the most plausible explanations will be given.

Possible Interpretations of 1 Corinthians 15:29

Of the scores of proposed interpretations for 1 Corinthians 15:29, only those views enjoying the widest acceptance and greatest support will be considered in this discussion. Three major categories encompass the views suggested by various commentators.[5] These categories are (a) vicarious baptism, that is, water baptism undertaken by a living individual for the benefit of a dead person who had died without being baptized; (b) metaphorical baptism, which refers to either martyrdom or Paul's sufferings; and (c) Christian baptism, water baptism of new believers.

VICARIOUS BAPTISM

Most commentators hold to some version of this interpretation, in which the beneficiaries of the baptism were catechumens or family members who had died without having been baptized.[6] Fee speculates that those involved in this practice felt that baptism was necessary for entrance into the eschatological kingdom, while Orr suggests that they felt that baptism was necessary for salvation.[7]

The strongest argument for this interpretation is that it is easily derived from the plain reading of the verse, since the words βαπτίζω, νεκρός, and ὑπέρ are understood according to their most common usages.[8]

However, this view faces two significant problems. First, apart from this verse there is no historical or biblical evidence of such a practice in Corinth or elsewhere during the first century. Although there is reference to this practice in the late second century, the practice was apparently limited to heretical groups. Apparently these groups had instituted this practice because of a misinterpretation of the passage in question.[9] Second, it is doubtful that Paul could appeal to a practice so contrary to his theology without commenting on it.[10]

METAPHORICAL BAPTISM

The commentators who understand baptism in a metaphorical way arrive at different conclusions regarding the interpretation of the passage. Two of the most recognized suggestions are the views that this baptism refers to martyrdom or to Paul's suffering for the gospel.

Martyrdom. Godet proposes that "baptized" means martyred and that "for the dead" means "for entering the place of the dead."[11] According to this view, Paul referred to those who had been "baptized by blood" (martyred) with the hope of the resurrection as evidence for his argument that the resurrection is sure. In support of this, Godet cites Jesus' use of βαπτίζω in Mark 10:38 and Luke 12:50, in which He spoke of the baptism He must endure, an apparent reference to His death. This view seems to suit the context well as Paul spoke in 1 Corinthians 15:30–32 of his suffering unto death for the gospel. However, this view has some insurmountable weaknesses. First, there is no evidence of persecutions or martyrdoms in the church at Corinth at that time.[12] Second, while Jesus used βαπτίζω in the metaphorical sense of "suffering" or "martyrdom," Paul did not do so.[13] Third, Godet's rendering of ὑπέρ as "for entering" is without parallel in Greek literature.[14]

Paul's sufferings. Murphy-O'Connor proposes that the phrase "baptism for the dead" was a slogan used by troublemakers in Corinth who were denying the resurrection in order to make light of Paul's efforts for the unenlightened or spiritually dead. Here the metaphorical understanding of βαπτίζω points to Paul's trials and suffering for the gospel while νεκρός refers to the "spiritually dead" or "spiritually unenlightened." The verse would then be rendered, "Why are they (Paul and other apostles) being destroyed while working for the sake of the lost? If dead believers are not raised, then why are they suffering for the lost?"[15]

In support of this view is the fact that it circumvents the theological problems of vicarious baptism. Also it fits the context well in that Paul referred to his sufferings in the following verses (15:30–31).[16]

However, this position faces some major difficulties as well. First, this view calls for differing nuances of νεκρός in the immediate context.[17] In its first occurrence νεκρός would be taken metaphorically as "the spiritually dead" but in its second occurrence it would have to be understood literally as "the physically dead." A writer would probably not utilize different nuances in the same sentence without indicating that intention.

Second, it is unclear how an appeal to this alleged slogan would strengthen Paul's case for the certainty of the resurrection. If the point of the alleged slogan was to demean Paul's efforts for the spiritually dead, as Murphy-O'Connor suggests, then why would the apostle include the slogan in a context where his struggles for the spiritually dead are given as evidence for the certainty of the resurrection?

Third, little evidence exists that the phrase "baptized for the dead" in verse 29 is a slogan, for it lacks some of the key characteristics of slogans, such as brevity, sustained qualification, and an unambiguous response.[18] Murphy-O'Connor's suggestion meets the first characteristic but falls short on the rest, as Paul is seen as agreeing with the basic premise of the alleged slogan rather than qualifying it.[19] Also there is no adversative to distinguish the Corinthian's slogan and Paul's response to that slogan.[20] And, as Fee suggests, the assumption of Philo's influence on the Corinthians in order to prove that the Corinthians would have used νεκρός in the sense of "spiritually dead" is "questionable at best."[21]

CHRISTIAN BAPTISM

Several commentators argue that 1 Corinthians 15:29 refers to Christian baptism in the normal sense of the initiation rite symbolizing the believer's identification with Christ. This category includes a variety of interpretations that can be grouped in six major subviews.

Because of dead believers. This view is one of the most widely supported alternatives to vicarious baptism. The phrase "baptism for the dead" is understood in the sense of unbelievers being baptized "because of" believers who have died.[22] In this interpretation unbelievers decide to become Christians and be baptized because of the influence of a believer who had recently died.

Several arguments support this view. First, Paul used νεκρός with and without the definite article consistently in 1 Corinthians 15 to differentiate between "Christian dead" and "the dead in general."[23] Thus it is argued that τῶν νεκρῶν refers to dead Christians. Second, the preposition ὑπέρ with the genitive can have the causal sense of "because of."[24] Third, this interpretation fits the context with Paul returning to his former argument on the absurdity of denying the believers' resurrection, which he concluded with a specific discussion of the Christian dead.[25]

A few arguments have been presented against this view. Some have suggested that if Paul had meant "Christian dead" he would have clarified his intention when referring to "the dead" with more specific phrasing such as "dead friends" or "dead relatives."[26] Also Paul usually used ὑπέρ with the sense of "on behalf of" when the object of the preposition is a person.[27]

In order to be united with the dead at the resurrection. With a slight modification of the former view, some have suggested that the preposition ὑπέρ is functioning with the final sense of "for."[28] Jeremias, building on the work of Raeder, argues that verse 29 refs to "pagans who take baptism upon themselves ὑπὲρ τῶν νεκρῶν with the purpose of becoming united with their deceased Christian relatives at the resurrection."[29] Although this preposition may have a final sense, this usage seems uncommon in the New Testament.[30] In addition this interpretation requires filling a significant ellipsis in order to convey this sense, such as "baptized in order to be united with their deceased Christian relatives at the resurrection."[31]

To take the place of dead believers. Another suggestion is that the apostle was referring to individuals who were converted and baptized to take the place of deceased believers.[32] In addition to understanding "baptism" and "the dead" in accord with consistent Pauline usage, this position maintains the common substitutionary sense of ὑπέρ without implying that this action is vicarious or beneficial for the dead.[33]

The major difficulty with this interpretation is that the notion of new believers coming in to replace believers who had died is not immediately evident in this context.[34]

With reference to the resurrection of the dead. A fourth interpretation understands "baptism for the dead" to refer to the general baptism of all believers in which they are baptized "with reference to the resurrection of the dead."[35] This view normally holds to an implied ellipsis of "resurrection" in order to yield the meaning of "baptism with reference to the resurrection of the dead."

There is little support for this view other than the fact that it alleviates the theological problems of vicarious baptism and that Christian baptism has the symbolic sense of being united with Christ in His death and resurrection (Rom. 6:3–5). Additional support includes the fact that Paul elsewhere used the preposition ὑπέρ to mean "with reference to" (2 Cor. 1:7; 8:23).[36] The major argument against this view is that the implied ellipsis of "resurrection" in the phrase "baptized with reference to the resurrection of the dead" is too violent.[37] Paul probably would have included "resurrection" if this is what he meant.

For their dying bodies. A fifth suggestion argues that 1 Corinthians 15:29 makes reference to Christian baptism in which an individual is baptized for the benefit of his own "dying" body. Several early church fathers including Tertullian and Chrysostom ascribed to this position, which was later held by Erasmus.[38] Calvin suggested a more specific nuance of unbelievers repenting and being baptized on their death beds.[39] O'Neill has most recently espoused this position, citing additional evidence based on a tenuous deduction from textual evidence.[40] This view has little support other than the fact that it avoids the theological difficulties of vicarious baptism and understands βαπτίζω and ὑπέρ in accord with common Pauline usage. The major problem is that viewing νεκρός to mean "dying bodies" is without parallel in the New Testament.[41]

Christian baptism based on alternative punctuation. Some scholars have proposed that the solution to the interpretation of 1 Corinthians 15:29 is found in changing the punctuation of the verse.[42] Foschini argues that verse 29 consists of four rhetorical questions: (1) Ἐπεὶ τί ποιήσουσιν οἱ βαπτιζόμενοι, "If there is no resurrection, what is the point of being baptized?" (2) ὑπὲρ τῶν νεκρῶν, "Is it only to be united with the dead?" (3) εἰ ὅλως νεκροὶ οὐκ ἐγείρονται, τί καὶ βαπτίζονται, "If the dead do not rise again, why are they baptized?" (4) ὑπὲρ αὐτῶν, "Is it only to be united with them (i.e., with the dead who will never rise)?"[43] Thompson suggests that verse 29 consists of two questions: (1) Ἐπεὶ τί ποιήσουσιν οἱ βαπτιζόμενοι ὑπὲρ τῶν νεκρῶν εἰ ὅλως νεκροὶ οὐκ ἐγείρονται, "Else what will they achieve who are baptized merely for the benefit of their dead bodies, if dead bodies never rise again?" (2) τί καὶ βαπτίζονται ὑπὲρ αὐτῶν, "And why do people get baptized for them?"[44]

Since paleography reveals that accents, breathing marks, and punctuation were not used during New Testament times, these proposed punctuation changes may or may not be legitimate.[45] However, there is one insurmountable difficulty with these interpretations: they still hinge on Foschini's and Thompson's understanding of the preposition ὑπέρ and the noun νεκρός.[46]

Exegesis of 1 Corinthians 15:29

THE CONTEXT

Paul had been addressing various problems in the Corinthian church, which had evidently been influenced by an overrealized eschatology and Hellenistic dualism.[47] Some in the church felt they were presently experiencing the kingdom in its fullness and were truly spiritual (1 Cor. 4:8–10). Also many in the church felt that the physical body was of little importance both in the present and in the future. This view led some to license (6:15–16) and others to asceticism (7:1–7). Some had evidently extended this view to deny the resurrection of believers (15:12). Having addressed these other problems, Paul then completed his letter by defending the doctrine of the resurrection.

Paul's argument in defense of the resurrection of believers includes three sections. First, he reaffirmed Christ's resurrection as a foundation for his argument that dead believers will be raised (15:1–11). Second, he demonstrated the absurdity of denying the resurrection of believers and he revealed the theological foundation that supports the resurrection of believers (vv. 12–34). Third, he affirmed that the resurrection is bodily, although he explained that the body will be transformed for an eternal existence (vv. 35–58).

Paul began the second major section of his argument (vv. 12–34) by demonstrating the absurdity of the position of those who deny the resurrection. Their position was contradictory, for they denied the resurrection of believers while affirming Christ's resurrection (vv. 11–12). His argument for the resurrection of believers then proceeded in three directions. First, he pointed out that their position implies that Christ was not raised from the dead, thereby destroying the foundation for their faith (vv. 12–19). Second, Paul reversed the proposition by arguing that the reality of Christ's resurrection guarantees the reality of believers' resurrection (vv. 20–28).

Third, Paul pointed out the incongruity of both their own behavior and the behavior of the apostles (vv. 29–34). By a series of rhetorical questions he pointed up the absurdity of various activities if there were no resurrection. The practice of baptism for the dead (v. 29) and the apostles' risk-taking behavior (vv. 30–32) were illogical if there is no resurrection of believers. In verse 31 he was probably emphasizing the truth of verse 30 that he daily faced the possibility of death. After giving a further concrete example of risk-taking in verse 32a, he quoted from Isaiah 22:13 to argue that it would make more sense to indulge in license than self-sacrificial behavior if there is no resurrection (1 Cor. 15:32). He concluded this section with some poignant words of advice, apparently designed to rebuke the Corinthians for associating with those who deny the resurrection (v. 34).

It is evident that verse 29 is only one small part of Paul's grand argument for the resurrection of believers. Verse 29 points out the incongruity of denying the resurrection of believers while at the same time participating in a certain religious practice.

CRITICAL EXEGESIS OF 1 CORINTHIANS 15:29

The wide variety of interpretations of 1 Corinthians 15:29 results from different suggested solutions to key exegetical problems. The meaning and referents of key terms such as οἱ βαπτιζόμενοι and τῶν νεκρῶν are the subject of some debate. However, the understanding of the preposition ὑπέρ and the resulting theological implications are the decisive issues in this *crux interpretum.*

οἱ βαπτιζόμενοι. This verse begins with the statement, Ἐπεὶ τί ποιήσουσιν οἱ βαπτιζόμενοι ὑπὲρ τῶν νεκρῶν, "Otherwise, what will those do who are baptized for the dead?"[48] As already stated, there are two basic suggestions for the meaning of βαπτίζω in this context. Some suggest that this word is being used metaphorically to describe martyrdom or Paul's sufferings for the gospel, while others hold that Christian baptism is in view. In favor of a metaphorical understanding is the fact that the figurative sense of "to perish" or "to suffer" is also evident in Greek literature,[49] including the New Testament (Mark 10:38–39).

However, this suggestion has a number of difficulties. First, apart from this verse there is no evidence that Paul used this term metaphorically to indicate suffering or martyrdom. Although Murphy-O'Connor's suggestion that the phrase "the ones being baptized for the dead" is a Corinthian slogan alleviates the problem of Pauline usage for the term βαπτίζω, his proposition seems doubtful, as previously discussed. Second, a figurative understanding of "baptism" would also require a figurative understanding of "the dead" (i.e., spiritually dead), in order to avoid a mystical view of suffering or of being killed for the benefit of the physically dead. A figurative view of "the dead" is improbable in this context, since Paul consistently referred to the physically dead throughout chapter 15 and even in the immediate context (v. 29b).[50] Third, there is no historical evidence of any believers being martyred in the Corinthian church at that time.[51]

Viewing βαπτίζω as referring to Christian baptism is most likely the correct understanding, since Paul consistently used this term with the literal sense of the Christian initiatory rite.[52] Also Paul's argument in verses 29–32 is more coherent if Christian baptism is in view, since Paul would be citing two different examples of activities that demonstrate the absurdity of denying the resurrection.[53]

Since βαπτίζω probably refers to literal Christian baptism in this context, οἱ βαπτιζόμενοι may be identified in one of two ways. Some identify this construction as a reference to all believers, while the majority hold that this construction refers to a specific group of individuals within the church. The third person present tense form of the verb βαπτίζονται (v. 29b) suggests that this activity was currently being practiced by a group of individuals and was probably well known by the Corinthians.[54] Thus the former suggestion is extremely doubtful, as Paul probably would have used the first person or second person plural form if he were referring to all believers or to the Corinthian believers (cf. vv. 17, 51). As Fee states,

> This is one of the rare instances in the letter where Paul addresses a community matter only in the third person plural. In other instances (e.g., 4:18–21; 15:12–19), even when "some" are specified, the rest of the argument is directed at the community as a whole in the second person plural. Since that does not happen here, one may surmise that this is the activity of only a few.[55]

τῶν νεκρῶν. Some suggest that νεκρός refers metaphorically to the spiritually dead in verse 29a.[56] Others suggest that the first occurrence of νεκρό" in verse 29 refers to "dying bodies."[57] The majority of commentators hold that this word refers to literally dead persons in both occurrences, with varying suggestions as to their identity.

The first suggestion is possible, as the word νεκρός is used both literally and figuratively in the New Testament and by Paul.[58] However, this interpretation is doubtful, since the literal sense is plainly in view throughout the entire context (15:12, 13, 15, 16, 32, 35, etc.). In addition Paul clearly used νεκρός literally in the immediate context (v. 29b). The suggestion that verse 29a is a Corinthian slogan may alleviate some of the difficulty with the occurrence of two distinct nuances within verse 29, but this hypothesis is doubtful for reasons already enumerated.

Similarly, the second suggestion is likewise doubtful as this understanding of νεκρῶν as "dying bodies" is without parallel in the New Testament and would differ with consistent Pauline usage in chapter 15.[59] In addition, this understanding requires an ellipsis such as τῶν νεκρῶν (σωμάτων) or a tenuous connection of νεκρός with a derivative found in classical Greek in order to produce the sense of "corpses."[60]

Since Paul consistently used νεκρός in a literal sense throughout 1 Corinthians 15 and since the literal sense is apparent in the second half of verse 29, a literal understanding of νεκρός as referring to "dead individuals" is preferred.

Who are τῶν νεκρῶν? Was Paul referring to dead believers,
unbelievers, or catechumens who died before being baptized?
Grammar suggests that the articular construction τῶν νεκρῶν
refers to a specific group of dead individuals (with the anarthrous
noun νεκροὶ referring to the dead in general).[61] Pauline usage in
chapter 15 confirms this. Paul seems to have been distinguishing
between the dead in general (vv. 12–13, 15–16, 20–21, and 29b)
and Christians who had died (vv. 29a, 35, 42, and 52).[62]

For example later in the chapter the resurrection of dead believers
is clearly in view as indicated by the references to "a heavenly
body" (vv. 40, 47–49), "a spiritual body" (vv. 44, 46), and a body
"raised in power" (v. 43). However, in verses 12–29, the anarthrous
construction is used consistently to denote the general concept of
"the dead" in speaking of Christ being resurrected from the dead
(vv. 12, 15, 20) and the general resurrection of the dead (vv. 13, 15,
16). In addition verse 29 seems to resume Paul's former argument
in which he demonstrated the absurdity of denying the resurrection
of dead believers and which he concluded by referring specifically
to deceased believers (vv. 18–19). Based on Paul's apparent
distinction between "dead believers" and the "dead in general," the
object of the preposition ὑπὲρ is probably dead believers.

This observation leads to the question of whether these believers
had been baptized or were catechumens who died before being
baptized. The latter suggestion depends on the existence of an
initiatory procedure in Corinth that historically developed much
later. The normal practice in the early church was for baptism to
follow immediately after conversion (Acts 10:47–48; 16:31–34;
18:8; 19:5).[63]

Thus the possibility of a convert dying before being baptized
was improbable, contrary to what some have suggested.[64] Added
to this improbability is the fact that this activity in Corinth involved
more than one individual and would have had to be well known to
the Corinthians for Paul's argument to have force. Rather than
referring to an exceptional case where a convert died before
baptism, Paul was most likely referring to the more common case
of dead believers who had already been baptized.

ὑπὲρ. The prepositional phrase ὑπὲρ τῶν νεκρῶν has been the
major focus in the controversy on this passage. The preposition
ὑπὲρ with the genitive normally has the meaning of "on behalf of,"
emphasizing representation (e.g., Eph. 5:2, 25; 1 Thess. 5:10; Titus
2:14), or "instead of," emphasizing substitution (e.g., John 11:50;

2 Cor. 5:14–15; Gal. 3:13; Philem. 13),[65] with the person as the object of the preposition (also see Rom. 5:6, 8; 8:32; Gal. 2:20).[66] In this case the preposition is used to express favor or advantage accrued to a person. As a result most contemporary commentators view the phrase ὑπέρ τῶν νεκρῶν as denoting an esoteric practice of vicarious baptism in which an individual was apparently baptized as a substitute for the benefit of a dead person.[67]

Although this is a natural rendering of the text, the major difficulties with this interpretation are the complete lack of historical evidence for this alleged practice in the first century and the theological problem of Paul appealing, without qualification, to a practice that implies that baptism has saving efficacy.[68] In addition, since the object of the preposition τῶν νεκρῶν probably refers to dead believers, the interpretation of vicarious baptism is doubtful, as these dead believers had most likely observed the rite of baptism before their death.

Another suggestion that maintains the substitutionary sense of ὑπέρ is that Paul was referring to individuals who were converted and baptized to take the place of deceased believers.[69] This sense would be parallel to Philemon 13, in which Paul spoke of Onesimus as "ministering in the place of Philemon." Here the emphasis is more on substitution than on any benefit accrued by Philemon (cf. Col. 1:7).

The preposition ὑπέρ can also be used to denote the cause or reason of an action as in the sense of "for," "because of," or "on account of" (see Rom. 15:9; 2 Cor. 12:8).[70] In the New Testament this preposition is used to indicate the cause of suffering or slander (Acts 9:16; 21:13;[71] 1 Cor. 10:30; 2 Cor. 12:10; Phil. 1:29; 2 Thess. 1:5), the cause of praise and thanksgiving (Rom. 15:9), and the reason for prayer (2 Cor. 12:8).[72] In the passage in question, the resulting sense would be that some new believers were being baptized because of the influence of dead believers.[73] The chief criticism of this view is that Pauline usage prefers the sense of "on behalf of" with a person as the object, whereas the sense of "because of" or "on account of" is preferred when the object is a thing.[74] The causal sense of ὑπέρ is, however, used by Paul with a person as the object either explicitly or implicitly on at least a few occasions (Acts 9:16; 21:13; Rom. 15:9; Phil. 1:29).[75]

Closely related to this understanding of ὑπέρ is the suggestion that this proposition is functioning in 1 Corinthians 15:29 with the final sense of "for": being baptized "with the purpose of becoming united with their deceased Christian relatives at the resurrection."[76] This understanding of ὑπέρ with a final sense is evident in the context of Paul's sufferings for the Corinthians' comfort (2 Cor. 1:6), although this usage seems to be uncommon.[77] The major problem with this view is that the phrase ὑπέρ τῶν νεκρῶν would require a significant ellipsis or additional explanation to arrive at a coherent interpretation.[78] However, other passages utilizing the final sense of ὑπέρ similarly have to be filled out by the exegesis of the text.[79]

Others have suggested that the preposition demonstrates the local sense of "over" as in "over the graves of the dead."[80] This understanding is doubtful, as there is no historical evidence for this practice in the first century. Also this local sense of the preposition, although common in classical Greek, is applied only figuratively in the Koine period.[81]

Still others suggest this preposition is used in 1 Corinthians 15:29 with the sense of "concerning" or "with reference to," as in believers being baptized with reference to the resurrection of the dead.[82] This interpretation is doubtful, since it requires a significant ellipsis such as "baptized with reference to [the resurrection of] the dead."[83]

Although the first understanding of ὑπέρ is most in keeping with Pauline usage with persons as the object,[84] the theological difficulties presented by Paul's nonqualification of an erroneous practice suggest that this occurrence may involve a different nuance such as "because of the influence of dead believers," "in order to be united with dead believers at the resurrection," or perhaps even the understanding of new converts "taking the place of dead Christians."[85]

Conclusion

Having examined 1 Corinthians 15:29, a number of conclusions can be made. First, the baptism referred to is probably literal water baptism of Christians. Second, the phrase "the ones who are baptized" most likely refers to a small group of individuals rather than the church as a whole. Third, "the dead" for whom some individuals were being baptized were in all probability dead believers. Fourth, these dead believers had presumably experienced Christian baptism before they died. If these four observations are true, it is extremely improbable that the proposition ὑπέρ denotes vicarious baptism for the benefit of the dead, as there would be no value in such a practice, since the dead in question would already have been "saved" and probably baptized. With the additional problem of vicarious baptism and Pauline theology, the improbability of 1 Corinthians 15:29 referring to vicarious baptism becomes insurmountable.

Therefore only three of the more than two hundred interpretations of 1 Corinthians 15:29 remain strong possibilities. One view translates ὑπέρ with the sense of "in the place of" as in new believers' being baptized to take the place of dead Christians. A second possibility translates ὑπέρ with the final sense: "in order to be reunited with their loved ones at the resurrection." A third view translates ὑπέρ with the sense of "because of": new believers' being baptized "because of the influence of deceased Christians." The first suggestion is perhaps less convincing, since it could be said that all believers take the place of deceased believers and yet Paul was evidently referring to a select group within the church. The final two suggestions are closely related semantically and fit the context well, as they both refer to a select group within the church and include an emphasis on the resurrection as the implied motive for these practices.

Perhaps the most plausible interpretation is the third option, since it makes sense without a significant ellipsis. No doubt many individuals in the early church were influenced by the testimony of other believers who had recently died or who were martyred. For example Paul may have been influenced by Stephen's testimony when Stephen was arrested and stoned (Acts 7). Although all three interpretations are not immediately evident from initial readings of the text, all three respect the contextual framework of Pauline usage and theology.

In light of the minor role this verse plays in the overall argument of 1 Corinthians 15, it is ironic that the verse has received so much attention in the literature. This disproportionate attention is justified, however, if this passage refers to a practice implying the saving efficacy of baptism. Was Paul referring to a practice fundamentally opposed to his theology of salvation by faith alone as the majority of modern commentators suggest? According to the evidence revealed by this study, this is highly improbable.

In addition there is no biblical warrant given in this passage for instituting the practice of baptism for the dead. Both the ancient and modern practices of baptism for the dead are apparently founded on misinterpretations of this verse.

CHAPTER 11

Tongues and the Mystery Religions of Corinth

H. Wayne House

Of all the controversial subjects discussed in Christian circles, probably few have received more attention than the subject of glossolalia. Though the material written on this subject is enormous, much confusion still pervades the issue. Since the Corinthian assembly gave undue preeminence to "speaking in tongues," it is only to be expected that a person seeking to understand the Corinthian phenomenon should desire to know the reason for this stress. This chapter seeks to demonstrate that some of the Corinthian Christians brought aspects of their pagan background into their worship and theology. These false perspectives and practices were characteristic of the contemporary religious setting in Corinth from which they had been converted. This chapter also seeks to show that the apostle Paul, in seeking to rid the church at Corinth of these ideas, used various means of argumentation to combat these practices, even using some of their terminology for the purpose of argument.

Statement of the Problem

Pagan forces were hard at work in the church at Corinth, but their identity and to what degree they influenced that congregation is a matter of debate. Scholars of the History of Religions school earlier in this century believed that Christians, including those at Corinth, were affected by the Hellenistic mystery religions.[1] On the other hand Schmithals and others have posited Gnostic influence in the church at Corinth.[2]

Religious ecstasy, particularly glossolalia, is found in the mystery religions or the religion of Apollo, rather than in Gnosticism as Bultmann and others have argued. Some of the characteristics of Gnosticism were already present in the general religious attitudes in the first century A.D.; but since Gnosticism was a later Christian heresy,[3] it would be anachronistic to see Gnosticism in Corinth. Whatever the cause, the church in this hub of pagan perversity was in grave trouble; the church abounded in nonbiblical and immoral practices.

Proper Methodology in Approaching the Problem

Scholars have differed in their view of the extent of the mystery religions' influence on Christianity. Clemen argued that Christianity acquired forms, concepts, and rites from the mystery sects.[4] Likewise Heussi said that undoubtedly the language and piety of the mysteries influenced the church.[5]

Pahl has a more cautious view. "The Mysteries may have exerted limited formal influence on certain subsequent developments of Christianity but they had no influence whatever on the Origin of Christianity."[6] Similarly, Geden says that most likely the Mithras doctrines and ritual had an unconscious effect on the language and teaching of some of the Christian apologists.[7]

Schweitzer argued that Pauline Christianity was not influenced by the mysteries.[8] Pruemm also seems to support the view that the mystery religions had no influence on Christianity.[9]

Another view, posited by Metzger, is that the mystery religions may have borrowed from Christianity.[10] This writer concurs with Metzger and contends that early Christianity did not borrow its theology from the mystery religions, though certainly early Christians individually may have been affected by them (which may have been true at Corinth).

The basic problem in discussing the mystery religions is that so many centuries have separated the inquirer from the subject of inquiry. Grant spoke of this problem when he wrote about the study of Greek religion in the Hellenistic-Roman world.

> And yet we are still on the outside, and have only the records, descriptive or interpretative, literary or archeological, which a few men here and there in that ancient world left behind them. How shall we ever get really inside that ancient faith, or complex of faiths, and see the world as men saw it then? There is no other way, I believe, than by a conscious effort of the imagination, by reading and thinking and in a sense dreaming our way back into it. And there is one caution we simply must never ignore—like the warnings to persons with magic gifts in many an old tale—we must not let our imaginings and our dreams conflict with the reality recorded in the books, the inscriptions, and the surviving rites; our indispensable guide must be a thorough knowledge of the facts so far as they have come down to us, all the facts, not just a pleasing little selection made to fit some theory or other![11]

A Look at the Origin and Philosophies of the Mysteries

ROMAN-HELLENISM AND RELIGIOUS SYNCRETISM

When the church began, the state religions in the Roman Empire, though given proper outward honor, had somehow lost their grip on individuals. One reason for this may be that since the philosophers had found the gods wanting, the fear of the gods had been removed. Furthermore in view of Roman domination over different countries and cities, the impotency of the gods became pronounced, and this realization was sensed by individuals. If the gods could not help the city, how could they meet an individual's needs?

The constant flux seen in the pantheon of Greek and Roman gods offered individuals little hope. People turned from thought to experience as the basis of religion, from rational content to emotional yearning.[12] Their contact with the Near East, especially from the time of Alexander, brought in new ideas which found favor with the peoples of the western Mediterranean world. The mystery religions swiftly spread in a world in which travel was relatively easy and in which soldiers, who believed in these mystery religions, moved from place to place. The people were seeking a change of some sort, which the dynamic of the religious syncretism provided. The key attraction of the mystery cults is captured by Gardner.

> Why were the priests able to attract the men and women who were dissatisfied with their lives and anxious for a better hope? What could they offer to the votaries? The best answer maybe given in a single word. The great need and longing of the time was for salvation, *soteria*. Men and women were eager for such a communion with the divine, such a realization of the interest of God in their affairs, as might serve to support them in the trials of life, and guarantee to them a friendly reception in the world beyond the grave. . . . The communion with some saving deity, then, was the [goal] of all practice of the mysteries.[13]

One must not suppose that the mystery religions were all alike. The Greek world abounded with all sorts of private associations with their respective gods. Even these varied in their myths, dramas, and practices. For example, the Eleusian variety, heard of at Eleusis near Corinth and Athens, had agricultural worship at its center. The Dionysian mystery was excessive in its religious practices, including uncontrollable ecstasy, eating of raw flesh, and orgies. A third important cult was that of Orpheus. It had an early influence on the people of Greece, being possibly a revised version of the cult of Dionysus. Its power was waning even by the time of Plato, who may have encountered it.

Three sources are the most probable candidates for the ecstatic phenomenon seen at Corinth: the Cybele-Attis cult, the Dionysian cult (both mystery religions), and the religion of Apollo.

The worship of Cybele-Attis was accepted by the Greeks in approximately 200 B.C. The rites of this cult were extreme in nature. Priests who were stirred by clashing cymbals, loud drums, and screeching flutes, would at times dance in a frenzy of excitement, gashing their bodies. Even new devotees would emasculate themselves in worship of the goddess.

The Cybele-Attis mystery religion existed in the first century A.D. Emperor Claudius (A.D. 41–54) introduced a festival of Cybele-Attis that focused on the death and resurrection of Attis.[14] Montanus, a second-century Christian heretic, known for his ecstatic excesses, was a priest of Cybele at one time.[15] However, no evidence this writer examined indicated that a temple of Cybele-Attis was in Corinth during the first century, though the Corinthians may have been familiar with that cult.

Dionysus, the god of wine, became one of the most popular gods of the Greek pantheon. The pine tree became identified with him, and the Delphic oracle commanded the Corinthians to worship a particular pine tree out of which two images of the god were made.[16] Hoyle describes the nature of this worship.

> Following the torches as they dipped and swayed in the darkness, they climbed mountain paths with head thrown back and eyes glazed, dancing to the beat of the drum which stirred their blood. . . . In the state of *ekstasis* or *enthousiasmos*, they abandoned themselves, dancing wildly. . . . and calling "*Evoi!*" At that moment of intense rapture they became identified with the god himself. . . . They became filled with his spirit and acquired divine powers.[17]

In 187 B.C. the Roman senate sought to ban the Dionysian cult but was never fully successful. It was revived under Julius Caesar and remained in existence at least until the time of Augustine (A.D. 354–430).[18] The question remains whether it was widely active during the first century A.D. and especially in Corinth. Rogers has argued that the Dionysian cult had permeated the Mediterranean world at the time of Paul, and was a background to Paul's words in Ephesians 5:18.[19] But would it have been popular at Corinth also?

Broneer has demonstrated that Dionysus was worshiped in
Corinth as early as the fourth century B.C. with a temple located in
the Sacred Glen. This most likely indicates that the cult of Dionysus
may have been in Corinth at the time of Paul.[20] Dionysus was
worshiped at Delphi across the gulf from Corinth, substituting for
Apollo when supposedly he was spending the winter with the
Hyperboreans.[21] This continued at least during the time of Plutarch
(A.D. 46–120),[22] so the Dionysian religion probably would have
had some influence on Corinth.

The third major cult that may have had influence on the
Corinthians was that of Apollo. Several temples in Corinth were
for the worship of Apollo,[23] and the famous shrine at Delphi was
primarily that of Apollo. The slave girl Paul encountered in
Philippi on the way to Corinth had a spirit of Python, or one
inspired by Apollo.[24] The ecstatic tongues-speaking of the oracle
and the subsequent interpretation by the priest at Delphi are
widely known. The cult of Apollo was widespread in Achaia, but
especially around the temple of Delphi across from Corinth. This
religion easily could have provided the kind of impetus for spiritual
experience found in the Corinthian church.

> Greece had long experience of the utterances of the Pythian prophetess at
> Delphi and the enthusiastic invocations of the votaries of Dionysus. Hence
> Paul insists that it is not the phenomenon of "tongues" or prophesying in
> itself that gives evidence of the presence and activity of the Holy Spirit,
> but the actual content of the utterances.[25]

With the ecstacism of Dionysianism and the emphasis on
tongues-speaking and oracles in the religion of Apollo, it is not
surprising that some of the Corinthians carried these pagan ideas
in the church at Corinth, especially the practice of glossolalia for
which both of these religions are known (though the Dionysian
cult did not include interpretation of the glossolalia as did that of
Apollo) .

THE FAITH AND PRACTICES OF THE MYSTERIES

The mystery religions were cults whose practices and secret
beliefs were not shared with the uninitiated. "In view of their great
importance, it is extraordinary that we know almost nothing about
them. Everyone initiated had to take an oath not to reveal them
and their influence was so strong that apparently no one ever
did."[26]

Gardner is severely skeptical about reading too much into the historical data. The writers of the ancient world, the art, and inscriptions give, at most, the public and outward rites rather than the inward secrets the initiates possessed.[27]

The major teaching in the mystery religions was rebirth and immortality of the initiates. Their rites were baptism, dedication, and the sacramental meals. These are discussed in several sources.[28] The primary concern in this chapter is the ecstatic nature of their worship. Fortunately, since ecstasy was not part of their secret rites, a fairly accurate knowledge of this aspect of the cults is available.

"The mystery-cults of the empire were designed to induce both higher and lower forms of ecstatic feeling."[29] The expression of the ecstatic state took various forms, such as gashing one's flesh, dancing nude in a frenzy, and speaking in ecstatic utterance. The latter was the means whereby the devotees sought to have communion with the saving deity. Here the significance of the term "glossolalia," or "speaking in tongues," comes to the fore.

The gift of tongues and of their interpretation was not peculiar to the Christian Church, but was a repetition in it of a phrase common in ancient religions. The very phrase *glossais lalein*, "to speak with tongues," was not invented by the New Testament writers, but borrowed from ordinary speech.[30]

The Influence of the Pagan Cults on Glossolalia in the Corinthian Church

To what degree did the mystery cults affect thinking and worship of the Corinthian church, and how did that influence Paul's discussion in 1 Corinthians 12–14?

If the church was affected by these pagan cults, one would expect to see evidence of these in Paul's letter, such as for example, certain allusions or terms that the Corinthians or Paul used. One must not assume that Paul was fluent in mystery terminology, but he certainly was aware of those terms that were in common circulation.

> We cannot picture [Paul] engrossed in the cure of souls without recognizing that he must have gained a deep insight into the earlier spiritual aspirations of his converts, and the manner in which they had sought to satisfy them. Even apart from eager inquirers, a missionary so zealous and daring would often find himself confronted by men and women who still clung to their mystic ritual and all the hopes it had kindled. It was inevitable, therefore, that he should become familiar, at least from the outside, with religious ideas current in these influential cults.[31]

SIMILAR TERMINOLOGY WITH THE MYSTERIES

Instruments in worship. Paul wrote that the ability to "speak with the tongues of men and of angels" without love is no better than his being "a noisy gong or a clanging cymbal" (1 Cor. 13:1). This may be an allusion to the use of these instruments in the mystery cults. These instruments were used to produce the ecstatic condition that provided the emotional intoxication needed to experience the sacramental celebration.[32] This is especially true in Dionysianism.[33] Failure to evidence love in the expression of the gifts would be as meaningless as their former pagan rites.

The spiritual one (πνευματικός). Paul contrasted the πνευματικός, one who has the Spirit, with the ψυχικός, one who is devoid of the Spirit (1 Cor. 2:10–3:4). The pneumatic character of worship in the mystery religions was always connected with states of ecstasy, whereas Paul never made this connection. To him the possession of the πνεῦμα is the normal, abiding condition of the Christian. The special meaning of πνευματικός and πνευματικά to the Corinthians was mainly due to their ecstatic emphases, especially the phenomenon of speaking with tongues.

Mystery (musthvrion). The term "mystery" is used in the New Testament but with a different force (except for possibly 1 Cor. 14:2). Hay clarifies the difference between these two usages.

> In the New Testament it refers to the things of God that could not be known by man except through revelation from God. The revelation given of these things by the Holy Spirit is not obscure but clear and is given to be communication to God's people (1 Cor. 2:1–16). It is not given privately in unknown words. In heathen religions this word referred to the hidden secrets of the gods which only the initiated could know. Those initiated into such mysteries claimed to have contact with the spirit world through emotional excitement, revelations, the working of miracles and the speaking of unknown words revealed by the spirits. In the New Testament Church every Christian is initiated.[34]

Possibly Paul spoke of these mysteries when he wrote that "one who speaks in a tongue . . . speaks mysteries" (1 Cor. 14:2). If this is not an allusion to mystery terminology, it is certainly not a commendation from the apostle.

SIMILAR ATTITUDES IN WORSHIP

Self-centered worship. Ecstatic religion by its very nature is self-oriented. Christians were to use their Christian χαρίσματα for the common good, but the pagans were totally concerned about their own personal experience, an attitude also prevalent among Corinthian Christians.

Women in worship. Women had an important place in the mystery cults, especially in the emotional and vocal realm. This was especially true in the Dionysian cult. Livy (59 B.C.–A.D. 17) in his *History of Rome* wrote that the majority of Dionysian worshipers were women.[35] The practice in the early Christian church and in the synagogue from which the church derived much of its order was for the women not to participate much in the vocal activities of the community. This aspect of the pagan cult could be what Paul was counteracting in 1 Corinthians 14:33b–36.[36] The believers were to conform to the practice of all the congregations of God in having vocal expressions limited to men. Also the use of ἄνδρας ("males") rather than ἄνθρωπους ("men") in regard to public prayer (1 Tim. 2:8) may give evidence of the consistency of this custom.

The Daemon (δαιμόνιον). The desire or at least reverence for the δαιμόνιον may be seen in the Corinthian church. In their pagan past the spirit would enable them to come into contact with the supernatural and to experience a oneness with the god in the state of ecstasy. These same attitudes existed among believers at Corinth. They had difficulty in accepting the fact that an idol (behind whom was a δαιμόνιον) was nothing and that meat sacrificed to an idol was just meat (1 Cor. 8:1–7). They were zealous for spirits (14:12). Some have said that πνεῦμα here is synonymous with "spiritual gifts," but this is an unlikely use of πνεῦμα. Also 1 Corinthians 12:1–3 demonstrates that they were not distinguishing the difference between speaking by the Spirit of God and speaking by means of the δαιμόνιον in their previous pagan worship, by whom they were led to false worship.

Ecstasy. Ecstasy was common in all mystery religions. The reason for this common experience is well stated by Nilsson.

> Not every man can be a miracle-worker and a seer, but most are suscepti-ble to ecstasy, especially as members of a great crowd, which draws the individual along with it and generates in him the sense of being filled with a higher, divine power. This is the literal meaning of the Greek word "enthusiasm," the state in which "god is in man." The rising tide of religious feeling seeks to surmount the barrier which separates man from god, it strives to enter into the divine, and it finds ultimate satisfaction only in that quenching of the consciousness in enthusiasm which is the goal of all mysticism.[37]

Unquestionably the Corinthian church was involved in ecstasy though many scholars today would not concede that they spoke ecstatic utterances.

GLOSSOLALIA IN THE CULT AND IN THE CHURCH

Speaking in tongues was not unique to the Christian faith. This phenomenon existed in various religions.

> There also the *pneumatikos*, by whatever name he might be called, was a familiar figure. As possessed by the god, or partaking of the Divine *pneuma* or *nous*, he too burst forth into mysterious ejaculations and rapt utterances of the kind described in the New Testament as *glossai lalein*.[38]

Possibly the carnal Corinthians, recent converts from the pagan religions, were failing to distinguish between the ecstatic utterance of their past and the true gift of tongues given supernaturally by the Holy Spirit.

There can be little question that the glossolalia in the Book of Acts were languages. The problem lies in the nature of tongues in 1 Corinthians. Gundry has forcefully argued that tongues in Acts and 1 Corinthians are intelligible, human languages.[39] The major problem with this view, in reference to Corinth, is given by Smith:

> If speaking in tongues involved a supernatural speech in a real language, then every such utterance required a direct miracle by God. This would mean, in the case of the Corinthians, that God was working a miracle at the wrong time and wrong place! He was causing that which He was directing the Apostle Paul to curtail.[40]

Is there a point of reconciliation for this contradiction? One may be that Paul used γλῶσσα for both ecstatic utterance and human language in 1 Corinthians, much as people do today with the term. One may wonder why Paul did not use μάντις when he referred to ecstatic utterance, but his method of argumentation may give the answer to this. Another possibility is given in Gundry's own article: Even if it were admitted that ecstatic utterance such as was practiced in Hellenistic religion was invading Corinthian Church meetings, *Paul would be condemning it by presenting normative Christian glossolalia as something radically different in style as well as in content.*"[41]

Pneumatika and Charismata in Paul's Theology

PAULINE ARGUMENTS

In seeking to lead the Corinthian Christians to a proper

understanding of the workings of the Spirit, especially the gift of tongues, Paul used several methods of argumentation. Rather than speaking immediately against their practice in the meetings, he desired to find a common ground of departure, endeavoring to bring them to his position at the end. This procedure was recognized by Chadwick.

> The entire drift of the argument of 1 Cor. xii-xiv is such as to pour a douche of ice-cold water over the whole practice. But Paul could hardly have denied that the gift of tongues was a genuine supernatural *charisma* without putting a fatal barrier between himself and the Corinthian enthusiasts . . . . [for] the touchstone of soundness in the eyes of those claiming to be possessed by the Spirit was whether their gift was recognized to be a genuine work of God. To deny this recognition was to prove oneself to be altogether lacking in the Spirit. That Paul was fully aware of this issue appears not only from 1 Cor. ii. 14–15, but also from 1 Cor. xiv. 37–8, a masterly sentence which has the effect of brilliantly forestalling possible counter-attack at the most dangerous point, and indeed carries the war into the enemy camp. To have refused to recognize the practice as truly supernatural would have been catastrophic. Paul must fully admit that *glossolalia* is indeed a divine gift; but, he urges, it is the most inferior of all gifts. But Paul does more than admit it. He asserts it: *eucharisto to theo, panton humon mallon glossais lalo* (xiv 18). No stronger assertion of his belief in the validity of this gift of the Spirit could be made; and in the context it is a master touch which leaves the enthusiasts completely outclassed and outmaneuvered on their own ground.[42]

Many of Paul's statements, then, should perhaps be recognized as conciliatory rather than commendatory. The statement, "One who speaks in a tongue edifies himself" (1 Cor. 14:4) is not commendatory. Paul merely conceded a point here for argument. He did not affirm the legitimacy of that believer's experience as from the Holy Spirit. One might even say that irony is to be found in Paul's statement.

> It should be carefully noted that if Paul is not using irony here, then he is crediting very carnal believers with an intimacy with the Holy Spirit and with God, with deep spiritual experiences, that all his other writings, and all the rest of Scripture, teach most emphatically can never be entered into by a carnal believer. . . . He is using irony as a weapon to lay bare the emptiness of the claims of carnal believers.[43]

In addition, if Paul's statement is one of truth, not irony, then it contradicts 1 Corinthians 12:7, that grace-gifts (χαρίσματα) are "for the common good," and also 13:1–3, that gifts are not to be self-centered. Paul also used irony in 1 Corinthians 4:8–10.

Usually scholars have taken the πνευμάτικοι in 1 Corinthians

12:1 to refer to the spiritual gifts Paul mentioned in that chapter (vv. 8–10, 28–30). There is good reason, though, to consider it instead as a technical term of the Corinthians for "one who speaks in tongues" or "speaking in tongues." Paul adopted the Corinthian terms and clichés at other points, it appears,[44] and it would seem to be equally true here. In other places (1 Cor. 2:14–15) Paul referred to all Christians as πνευμάτικοι and non-Christians as ψυχικοί, but here (1 Cor. 12) the word takes on a special meaning that probably reflects the enthusiasts' use of the term for one who speaks in tongues.

Certainly such use is in harmony with usage in the mystery cults, from which these Corinthians derived their initial religious thinking. A further evidence of this specific meaning for πνευματικός is that 1 Corinthians 12:2–3 concern "speaking by the Spirit of God." Also, the term is used again in 14:1–3, to contrast the one who prophesies with the one who speaks in tongues. In addition, 14:37 without doubt uses πνευματικός as a definite term for a tongues-speaker. The verse could be translated, "The prophet or the one with the gift of tongues. . . .," since this is the contrast throughout Paul's argument.[45]

Paul sought to demonstrate that the specific pneumatic utterances of the Corinthians should conform to the χαρίσματα of the Holy Spirit. Tongues, as a χάρισμα, had a specific purpose in God's program (14:21–22) but not for personal edification or to show "possession by the god, as the Corinthians supposed."

PAULINE CORRECTIVES

One would not want to intimate that all tongues-speaking in the church at Corinth was illegitimate. Ervin poignantly speaks to those who would categorically parallel glossolalia at Corinth to the mysteries. "Behind this glib assumption is the erroneous a priori that superficial correlation proves mutual causation."[46]

Though Ervin is basically correct in his observation, nevertheless there is good evidence that the Corinthian church included members who were affected by their pagan past. Paul prefaced his answer to the Corinthians' question about "spirituals" (περὶ δὲ τῶν πνευματικῶν) with a reference to their religious history. He did not want them to be ignorant of the spirituals, "because you know that when you were led away toward speechless idols as you would be unconsciously led" (1 Cor. 12:21, author's translation). Since the Corinthians had a background of ecstatic (and so-called "spiritual") religion, the apostle felt it necessary to instruct them that the spirituals of which he would be writing were not of the same class.

> The very characteristic of the Corinthians' heathen past, [Paul] argues, was the sense of being overpowered and carried away by spiritual forces. . . . "There is no doubt at all," Schrenk comments, "that Paul intends to say here, The truly spiritual is not marked by a being swept away . . . that was precisely the characteristic of your previous fanatical religion." It is important to notice that Paul places this valuation of the spiritually "sweeping" at the very outset of his treatment of "spiritual things" in Corinth. As the superscripture to his essay in chapters twelve to fourteen Paul has written: Seizure is not necessarily Christian or paramountly spiritual.[47]

That the Corinthians leaned toward their pagan past in the mysteries as a means of spiritual expression maybe also seen in 1 Corinthians 14:12, "Since you are zealous of spiritual gifts" (lit., "spirits," πνευμάτων). Gerlicher rightly observes, "This implies that their present devotion was to spiritual matters per se, independent of Christ-centered worship and congregational-oriented edification."[48]

Did the apostle recognize any of the tongues-speaking at Corinth as being genuine? Was there, in other words, a genuine gift of tongues distinguishable from the counterfeit manifestations (that were demonic in nature)?

Paul gave several guidelines for glossolalia, showing how to differentiate between the true and false manifestations. In light of his statement that the Corinthians had been uncontrollably driven in their pagan worship, Paul wrote, "Wherefore I am making known to you that no one speaking in the Spirit of God says, Jesus is Anathema" (1 Cor. 12:3, author's translation). In their former pagan frenzies they did not have control over themselves and so some might have felt that now speaking (presumably) in the Spirit of God (in this context glossolalia) they would call Jesus cursed. However, this mystery cult practice was to be exposed by Paul.[49] Whoever says "Jesus is Anathema" is obviously not being controlled by the Spirit of God. The lordship of Jesus is the criterion by which pneumatic utterances are to be judged as genuine or false.[50]

In the pagan glossolalia, no thought was given to the harmony of participants in group worship. Only the individual experience was important. Paul wrote that unity is a sign of the Spirit's activity. "All do not speak with tongues, do they?" (1 Cor. 12:30). "If anyone speaks in a tongue, it should be by two or at the most three, and each in turn, and let one interpret" (14:27). A true manifestation by the Spirit would be orderly, "for God is not a God of confusion but of peace" (14:33).

Another method of discerning genuine from cultic or demonically inspired ecstasy was self-control.

> Tongues were to be manifested in the public worship when accompanied by the companion gift of interpretation. Prophesying was subject to the discernment of the order of prophets. In every case, self-control is the dominant note, for "the spirits of the prophets are subject to the prophets." Contemporary descriptions take note of the fact that such self-control was totally lacking in the orgianistic ecstasies of the mystery cults. Hence, these safeguards would protect the church by distinguishing the counterfeit from the genuine manifestations of the Holy Spirit.[51]

Another factor that distinguishes the true from the false concerns the person who speaks in tongues. Paul wrote, "If anyone seems to be a prophet or a glossolalist, let him recognize what I am writing that it is a commandment of the Lord. If anyone does not know (ἀγνοεῖ), he is without knowledge (ἀγνοεῖται)" (1 Cor. 14:37–38. author's translation). Paul was possibly being satirical here since pneumatics felt themselves spiritually and knowledgeably superior. If anyone did not submit to the apostolic Word, it was proof that his manifestations were false.

Paul gave the previous safeguards so that the spurious tongues would fall away, since they would be recognized as false by not agreeing with the guidelines he set. The true gift of tongues would then properly operate in alignment with the other gifts of the Spirit and edify the body of Christ.

One might ask what proof there is that there really was a legitimate gift of tongues in the Corinthian church. First, Paul gave rules to regulate the gift. Why give rules for it if it were not even in existence? Since there was a mixture of the true and the false, Paul gave a way to distinguish them rather than forbidding tongues outright.

Second, in 14:26 he showed how χαρίσματα involves more than tongues. "When you gather together, each one has a psalm, each one has a teaching, each one has a revelation, each one has a tongue, each one has an interpretation" (author's translation).[52]

Third, Paul gave the injunction "Stop forbidding speaking in tongues" (14:39). Paul wanted tongues, which seemed to be the main problem at Corinth, to continue. Moffatt says, "Some soberminded Christians in the local church, as at Thessalonica, evidently were shocked; they desired to check the habit (xiv. 39)."[53] In light of the mystery religions Ervin presents a more plausible viewpoint.

> There is another possible reconstruction of events in Corinth that fits the facts. It is not beyond the realm of possibility that the "sober-minded Christians," postulated by Dr. Moffatt, with or without the cooperation of Gnostic elements of more speculative bent of mind, may have initiated the prohibition of tongues in the worship of the assembly. Alarmed at the patently unspiritual excesses of Gnostic [?] "ecstatics," and not being able to cope with such counterfeit manifestations, they may have consented to the radical expedient of forbidding all "spiritual" manifestations. The expedient may have represented a counsel of despair which Paul sought to counter by reinstating tongues and prophesying to their proper place in the worship of the church where "each one hath a psalm, hath a teaching, hath a revelation, hath a tongue, hath an interpretation."[54]

Conclusion

Corinth was experience-oriented and self-oriented. Mystery religions and other pagan cults were in great abundance, from which cults many of the members at the Corinthian church received their initial religious instruction. After being converted they had failed to free themselves from pagan attitudes and they confused the true work of the Spirit of God with the former pneumatic and ecstatic experiences of the pagan religions, especially the Dionysian mystery or the religion of Apollo. By careful and delicate argumentation Paul sought to help these believers recognize their errors and operate all the χαρίσματα (gifts of the Spirit) not just the πνευματικά (tongues). Also he desired that they perform the χαρίσματα for the edification of the body of Christ, not self.

CHAPTER 12

Who Were Paul's Opponents in Galatia?

Walter B. Russell

Why Is the Identity of Paul's Opponents an Issue?

Paul's opponents in Galatia are central to the argument of the Book of Galatians because the epistle is essentially a response to their threat to the churches of Galatia. Therefore it is not surprising to see that the opponents are mentioned in every chapter (1:6–9; 2:4–5; 3:1; 4:17; 5:10, 12; 6:12–13). Conservative scholars have historically assumed that these foes were Judaizers and have interpreted the text in that light. However, in the last 70 years a persistent critique now gaining widespread acceptance says the Judaizer identity is totally inadequate in explaining crucial verses like Galatians 5:13, "For you were called to freedom, brethren, only do not turn your freedom into an opportunity for the flesh, but through love serve one another."

While Paul was apparently addressing some sort of Judaistic aberration in Galatians 3–4, these critics argue, he was also overtly attacking an antinomian aberration in Galatians 5–6, and the Judaistic identity cannot encompass this additional aberration. Therefore an increasing number of New Testament scholars are advocating a different identity for Paul's opponents in Galatia. Evangelicals should not blithely continue to assume the correctness of the Judaizer identity. They must see if their assumptions need revision and if this will aid in understanding the latter part of Galatians.

The Three Major Views of the Opponents' Identity

Three major views of Paul's opponents in Galatia encompass numerous minor views. The *traditional view* is that the opponents were "Judaizers" pressuring Gentiles to live as if they were Jews. The *two-opponent view* holds that both Judaizers and libertinistic "pneumatics" plagued Paul in Galatia. The *Gnostic/syncretistic*

Jewish Christians view is that there was one group of opponents with both Judaistic and libertinistic traits in some of the peripheral groups within Judaism and Asia Minor.

THE TRADITIONAL VIEW: JUDAIZERS

Since the second-century Marcionite *Prologues to Galatians* (preserved only in Latin translations), it has been inferred that Paul's opponents were overzealous Jewish Christians from Jerusalem. They advocated in Galatia the traditional Jewish proselyte model by requiring Gentile Christians to attach themselves to ethnic Israel. This identification was carefully confirmed by Calvin[1] and more casually assumed by Luther.[2] Since Calvin's and Luther's day the majority of Protestant scholars have identified Paul's opponents in some way with the Jewish Christians from Jerusalem.

This identity was solidified in the 19th century by F. C. Baur of the Tübingen School, who made these opponents a decisive interpretive key to all Paul's writings. Baur's reconstruction of the history of the early church does not so much pit Paul against the Jerusalem apostles, as is popularly understood, but against the party of Jewish Christians identified with James and the Jerusalem church.[3] These Judaizers had an Ebionite tendency and had not broken out of the limits of Judaism in their understanding of Christianity and the sufficiency of Christ's ministry.[4] To Baur, the Epistle to the Galatians was a microcosm of the massive struggle between Pauline and Jewish Christianity. So while Baur never wrote a commentary on Galatians, his central and emphatic identification of Paul's opponents in Galatia became the almost unquestioned standard, even to those who opposed major portions of Baur's reconstruction of early events.

Schmithals summarized the situation as follows.

> There are few problems in the realm of New Testament introduction in which the scholars of all eras are so unanimously and indisputably of one mind as here.
> The heretics in Galatia are Judaizers, that is, Christians who demand the observance of the Jewish law on a greater or lesser scale, but in any case including circumcision: thus they are Christians in whose opinion membership in the eschatological community of the Messiah who has appeared in Jesus depends upon membership in the national cultic union, constituted through the rite of circumcision, of the ancient people of the covenant. This thesis is the presupposition of the exegesis of the Galatian epistle in the commentaries, not its conclusion; and it can be such a presupposition because no one would deny it.[5]

Schmithals himself denies the traditional identity of Paul's opponents, holding, instead, that they were Gnostics. Before Schmithals wrote in the 1970s and 80s, the status of the Judaizers identity was generally unquestioned. Ironically some recent New Testament introductions have assumed some form of *his* position.[6]

Viewing Paul's Galatian opponents as Judaizers seems supported by strong internal evidence. Those who "distort the gospel" in the churches seem to have come from the outside (1:7) and they confused the churches (1:7; 5:10, 12). They seem to have been Christians, since they were offering "a different gospel" (1:6) and desired to avoid persecution from the Jewish community (6:12). Paul's focus on Jerusalem and Judea in Galatians 1–2 and 4:21–31 seems to point to the opponents' origin from this area, though this is not held as firmly as other aspects of their identity. Their Jewish roots seem unassailable given their emphasis on circumcision (5:2; 6:12–13), observance of the Mosaic Law (3:2; 5:4) and certain festivals (4:10), and apparent interest in being "sons of Abraham" (3:6–29; 4:21–31). With its straightforward reading of Galatians and its correlation with Acts 15, many scholars continue to espouse this traditional view in standard New Testament introductions,[7] technical monographs,[8] commentaries on Galatians,[9] and journal articles.[10]

Worthy of inclusion under this major view is the position argued by Johannes Munck.[11] While he was reacting against Baur's bifurcation of the early church into competing Pauline and Jewish segments, Munck nonetheless saw Paul's Galatian opponents as Judaizers. The uniqueness of his view is that he saw these Judaizers as *Gentile* Christians from within Galatia.[12] They had only recently been circumcised, according to Galatians 6:13, in which Paul used the present participle οἱ περιτεμνόμενοι to describe them.[13] While Munck perceived himself to be opposite Baur with this particular view, his identifying of Paul's opponents does not lead to any substantial difference from Baur's in interpreting the epistle as a whole. The same can be said of the similar position of Harvey,[14] who identifies Paul's opponents as "not Jews by birth, but Gentiles who have only recently become Jewish proselytes, or who are still contemplating doing so."[15] The uniqueness of Harvey's view is that he argues that these proselytes were pressuring fellow Christians to avoid persecution from the synagogue by adopting *Jewish practices,* not Jewish theology. Harvey reasons that this is so because of the Jewish emphasis on strict adherence to Jewish practices, rather than to Jewish orthodoxy.[16] Paul's tactic was to show the theological consequences of embracing Jewish practices (Gal. 6:12–13).

THE TWO-OPPONENT VIEW: JUDAIZERS AND ANTINOMIANS

In reaction to Baur's dominant reconstruction of the early church, Lütgert[17] opposed the one opponent/Judaizers view by arguing for the additional resistance of a second group in Galatia. While conceding the existence of the Judaizers, Lütgert was convinced that an even more threatening group was the primary focus of Paul's attack in Galatians. Like Luther before him,[18] though seeing them more as an organized party, Lütgert identified this second group of Christians as antinomians.[19] The thread that holds Galatians together as Paul addressed this two-front battle is the subject of the Law.[20] Paul's arguments with both the Judaizers and the antinomians involve the Law and its relationship to the Christian life. Therefore, Lütgert argued, Paul vacillated between addressing these two groups as he wrote Galatians. For example while Galatians 3–4 is primarily concerned with the Judaizers, Paul's focus on them ends at 5:6 and he began to address the antinomians' abuses of the Law in 5:7.[21] The majority of Galatians 5–6 is no longer seen as Paul's defensive limitation of the boundaries of freedom in light of possible Judaizers' criticism, but rather as a much more aggressive and overt attack on the antinomians' real abuses.[22]

Lütgert's views were not broadly disseminated until Ropes championed them in a small monograph in 1929.[23] Ropes made only minor adjustments to Lütgert's thesis and sought to demonstrate it by briefly but systematically going through Galatians chapter by chapter. Interestingly enough, he perceived the break from the lengthy Judaizers' discussion of Galatians 3–4 to be at 5:10, not 5:6 as Lütgert had argued. Ropes suggests that Paul began the practical section with 5:11. "The transition to the next topic is an important one, sharper than any other transition in the epistle. Our theory requires the break to be made after verse 10, not after verse 12."[24] As Fletcher has wryly noted, "For such a sharp division, it does not seem that it would be necessary to rely upon one's presuppositions to discern it."[25] Weaknesses like this have hindered acceptance of Lütgert's and Ropes's two-opponent view. Nevertheless their emphasis on the presence of libertinistic "pneumatici" or "spiritual persons"[26] helped shape the next reaction to the traditional view.

THE GNOSTIC/SYNCRETISTIC JEWISH CHRISTIAN VIEW

Though the identification of Gnostics as Paul's opponents in Galatia tends to be associated with Schmithals, other scholars had previously written of a Gnostic presence in Galatia.[27] However, it is Schmithals who firmly ties Paul's ministry to the combating of some form of first-century Gnosticism.[28] Schmithals follows the Corinthian/Galatian epistles' order of Lütgert's study and his identification of Gnostics in both communities. Like Lütgert, Schmithals considers that "the picture of the Galatians heresy is to be filled out in details from the Corinthian epistles."[29] While building on Lütgert's and Ropes's identification of libertinistic pneumatics in Galatia, Schmithals (and others after him) significantly deviates from that theory by positing a *single* battlefront in Galatia. The questionable audience theory of the two-opponent view is rightly criticized and rejected as unsatisfactory.[30] In its place is offered a single group of opponents who manifest both sets of characteristics previously attached to the Judaizers and antinomian pneumatics.

Rather than refuting the traditional view of Judaizers in Galatia, Schmithals' strategy is to develop a coherent picture of Gnostics in Galatia and demonstrate how this best explains the details in Galatians. To do this, however, involves some question-begging on his part. For example in the traditional view Galatians 3–4 is seen as the heart of the argumentation against the Judaizers. Rather than contesting the particulars of the Judaizer interpretation of this section, however, Schmithals virtually ignores it and alleges that Paul did not really understand his Gnostic opponents or he would not have argued in this manner.[31] Others who adhere to this Gnostic identification find that they too must assert that their knowledge of the Galatian opponents exceeds Paul's because in Galatians 3–4 he argued about the Law "in such a way as he might have done if his opponents had been Pharisaic Judaists, which they obviously were not."[32] It is *possible* that a critic's knowledge can exceed an author's knowledge of the *subject matter,* but this is not to be confused with the critic's thinking that his knowledge of the author's *meaning* is superior.[33] Schmithals and some who have followed him seem to lapse into this hermeneutical error at times.

Before looking at support for this view of Paul's opponents, the closely related identity of syncretistic Jewish Christians should be discussed. This view came into particular prominence through the writing of Crownfield.[34] He identified Paul's Galatian opponents as a group that combined Christianity with a mystical understanding of following Torah and Jewish legal practices.[35] The "Judaizers" and "spirituals" were actually the same group. The leaders of this group are theorized to have been early converts to Christianity, and although not followers of the earthly Jesus, were nonetheless connected with Jerusalem. Crownfield conjectured that they were adherents of Jewish mystery cults seeking spiritual illumination through legalism. As he built on Lütgert's thesis to develop his view, Schmithals also built on Crownfield's work and specified it to Gnostic groups. Both writers tended to correlate the Colossian errorists with those of Galatia who combined some Jewish rites with laxity in morals.[36] A similar view is held by Schlier in his commentary on Galatians.[37] He embraces an identity for the opponents that explains their nomism coupled with their libertinistic tendencies as an early stage of Gnosticism demonstrating a sort of Jewish apocalypticism similar to that found at Qumran.[38] This is not far from the view of Brinsmead, who sees Paul's opponents as possessing an Essene theology and ethics that espoused a "nomistic enthusiasm."[39] Brinsmead's elaborate picture of the Galatian intruders has been devastatingly criticized by several scholars.[40]

Following this trajectory Georgi sees the troublers of the Galatian churches as pneumatics using Christian elements as the ultimate completion of a Jewish syncretism previously enriched with Gentile motives.[41] Against Schmithals, who sees Paul's opponents as Jews who were never baptized,[42] Georgi views these false brethren as a faction within the Jerusalem church pressing for the circumcision of Gentile Christians. This faction viewed the Law as a source of speculative wisdom, not simply for the Jews, but as the norm for the universe. However, their goal was the attainment of pneumatic completion through individualistic and ascetic religious experiences.[43] Wegenast holds a view similar to that of Georgi and underscores the importance of circumcision and the Law to these opponents.[44] This represents a basic following of the general thesis of Crownfield *in this area* against Schmithals, while still working within the general Gnostic identity championed by the latter.

Both the Gnostic and the syncretistic Jewish Christian identifications consider that Paul was primarily addressing the conduct of his opponents and that this libertine lifestyle, not the legalistic theology, was the basic threat facing the Galatians.[45] Following Lütgert, Schmithals focuses on passages like Galatians 4:9 and 5:1 that seem to point to this threat. However, of particular importance are these verses.

> "And I testify again to every man who receives circumcision, that he is under obligation to keep the whole Law" (5:3).

> "For you were called to freedom, brethren; only do not turn your freedom into an opportunity for the flesh, but through love serve one another" (5:13).

> "But I say, walk by the Spirit, and you will not carry out the desire of the flesh" (5:16).

> "For those who are circumcised do not even keep the Law themselves, but they desire to have you circumcised, that they may boast in your flesh" (6:13).

Following Schmithals's basic identification Betz asserts that the fundamental problem facing the churches of Galatia was the conflict of the Spirit and the flesh. He proposes that the churches were wrestling with how being ἐν πνεύματι conflicted with life's daily realities. "How can the πνευματικός coexist with 'trespasses' in his daily life?"[46] Paul's opponents were answering this question with the security that Torah offered. By accepting Torah and circumcision, the Galatians would then become partakers of the safety offered by the Sinai Covenant.[47] One can see with this reconstruction and emphasis that Galatians 5–6 becomes the specific recommendation that Paul made to the Galatians. The focal point of Galatians in Galatians 3–4, associated with the traditional view of Judaizing opponents, has shifted to a focal point in Galatians 5–6 in this third major view. Methodologically the procedure is to seek to wrap the remainder of Galatians around the primary core in chapters 5–6. While Betz essentially subscribes to this third view (though not emphasizing the opponents' identity in his exposition), his masterful literary analysis of Galatians locates the body of the epistle in chapters 3–4.[48] This runs contrary to his belief that chapters 5–6 have real force for the Galatians' problems. The mere polemic against accepting circumcision and Law in 2:15–5:12 "does not do justice to the Galatian trouble."[49] However, the force of Betz's identification of the problem in Galatia is offset by the weight of his literary analysis, as Fletcher has noted.[50] A similar problem is shared by Schlier, who accepts a conservative version of the Gnostic identity, but interprets Galatians as if Paul were addressing Judaizers.[51]

Solving the Identity Crisis

The goal in identifying Paul's opponents in Galatia is to account for all the particulars of the epistle in the most comprehensive way. In seeking to do this Barclay has delineated three major problems in this kind of "mirror-reading": (1) Paul did not directly address his opponents but talked to the Galatians about the opponents. (2) Galatians is a fierce polemic and the intense rhetoric may tend to distort the opponents' actual positions. (3) Readers encounter the linguistic distortion of hearing only one partner in the conversation.[52]

Barclay then describes four dangerous pitfalls in recent attempts to mirror-read Galatians. (1) The danger of *undue selectivity* (deciding which of Paul's statements are particularly revealing about the opponents' message). (2) The danger of *over-interpretation* (imagining that every statement of Paul rebuts an equally vigorous opponents' counterstatement). (3) The danger of *mishandling polemics* (making more out of Paul's attacks than is warranted with polemical language). (4) The danger of *latching onto particular words and phrases* (using these brief bits of data as the flimsy pegs on which the whole thesis should hang).[53]

Keeping in mind the seven methodological criteria that Barclay suggests,[54] this writer will attempt to weigh the particulars of Galatians and to sift through the three major views.

In agreement with the first and third views, it seems that the problems raised by Paul's opponents are of a unitary nature. Gordon's observation is on target.

> An examination of the variety of connecting terms and particles reveals that Galatians is, essentially, a single argument. We do not find in this epistle indicators of a shift in topic such as we find in First Corinthians. One does not have to agree with every dimension of Betz' argument to recognize the validity of his claim of unified rhetoric. At least by literary canons, Galatians is not a series of arguments about different matters but a series of sub-arguments about essentially one matter (which itself may, of course, have many ramifications).[55]

In lieu of in-depth analysis, two significant structural observations will suffice at this point. The first is the bracketing of the epistle to the Galatians with the prescript (1:1–5) and the postscript (6:11–18). Bullinger noticed the similarity between 1:1–5 and 6:17–18 and labeled it "complex correspondence of repeated alteration."[56] Betz calls it "the epistolary framework" and notes that "it appears almost as a kind of external bracket for the body of the letter."⁵⁷ Betz observes the structural ramifications of this bracketing effect when he comments on the nature of the prescript (1:1–5): "It is also interesting that at several points there are interrelations between the preface and the body of the letter. It is at these points that the theological tendencies and the purpose of the letter can be observed."⁵⁸ He notes that the postscript (6:11–18) serves a similar purpose: "It contains the interpretive clues to the understanding of Paul's major concerns in the letter as a whole and should be employed as the hermeneutical key to the intentions of the Apostle."⁵⁹

Given the significance of these beginning and ending paragraphs for determining the purpose of Galatians and Paul's intentions, noting their three common topics should prove insightful.

First, the issue of *Paul's threatened apostolic authority* occurs in both passages. He used several Greek prepositions in describing his apostleship in 1:1: Παῦλος ἀπόστολος, οὐκ ἀπ' ἀνθρώπων οὐδὲ δι' ἀνθρώπου ἀλλὰ διὰ Ἰησοῦ Χριστοῦ καὶ θεοῦ πατρὸς. Such a definitive description of his apostleship is unique among the salutations of the traditional 13–epistle Pauline corpus. Paul ended on an even more picturesque note of his authoritative identity in 6:17, in which he flatly stated that he bore in his body the στίγματα τοῦ Ἰησοῦ. He began and ended Galatians with unique claims of association with both the Person and ministry of Jesus.

Second, *the fatherhood of God* is emphasized in both the prescript and postscript of Galatians. Again among the salutations of the Pauline corpus this emphasis is unique in that θεοῦ πατρὸς (ἡμῶν) is mentioned three times. In the salutations of 11 of the epistles God's fatherhood is mentioned only once, and 2 Thessalonians has two occurrences (1:1–2). But Galatians is unusual with its threefold repetition within the opening verses (1:1, 3–4).

Apparently the underscoring of God's fatherhood over the Galatian ἀδελφοί (v. 2) weighed heavily in Paul's thoughts as he began this epistle. If the Galatians questioned Paul's apostolic status and therefore his gospel, then they probably questioned whether Paul's gospel really did bring them into the family of God. It seems that Paul began to provide reassurance of God's paternity from the very beginning of this epistle. It is from θεοῦ πατρὸς ἡμῶν καὶ κυρίου Ἰησοῦ Χριστοῦ that "grace and peace" come, in Paul's typical salutation (v. 3). In 6:16 the conditional blessing of "peace and mercy" is on those who walk by the rule (τῷ κανόνι) that Paul just explained in 6:14–15. It is also these who are appositively called τὸν Ἰσραὴλ τοῦ θεοῦ. They deserve this term denoting God's chosen people. He is *their* Father.

Third, *deliverance from the present evil age* (αἰῶνος) is associated with the death of Jesus Christ and promised to His people in both the prescript and postscript. In 1:4 Christ's giving of Himself was for the purpose (ὅπως as a conjunction with the subjunctive) of delivering people from the present aeon. In 6:14–15 Paul associated deliverance from the κόσμος with the cross of Christ and having a new life (6:12–13). Apparently Paul's opponents offered an alternative means of deliverance from the tug of the aeon or cosmos. That means was apparently connected to being identified with Israel by means of circumcision. In contrast the deliverance Paul preached identified the Galatians primarily with the death of Christ that created a new creation. As both Martyn[60] and Brinsmead[61] have observed, bracketing the epistle with this apocalyptic language gives the epistle an apocalyptic tone. "Thus the subject of his letter to the Galatians is precisely an apocalypse, the apocalypse of Jesus Christ, and specifically the apocalypse of his cross."[62]

The point of this sketchy picture of prescript and postscript parallelism is that Paul began and concluded his letter by expressing concerns about his threatened apostolic authority, the fatherhood of God, and the deliverance from this present age. If these are reflecting Paul's major concerns in the letter as a whole, then the body of the letter between these brackets must give primary attention to the development of these three points. This in turn should reflect the major questions of the Galatians and should thereby give some indication of the identity of the opponents who raised those questions.

If the first structural clue comes from the bracketing effect of the prescript and postscript that underscores the unity of the problem in Galatia, then the second structural clue flows out of the first and also helps establish the identity of Paul's opponents. This second structural insight is simply that Galatians 3–4 must be considered a significant part of Paul's argument. These two chapters cannot be brushed aside as Schmithals does when he says Paul did not really understand his opponents' theology so that "it is indeed characteristic that this middle section of the Galatian epistle [3:1–5:12], in contrast to all other sections, contains hardly any direct references to the situation in Galatia."[63]

Betz realized that this section was the core of Paul's argument. Galatians 3–4 was the *probatio* that followed the *propositio* of 2:15–21 and preceded the *exhortatio* of 5:1–6:10.[64] Betz had no other alternative in light of the structure of the epistle that emerged from his rhetorical analysis. Therefore he was left to criticizing the persuasive value of rhetoric itself since "*no* kind of rational argument can be adequate with regard to the defense Paul must make."[65] Betz's solution is to see the epistle as a "magical letter," since Paul began it with a curse and ended it with a conditional blessing.[66] Since Paul allegedly "does not leave things to be decided by the reasonableness of the Galatians,"[67] then the value of Galatians 3–4 in his argumentation is greatly diminished in Betz's analysis. However, at best, this seems to be a questionable view of chapters 3–4. Is it legitimate to appeal to the genre of a magic letter that is supposedly acting as some "supra-genre" at the *real* level of the persuasion of the Galatians? Indeed, is this legitimate when Betz himself admits that "no satisfactory investigation of the genre [of magical letter] exists"?[68] Is this not similar to Schmithals's response that final appeal rests with an extratextual entity to which there is no access?

Would not a simpler and more credible conclusion be that Galatians 3–4 is important in Paul's argumentation, since it is the structural middle of his epistle? Even more importantly it contains significant discussions of two of the three bracketing themes: the fatherhood of God and deliverance from the present evil age. The fatherhood of God permeates chapters 3–4 as the metaphoric umbrella of the section that covers the themes of sonship (3:15–29), heirship (4:1–7), and line of blessing (4:21–31). While the deliverance theme receives in-depth treatment in chapters 5–6, it is also a central part of Paul's argument in chapters 3–4 as he discussed possible perfection by the flesh (σαρκὶ ἐπιτελεῖσθε, 3:3). However, rather than deliverance, such a flesh-strategy will lead to the bondage of slavery in various forms (3:22–23; 4:1–11, 21–31). Without Galatians 3–4 Paul's beginning and ending concerns with the themes of God's fatherhood and deliverance from the present evil age would be dealt death blows. These chapters must be considered as primary data in the identification of Paul's opponents. If that is the case, then Jewett's assertion (following H. J. Holtzmann's) is probably correct "that their mottoes were σπέπμα ᾽Αβραάμ [3:16] and ᾽Ιερουσαλήμ ἥτις ἐστιν μήτηρ ἡμῶν [4:26]."[69] Both mottoes represent opposition to Paul's viewpoint about the three bracketing themes of apostolic authority, God's fatherhood, and present deliverance. Both mottoes are discussed by Paul in depth in chapters 3–4.

Some who hold the Gnostic/syncretistic Jewish Christian identity of Paul's opponents may be able to embrace all that has been proposed in reference to the three bracketing themes and the centrality of Galatians 3–4 in Paul's argumentation. However, this writer must part company with those holding the Gnostic/syncretistic view. First, the Gnostic identification is inadequate because it seems highly unlikely and extremely ill-fitting to assume the presence of Gnostics in Galatia.[70] Second, the more generic reason for separating from those who hold this third view is that this writer perceives the theory of the presence of antinomian or libertinistic elements in Paul's opponents to be fundamentally wrong. Therefore rooting the identity of Paul's opponents and centering the primary issue of Galatians around antinomianism and libertinism is fallacious. If this is true, then both the two-opponent view of Lütgert and Ropes and the third view that flowed out of it must be rejected.

In view of some widespread recent acceptance of the third view, how can it be so readily discarded? The answer is that the Gnostic/syncretistic Jewish Christian view is built on several verses that are all interpreted from the same faulty perspective. In particular, fundamental to this third view is the premise that these opponents of Paul did not want to keep all the Law, but only that part of it that served their purposes—circumcision and sacred days. Hence Paul reminded the Galatian believers of the unity of the Mosaic Law and the obligation to the whole Law if one places himself in submission to any part of it.

> "For as many as are of the works of the Law are under a curse; for it is written, 'Cursed is everyone who does not abide by all things written in the book of the Law, to perform them'" (3:10).
> "And I testify again to every man who receives circumcision, that he is under obligation to keep the whole Law" (5:3).

However, this is where the opponents apparently were caught in a serious conflict, since they did not want to keep the Law because of their basic antinomian and libertine desires.

> "For you were called to freedom, brethren; only do not turn your freedom into an opportunity for the flesh, but through love serve one another" (5:13).

"For those who are circumcised do not even keep the Law themselves, but they desire to have you circumcised, that they may boast in
your flesh" (6:13).

The evidence *seems* plain. These opponents mixed nomistic
theology with antinomistic lifestyles. But is this what Paul was
really saying? This writer thinks not. Paul never said his opponents
lacked a desire for obedience to all the Law. In fact he said just the
opposite. Paul's opponents apparently held forth the ideal of a
whole life under the protection of the Law, in that the Galatians
could be described as wanting to be under Law (4:21). They were
considering taking up the yoke (ζυγός) of the Law, which Paul
derisively described as a "yoke of slavery" (5:1). To take up a
yoke is a New Testament phrase for a life of submission. In
Matthew 11:28–30 it refers to identification with and submission
to Jesus. In Acts 15:10 Peter referred to identification with and
submission to the Law as "a yoke which neither our fathers nor we
have been able to bear." The term ζυγός itself is neutral and was
used throughout rabbinical literature as a symbol of obedience,
not of oppression.[71] The yoke of the Law was referred to as a
gracious blessing compared to other possible yokes. The following
statement about the yoke of the Torah from *Pirqé Avot* 3:5 is
attributed to Rabbi Nehunia ben Haqqaneh, who supposedly was
a disciple of Rabbi Yohanan ben Zakkai (A.D. 1–80): "Whosoever
accepts the yoke of the Law from him shall be removed the yoke
of the kingdom and the yoke of mundane care, but he that casts off
from him the yoke of the Law upon him shall be laid the yoke of
the kingdom and the yoke of worldly care."[72]

While the final form of this saying was probably completed
about A.D. 250,[73] scholars have no difficulty accepting that the
basic thrust of the original saying is at least as old as the first
century A.D.[74] Therefore Paul's reminder that the whole Law is
binding was probably not a negative statement within 1st-century
Judaism, and it certainly would not be a surprise to his opponents.
But was it not necessary if these opponents did not keep the Law
(6:13)? Yes, it was necessary to make his point, but for reasons
different from those assumed by the advocates of the third view.

They assume that reminders about the whole Law's binding
nature were because of the opponents' desire to disobey much of
the Law (e.g., 5:3 and 6:13). However, Paul explained why the
opponents did not obey the Law. It was not from lack of desire to
obey, but rather from an inherent inability to obey. Their failure

was due to identifying with a community that was not aided by God's Spirit (3:1–5). Therefore they were unable to meet the demands of the Law. In 3:19–4:11 Paul attributed this inability to an earlier, preparatory, more immature period in God's redemptive program in which enslavement to sin and failure were the norm (3:23; 4:3, 8–11).

Paul's opponents wanted to revert in an anachronistic fashion to this period by their intense nomistic emphasis. With their commitment to Torah-observance came the accompanying failure of the Law era—its shutting up under sin (3:22), its keeping in custody (3:23), its childish, slavelike state (4:1–3), and its enslavement to the elemental things of the world (4:8–10; cf. 4:3). Those who preferred this kind of childish failure, evidenced by receiving circumcision (5:2), needed to realize they were subjecting themselves again to a yoke of slavery (5:1), were putting themselves under the obligation of the whole Law (5:3), and were severing themselves from Christ, the only One who could set them free from the Law and failure (2:15–21; cf. Rom. 8:1–4).

Therefore the "opportunity for the flesh" in Galatians 5:13 is not turning the freedom in Christ into license or libertinism, but it is the *continued fleshly failure that characterized the Law era.* Paul explained further in 6:13 that his opponents could not keep the Law themselves, but they still wanted the Galatians to join them in this fleshly failure for the purpose (ἵνα) of "boasting in your σαρκί." The Law era and ἡ σάρξ go together as an inseparable twosome. This was expressed repeatedly by Paul in Galatians (e.g., 5:13–14; 5:17–18; 5:19–21, 23; 6:12–13). The failure to tie νόμος and σάρξ together has needlessly spawned this third view of Paul's opponents and has almost hopelessly muddied the waters about their identity. This failure has also greatly hindered a correct understanding of the σάρξ/πνεῦμα duality. An accurate, contextual understanding of the opponents should go a long way toward unraveling the second issue.[75]

The Identity of the Galatian Opponents

The traditional view seems correct: Paul's opponents were Jewish Christians who sought to "Judaize" the Gentile Christians of Galatia. In over 70 years of scholarly attacks, this identification of Paul's opponents has not been effectively overturned. The Judaizers' identity best satisfies the "mirror-reading" criteria and limitations. Barclay concludes that the troublers were probably

Jewish Christians who also questioned the adequacy of both
Paul's apostolic credentials and the gospel he preached.[76] They
apparently made circumcision the central issue among the Gentile
Christians of Galatia because it was the classic symbol for one
who was choosing to live like a Jew ('Ιουδαϊκῶς ζῇς and
'Ιουδαΐζειν, Gal. 2:14). "In fact Paul's concern about 'works of
the law' (3:1–10) and his extended arguments to prove the
temporary validity of the law (3:6–4:11), taken together with
remarks like 4:21, make it highly probable that the opponents
wanted the Galatians to observe the law as circumcised
proselytes."[77] Barclay concludes, "Taking the argument of the
letter as a whole, there is sufficient evidence that the Galatians
were informed of (and responded warmly to) the requirements of
Torah-observance as the hallmark of the people of God."[78]

Such a conclusion and the lack of viable support for a Gnostic
or libertine identity make assuming the presence of such opponents
in Galatia or the presence of a dual nomistic/libertinistic threat[79]
totally unwarranted and unnecessary. The struggles over ethics
and law in Galatians 5–6 can be explained more naturally and
holistically within the context of Galatians with a unified Judaizers'
threat in the background. As students of Galatians are tying
Galatians 5–6 more closely and logically to Galatians 3–4, the
underscoring of this traditional identification gets even stronger.
Increasingly it is becoming apparent that rather than stepping
back and defensively clarifying and limiting the boundaries of
Christian freedom in Galatians 5–6, Paul was actually continuing
his attack on the Judaizers in an overt and aggressive manner, but
(in chaps. 5–6) in the area of ethics and behavior. This heightened
sense of continuity greatly aids the Judaizer identity. Such
continuity also serves to undercut the predominant understanding
of the σάρξ/πνεῦμα internal duality which arose in part due to a
failure in understanding the proper linkage of chapters 3–4 with
chapters 5–6 in Paul's argument.

These conclusions do not mean that all questions about the
Judaizers' origin and motivation have been satisfied. Because of
the emphasis in Galatians 1–2 and 4 on Jerusalem and Judea, it is
possible to suspect some link to the Jerusalem church. Jewett
asserts that Jewish Christians in Judea, stimulated by Zealot
pressure in the forties and fifties, responded to this threat of
persecution (Gal. 6:12) and launched a nomistic campaign among
Gentile Christians in areas that included Galatia.[80] As Barclay

points out, the weakness of this thesis is the slender thread of Galatians 6:12 from which it hangs.[81] Fung more pointedly refutes it, based on the sharply antithetical relationship between the Zealots and the church at the outbreak of the Jewish War and based on the Zealots' lack of interest in bringing Gentile Christians to the "perfection" mentioned in 3:3.[82]

Perhaps a more viable origin and motivation is that the Judaizing threat came from a Law-observant mission among the Gentiles by Jewish Christian "Teachers" (not "opponents"):

> In the main it is not they who are reacting to Paul's theology, but rather he who is reacting to theirs. To be sure, the Galatians heard Paul's gospel first and only later that of the Teachers. But the finely formed theology of the Teachers is best understood on the hypothesis that the order of events in Galatia is for them atypical. Elsewhere they will have worked in virgin fields, impelled not by a desire to correct Paul, but by a passion to share with the entire world the only gift they believed to have the power to liberate humankind from the grip of evil, the Law of God's Messiah. In the full sense of the expression, therefore, they represent a law-observant mission to Gentiles, a mission inaugurated not many years after the death of Jesus.[83]

While this attractive thesis lessens the malevolence of the Judaizers' motives, it does not lessen their theological error. Nor can the thesis be validated based on 1st-century data, because it is reading from 2d-century Jewish Christian documents back into the first.[84] Therefore it must remain in the category of an attractive possibility. It does, however, highlight the fact that, whatever the specific motivation of these Jewish Christian opponents, they obviously viewed their cause as righteous and biblical. Their apparent use of the Abraham and Sarah-Hagar narratives seems to point to such a perspective, as numerous writers have observed.[85]

Given that the Judaizers considered it imperative that Gentiles be saved in continuity with Israel and in accord with the Law and customs of Moses by becoming Jewish proselytes, the issue of their geographical origin is worthy of some focus. There is no overwhelming consensus about their origin. Lake identified them as local Jews who were proselytizing the Gentile Christians.[86] Tyson correctly identifies the opponents as Jewish Christians, but follows Lake's lead in arguing that they were native to Galatia.[87] Munck's view of Judaizing Gentile Christians also places the opponents' origin within Galatia from within Paul's own ministry.[88] The difficulty with the Galatian origin, as many have observed,[89] is that Paul seems to have referred to the agitators as coming into the churches of Galatia from outside (e.g., 3:1–5; 4:8–16; 5:7–8) and that he underscored their "outsider" identity by referring to them in third person pronouns, while he referred to the Galatians in the second person (e.g., 4:17).

Based on the sketchy external and internal evidence, the best choice of the origin of these mistaken Jewish Christians is Jerusalem or possibly Judea. Externally, two passages in Acts point to the presence of these strong Law-observant attitudes in the Jewish Christians in Jerusalem and Judea. Paul arrived in Jerusalem on his collection visit after his third missionary journey (Acts 21:17–26). The next day James and the Jerusalem leaders told Paul of the local Jewish Christians' animosity toward him because of his perceived threat to traditional Jewish Christianity: "You see, brother, how many thousands there are among the Jews of those who have believed, and *they are all zealous for the Law;* and they have been told about you, that you are teaching all the Jews who are among the Gentiles to forsake Moses, telling them not to circumcise their children nor to walk according to the customs. What, then, is to be done? They will certainly hear that you have come" (Acts 21:20–22, italics added).

In light of the chronological work of Knox,[90] Jewett,[91] Luedemann,[92] and Hoehner,[93] Paul's final visit to Jerusalem is dated between A.D. 54 and 57. This visit could have been as much as eight years after the Jerusalem Conference of Acts 15. It demonstrates the continuation of a powerful, Law-observant wing in the Jerusalem church. Apparently these same Jewish Christians, who were "zealous for the Law," had caused trouble in Antioch a few years earlier. "And some men came down from Judea and began teaching the brethren, 'Unless you are circumcised according to the custom of Moses, you cannot be saved'" (Acts 15:1).[94]

After Paul and Barnabas disputed with these teachers (Acts 15:2), the Jerusalem Conference was convened to settle the issue. The discussion continued at the conference. "But certain ones of the sect of the Pharisees who had believed, stood up, saying, 'It is necessary to circumcise them, and to direct them to observe the Law of Moses'" (v. 5). After the conference decided against such a notion, the church leaders recorded their decision and addressed it to the Gentiles in the churches of Antioch, Syria, and Cilicia (v. 23), purposely distancing themselves from the troublers. "We have heard that some of our number to whom we gave no instruction have disturbed you with their words, unsettling your souls" (v. 24). While admitting to being home to these Pharisaic Jewish Christians, the Jerusalem church disavowed any authorization of them or their teaching. Since this external data sounds much like the problems in Galatia, it is reasonable to conclude that the Acts 15 and 21 troublers and the Galatian troublers shared a common origin and that "they represent a wider group of ritually strict Jewish Christians."[95]

Internally, the Epistle to the Galatians strongly supports such a correlation. Given Paul's recurring emphasis on Jerusalem and Judea in Galatians 1–2 and 4, it is not difficult to conclude that the Pharisaic troublemakers from Jerusalem and Judea kept going past Antioch, Syria, and Cilicia into Galatia. So Paul persistently struck at their home base and at those Jerusalem pillars (στῦλοι, 2:9) to whom they fallaciously appealed for support of their position (cf. Acts 15:24). This may also explain why Paul recounted the confrontation in Antioch that was so embarrassing to Peter and Barnabas (Gal. 2:11–21). His point is that the Judaizers' view had already been rejected at one of their prior stops, the most prominent Gentile church, Antioch of Syria. That rejection was *public in scope* (ἔμπροσθεν πάντων, 2:14), *apostolic in authority* (involving both Peter and Paul), and *apparently accepted as legitimate* (otherwise Paul would not have appealed to it as authoritative for the Galatian situation).

Another point to be made about these Jerusalem/Judea-based opponents involves the motive for their apparent claims against Paul. As King observed in his fine analysis of the situation,[96] these Pharisaic Judaizers made three main claims against Paul.

1. Paul was on their side but trimmed the demands of the gospel to please his hearers (1:10). . . .
2. He received his gospel from the same Jerusalem authorities who supported their mission (1:18–2:9; and 1:11). . . .
3. In Paul's work as a representative of the "pillars" (1:12, 15–19) he began a work which they had come to complete (3:3). . . . [97]

As King notes, these Jewish Christians from the sect of the Pharisees expressed a concept of revelation typical of second temple Judaism.[98] According to this view revelation flowed from the seat of authority (Jerusalem), where Jesus had left His disciples (the Jerusalem apostles) to carry on the line of tradition. Paul was a *tanna,* a rabbi, who had broken the chain of Jewish traditions by not faithfully or accurately passing on the tradition. Assuming that Paul was a pupil of the Jerusalem apostles, the Judaizers apparently accused him of failing in his duty to transmit the exact words of Jesus' tradition as it had been mediated to Paul by the apostles. Such "iterative incompetence" was viewed as one of the gravest offenses according to ancient rabbinical rules (e.g., m.'Ed. 1.3; b. Sabb. 15a; 'Avot 3:8 and 6:6). The Judaizers had to correct and complete Paul's breech of the "Jesus tradition" among the Galatians. It is to this attempt to correct and complete his gospel that Paul responded in Galatians. In light of these charges against him, Paul's purpose in Galatians 1–2 is now quite understandable:

> Contra the insinuations of the agitators, he maintained that his gospel was not of human origin; Christ had communicated it to him in person. He was also careful to assure his readership the pillars of the church in Jerusalem had recognized its truth and his right to preach it in its present form. He denied the charge of tanna-oriented dependency, but also maintained consistency with Jerusalem on all important matters.[99]

Paul's reasoning in Galatians 1:11–2:14 also reveals that in the 14 to 17 years following his conversion he spent time in Arabia and Damascus (1:17) and Syria and Cilicia (1:21). He had three contacts with some of the Jerusalem apostles in Jerusalem (1:18–20; 2:1–10) and Antioch (2:11–14). These contacts were too infrequent and too brief for the tannaitic process of tedious repetition and memorization to occur. This obvious fact coupled with Jesus Christ's direct teaching of Paul (1:11–12) and the Jerusalem acceptance of Paul's gospel (1:22–24; 2:7–10) powerfully refutes the Judaizers' claims against him. All the particulars of Galatians 1–2 can most simply and coherently be explained in light of this reconstruction.[100]

Conclusion

The identity of Paul's opponents in Galatia is a crucial issue in interpreting Galatians. While the last 70 years of scholarly study about the identity of these opponents have given rise to a more balanced view of their identity, it has not effectively overturned the traditional Judaizer identification. Bible students can rest secure that this identification is, in fact, the correct one.

CHAPTER 13

The Dionysian Background of Ephesians 5:18

Cleon L. Rogers, Jr.

I n Ephesians 5:18, Paul wrote, "And be not drunk with wine, in which is excess, but be filled with the Spirit" (AV). Why did he contrast drunkenness with the filling of the Holy Spirit? Often this question is answered by referring to one or more comparisons between drunkenness and the Spirit's filling, such as submission to and dominance by an outside control, loss of one's rational functions, etc. But is this really what Paul was saying?

Is it not possible that Paul was referring to something more explicit in his own culture? This chapter is a presentation of the view that the wild, drunken practices connected with the worship of Dionysus or Bacchus, the god of wine, form the general cultural background for Paul's two commands in Ephesians 5:18.[1]

Interpreting a passage of Scripture in its cultural setting is not new. It is a well-known and widely practiced axiom that any writing must be interpreted in the light of its cultural setting. Some obvious cultural or historical matters forming the background of the New Testament are clear and have been the subject of many profitable studies.[2] In addition to specific culturally couched terms, there is the general cultural New Testament background consisting of historical, social, economic, and religious conditions.

Some of these cultural matters form a tacit background to the New Testament writings, though they are not specifically mentioned by the New Testament writers—perhaps because they were so commonplace and well known that they did not need elaboration. For example Paul did not explicitly relate his injunctions against immorality to the cult of Aphrodite (e.g., 1 Cor. 6:18–19) or to the other pagan deities, but hardly anyone would doubt that such worship in the city of Corinth or in Ephesus forms the cultural background for the general commands against sexual sins.

In the same manner Paul may have had in mind the drunken activities of the Dionysian cult as he penned Ephesians 5:18.

After an examination of the support for this suggestion, the significance of the Dionysian cult to Paul's commands in Ephesians 5:18 will be discussed.

Support for the Dionysian Background

The two major supports to be considered are the widespread character of the cult and the worship of the cult.

THE WIDESPREAD CHARACTER OF THE CULT

The word "widespread" is used here to include temporal, geographical, social, and cultural aspects of the Dionysian cult. Although the exact beginnings of the deity are unknown, it is clear that Dionysus was known as early as the Homeric period (ca. 900 B.C.),[3] and as late as the church fathers.[4] The temporal span of Dionysus includes the New Testament period, during which time worship of him was quite active. It is generally acknowledged that Dionysus was not originally a Greek god, but probably had his origins in Thracia, Lydia, or Phrygia.[5] The name "Dionysus" seems to be the genitive of the word "Zeus" joined with the word "nysos" ("son") with the resultant meaning "son of Zeus."[6] Dianysius is also referred to by the Lydian name of "Bacchus."[7]

In spite of opposition[8] the worship of Dionysus spread throughout Asia Minor, Macedonia,[9] Greece, Italy, Egypt, Palestine, and even India. By the time of the apostle Paul the cult of Dionysus or Bacchus was well established in most of the major cities in which Paul preached. In Thessalonica, for example, the epigraphical and historical evidence is said to indicate that there was not only the Dionysian cult there, but also "a state priesthood of Dionysus existed in Thessalonica from the time of the founding of the city by Cassander."[10]

A Latin inscription from Philippi provides proof that the cult of Dionysus was active in that city.[11] In Athens the worship of this deity was prominent and his festivals very popular.[12] Pausanias describes the images of Dionysus which he saw at the marketplace in Corinth as being wooden images covered with gold, with the exception of the faces which were ornamented with red paint.[13]

The city of Ephesus was also filled, not only with the worship of Artemis (Diana), but also with the cult of Dionysus. When Anthony entered the city of Ephesus, Plutarch says, "women arrayed like Bacchanals, and men and boys like Satyrs and Pans led the way before him and the city was full of ivy and thyruswands and harps and pipes and flutes, the people hailing him as Dionysus, giver of Joy and Beneficent."[14]

Other major cities where the cult was prominent were Rome and its surrounding cities, and Smyrna, Pergamum, Philadelphia, Alexandria, and others.[15]

Palestine and the Jews did not escape the influence of Dionysus. The city of Beth Shean not only had certain links to Greek mythology in connection with Dionysus, but also it is highly possible that Dionysian worship was carried on there.[16] It was the infamous Antiochus Epiphanes who accused the Jews of being worshipers of Dionysus. He set up the "abomination of desolation"[17] in the temple, and imposed the cult of Dionysus on the Jews by compelling them during the feast of Dionysus to wear wreaths of ivy and to walk in the procession in honor of Dionysus.[18]

From these examples it can be seen that the cult had spread to practically every area of the Roman Empire. However, not only was the cult widespread geographically; it had also penetrated every level of society. It is common knowledge that women played a major role in Dionysian worship,[19] and it was becoming increasingly popular for both men and children to have an active part in the cultic practices.[20] The social levels ran from slaves to the rich, including nobility and even the emperor.[21] Of course, not every individual was a worshiper of Dionysus, but certainly everyone must have been aware of the great festivals which were also great social occasions.

The influence of Dionysus on the cultural aspects of the world is astonishing. He is the subject of drama, sculpture, paintings, music, poetry, and the like.[22] One only has to walk through the British Museum, or examine pictures of museum collections to see how many vases, paintings, sculptures, and household objects (such as plates, drinking vessels, and pitchers) have Dionysian motifs.[23] It would have been hardly possible to have visited an ancient city and to have remained any length of time without seeing Dionysus and his ever-present companions, the Satyrs, Silens, and Maenads.[24]

It would seem that the cult of Dionysus was so widespread and common that anything having to do with grapes, wine, ivy, or any other Dionysian motif was at once connected to Dionysus and his worship. Many pagans even accused the Jews of worshiping Dionysus, simply because certain things in Judaism appeared to have Dionysian motifs.[25] To talk of wine and drinking immediately brought Dionysian expressions in the conversation,[26] and to live a riotous, wanton, debauched, drunken life was characterized as a

"Dionysian mode of life."[27] The cult was so widespread that it was part of common everyday life in the ancient world.

THE WORSHIP OF THE CULT

Since the cult developed over the years and experienced many adaptations,[28] this study will touch on only certain salient features of the worship and consider their significance briefly.

The festivals celebrated in honor of Dionysus varied from place to place, but one common feature was the emphasis on fertility and sex.[29] The emphasis on the phallus (the male sex organ) in the so-called "Phallus Procession" along with such things as "the Phallus Song," certainly indicate the lewd debauchery connected with this worship.[30] The significance was evidently to please Bacchus so that he would grant fertility.

Another feature of the festivals was the wild, frenzied dancing and uncontrolled ravings, in connection with wine drinking and the music of flutes, cymbals, drums, or tambourines.[31] Along with this was the mountain dancing of the women, which sometimes took place in the dead of winter, and the devouring of the raw flesh of animals.[32] The purpose of the intoxication by wine and also the chewing of ivy, as well as the eating of raw animal flesh, was to have Dionysus enter the body of the worshiper and fill him with "enthusiasm" or the spirit of the god.[33] Dionysus was to possess and control such ones so that they were united with him and partook of his strength, wisdom, and abilities. This resulted in the person doing the will of the deity (either willingly or unwillingly)[34] and having the ability to speak inspired prophecy,[35] and was often thought to be the source of artistic or poetic ability.[36] During these festivals many unusual phenomena were to have occurred in the woods. Not only was Dionysus to have appeared in the form of various animals, but also milk, honey, and wine were seen bubbling out of the ground.[37]

In addition to such festivals, the mystery religion aspect of Dionysian worship had become popular in Hellenistic times. Although comparatively little is known about these rites, it seems that they had to do with unification with the deity as a preparation for the afterlife.[38]

The significance and appeal of the Dionysian cult to the ancient world is aptly described by Wilamowitz-Moellendorf. He points out that after having gone through the experience of a frenzied Dionysian orgy, one evidently felt a sort of release from the pressures and stress of the daily drudgery of life. It was especially the women who felt lifted above their lowly status in life and felt freed from the weary burden of their work.[39] When both the widespread character of the cult and the worship of the cult are considered, it seems difficult to doubt that Dionysian worship would not at least have been thought of when Paul gave the command, "Be not drunk with wine."

The Significance of the Dionysian Background

If the cultural background was Dionysian worship, then the two commands of Paul in Ephesians 5:18 and their context take on a new light. The several features to be considered are almost in themselves further support for a Dionysian background.

THE CONCEPT OF ἀσωτία

"Be not drunk with wine, wherein is excess, but be ye filled with the Spirit" (Eph. 5:18, AV). The word translated "excess" basically means "without health," or "incurable."[40] The word then refers to "one who by his manner of life, especially by dissipation destroys himself."[41] After discussing the various uses of the word, especially in the New Testament, Foerster concludes, "In all these passages the word signifies wild and disorderly rather than extravagant or voluptuous living."[42] Though not limited to Dionysian practices, this is certainly a fitting and descriptive term to describe the behavior of Dionysian worshipers. There was no salvation (σωτηρία) in being filled with the spirit of Dionysus; only wild behavior ἀσωτία accompanied such filling.

THE CONTRAST OF THE COMMANDS

It is obvious that there is a certain contrastive parallelism[43] in the commands "be not drunk with wine . . . but be filled with the Spirit." The grammatical parallels and contrasts reveal a close connection between the two commands. "Do not be drunk" is a present negative imperative prohibiting a manner of life, while the command "be filled" is a positive present imperative calling for a continued consistent manner of life.[44] The two datives with the imperatives have the same function, that is, instrumental ("with wine") and agency ("with the Spirit").[45] The parallelism may also indicate a certain equation in meaning. If the filling of the Spirit has to do with a supernatural infilling of the Spirit of the living God, it would only be logical to suppose that the "drunk with wine" could have a supernatural implication. The significance would then be a contrast with the filling of the "spirit" of Bacchus through wine and the filling of the true and living God by His

Spirit. The wisdom and power, the intellectual and artistic ability, the freedom from the drudgery of daily life, as well as a prophetic message from the true God, are not to be found in the Dionysian drunkenness, but in the control of the Spirit of the true God.

THE CONTINUING CONTEXT OF THE COMMAND

It seems significant that the things Paul wrote about in Ephesians 5:19–33 have to do with some matters that played a vital part in the Dionysian worship. First, there is the mention of singing (v. 19). This is the singing of spiritual songs (ᾠδαῖς πνευματικαῖς) to the Lord Himself, not the raving of drunken worshipers singing the praises of Dionysus. Second, there is the giving of thanks for all things (v. 20). Philo, in his appeal to Gaius, extols the positive benefits of Dionysus.[46] However, the true source of blessing is not Bacchus but the true God. Third, there is Paul's discussion of marriage and the responsibilities of each partner. Wild sexual debauchery is not the God-ordained way of conduct; instead, the marriage relationship is the means of fulfillment. Even more relevant is the instruction regarding the ordained order in marriage. Wives are to be in submission to their husbands (v. 22) and are not to be leaders in wild worship. The way to a fulfilled life of freedom and accomplishment is not through Dionysus but through the filling of the Spirit and submission to God's order.

Conclusion

This study has sought to identify a possible cultural background for Ephesians 5:18 and has suggested that it is the worship of the wine god Dionysus. This does not mean that the commands of Paul were necessarily directed primarily against the cult of Dionysus. It does, however, indicate that the Dionysian worship could well have formed the background against which Paul gave his general instructions. In answer to Barth's question regarding the "sudden reference to drunkenness,"[47] some have suggested that a general problem of drunkenness prevailed in the private lives of the saints, but another suggestion is that the saints attempted "to gain or to increase unity with the divine world by cultic inebriation as practiced in the Dionysus cult."[48] Perhaps both possibilities should be combined: Paul's command was given against the cultural background of Dionysian worship, and that command is valid for all times and all cultures. Spiritual strength, wisdom, and divine help to live a godly life are obtained by being controlled by the Spirit of God, not by any other means.

CHAPTER 14

The Theme and Structure of Philippians

Robert C. Swift

Among exegetes, Philippians has been sort of a "Rubik's Cube" of the Pauline literature. Many times it has been twisted, turned, and rearranged as scholars have attempted to make the best sense they could of it. Many have sensed that the book has no central theme systematically developed in a logical argument throughout the epistle. "Since the early days of historical critical research, exegetes have had difficulty finding any main theme or a line of argument in Philippians."[1]

While there have been exceptions,[2] this difficulty has generated three responses among interpreters.[3] With the exception of Lohmeyer,[4] most interpretations of the epistle can be categorized as follows.

First, many commentators hold that because of the emotional and hortatory nature of the letter, no central idea or inner logical coherence is really necessary. Being a personal and friendly letter, Paul skipped from one subject to another as various topics came to mind.

> To anyone reading this epistle as a familiar letter of Paul to a greatly beloved church, intended to inform them concerning his own circumstances, to thank them for their generous care for him, and to give such counsel as his knowledge of their condition might suggest, *its informal and unsystematic character* and its abrupt transitions from one theme to another will appear entirely natural.[5]

Eadie suggests, "The transitions depend upon no logical train— as the thoughts occurred they were dictated. And we can never know what suggested to the apostle the order of his topics."[6]

A more recent advocate of this same view is Hendriksen.

> Attempts have been made repeatedly to construct a formal outline for Philippians, a central theme with its subdivisions. . . . But such themes either lack distinctiveness . . . or comprehensiveness. . . . What we have here is a genuine letter from Paul to his beloved church at Philippi. The

writer passes from one subject to another just as we do today in writing to friends. . . . What holds these subjects together is not this or that central theme, but the Spirit of God, mirrored forth, by means of a multitude of spiritual graces and virtues, in the heart of the apostle, proclaiming throughout that between God, the apostle, and the believers at Philippi there exists a blessed bond of glorious *fellowship*.[7]

Most commentators who maintain that "joy in Christ" is the main theme also view the epistle as an "informal letter." This is so because few, if any, really seek to structure the epistle systematically around the concept of joy.[8] It is more accurate to maintain that joy is the prevailing *mood* of the epistle, not its central theme.

A second group of interpreters has difficulty accepting that the letter's "abrupt transitions from one theme to another . . . appear entirely natural." The epistle, they say, is best explained as the result of two or more documents being combined into one.[9]

If it could be shown that Philippians truly is unified by a central theme whose development generates a coherent structure, then this view would be difficult to maintain.[10] The reason such a "conflated-letter" view has arisen in the first place is because most exegetes have despaired of ever finding inner coherence in the epistle.

A third approach to the problem of the epistle's structure has been proposed by Martin.[11] In a form critical approach he follows the results of research done by White.[12] White, in turn, follows with some refinements, the lead of his teacher, Funk.[13] Martin concludes that Philippians is a unit as it stands and feels that the overall structure of the letter displays the characteristic structural elements of the Pauline letter form.[14]

Though this view is innovative, it too fails to solve the problem of the structure of Philippians. Three criticisms may be noted. First, the method accounts for the structure of the epistle by conforming it to an external set of formal criteria, not by discovering an inner thematic development and line of argument. Thus it bypasses the issue that has led to the Philippian problem in the first place. Martin holds that the epistle is a *unit*, but he does not see it *unified* internally. Second, the form critical tradition, to which Martin appeals in defense of the integrity of the epistle, has largely viewed the letter as a composite document. White, for instance, believes that 4:10–20 was originally another letter.[15] Schubert also has doubts about chapter 3.[16] Third, exegesis fails to support the scheme Martin proposes. Whether one agrees with the exegesis in this chapter, it is unlikely that many will agree entirely with Martin.[17] The epistle simply does not unfold according to that scheme. In fact Martin's outline of the epistle makes little attempt to follow the "overall structure" of the letter he suggests.[18] All three of these approaches to the book seek to explain the structure of the epistle based on something other than the systematic development of a central theme in a point-by-point argument.

By contrast the contention of this chapter is that (a) Philippians has one central theme that is broad enough to explain the details of the entire epistle, and that (b) the development of this theme follows a literary structure that is as systematic, coherent, and logical as that of any New Testament epistle.

The overall structure of the epistle is this. *After the salutation* in 1:1–2, the first major division is *the prologue* (the opening thanksgiving and prayer; 1:3–11). These verses are a true epistolary prologue because they not only introduce the central theme, but they also foreshadow all the other significant motifs developed in the letter.

The biographical prologue follows in 1:12–26. It is "biographical" because it discusses Paul's personal circumstances. It is "prologue" because in the argument of the book it has close conceptual ties with both the prologue proper (1:3–11) and with the body of the epistle which begins at 1:27. Thus it serves as a conceptual link between the prologue and the body of the letter, though it is much more than a mere transition section.

The body of the epistle extends from 1:27 through 4:9. The contents of this section are systematically and logically arranged.

The epilogue (4:10–20) balances the prologue (1:3–11). The book then closes with *the salutation* and *benediction* in 4:21–23.

The Prologue (1:3–11)

As stated previously, these verses serve as an epistolary prologue. What Schubert says in regard to the Pauline thanksgivings generally, is particularly true with regard to Philippians. "Generally speaking it may be said that the Pauline thanksgivings . . . serve as a rather formal introduction to the body of the letter."[19] More explicitly he later states, "Their province is to indicate the occasion for and the contents of the letters they introduce."[20] Conzelmann sharpens the point even further. "It is important to show that the epistolary thanksgiving is already part of the context and can even serve to usher in the main theme."[21]

This is exactly the case in Philippians. For the purpose of

thematic analysis, it is convenient to look at each of the three major syntactical units of the prologue separately.[22]

THE THANKSGIVING: THE THEME INTRODUCED (1:3–6)

In this opening thanksgiving, the main theme of the entire letter is introduced and summarized. Paul joyfully thanked God for the Philippians (vv. 3–4).[23] However, in all his fond memories of them, one particular feature is highlighted in verse 5. Later Paul developed this as the central theme of the epistle: *the Philippians' partnership in the gospel.*

Verse 6, when properly interpreted in relation to verse 5, provides a summary statement of the entire epistle.

Having spoken of their partnership in the gospel (κοινωνία . . . εἰς τὸ εὐαγγέλιον) in the past and present (v. 5), Paul then expressed his confidence that God would continue His work in them so that they might become even more effective partners. His confident hope was that God would perfect (ἐπιτελέσει) them in their work for the gospel and that it would bear fruit from then till the day of Christ. In brief, verse 6 speaks of the perfecting of the Philippians' κοινωνία ("partnership") and of them as κοινωνοί ("partners") in the gospel.

The ἔργον ἀγαθὸν ("good work") in verse 6 must be interpreted by the κοινωνία of the previous verse. This exegetical point is frequently noted by commentators, though few of them consistently restrict it enough to this sense.[24] This writer holds that verse 6 refers *restrictively* to the perfecting of the Philippians as workers for the gospel, and to the perfecting of their works in the cause of the gospel. Many exegetes, failing to note this, have thus failed to see that verses 3–6 contain a thematic summary of the entire epistle. When the first half of verse 6 is taken as suggested, then the rest of the verse ("perfect it until the day of Christ Jesus") should be seen as a reference to the outcome at the judgment seat of Christ, an interpretation fully in harmony with the eschatological reference in verses 10–11.

Verses 3–6, then, are a cameo of the entire epistle. They introduce the main theme, the Philippians' partnership[25] in the gospel. This theme is developed in the direction of God's perfecting of both them and their works for the gospel. The rest of the letter is concerned primarily with their development as κοινωνοί so that they may be blessed with a temporally fruitful, eternally rewardable partnership in the gospel.

Following Schubert, Jewett correctly suggests that this thanksgiving is "a formal device serving to announce and to introduce the topics of the letter. The epistolary thanksgiving is intimately connected with each succeeding section of the letter."[26]

THE BASIS FOR CONFIDENCE IN THEM: THE THEME EXPANDED (1:7–8)

These verses give a "subjective justification of the confidence expressed in verse 6."[27] They also relate to the theme of partnership in the gospel. Paul associated himself with the readers as συγκοινωνούς ("fellow partners"). They partake together of the special enabling grace that God supplies to those who confirm and defend the gospel.[28]

In addition, several subthemes are introduced in verses 7–8 that are developed later.

1. Verse 7 includes the first occurrence of the verb φρονέω, an important concept further developed in 2:1–5; 3:15 (and v. 16 if the reading of the majority of the Greek manuscripts is accepted), 19; 4:2, 10. Φρονέω refers to holding a mind-set that expresses itself in right action. For partners in the common cause of the gospel who are to progress toward perfection (1:6), nothing less would be appropriate. This attitude supplies the basis for the exhortation to unity through humility in chapter 2.

2. The work of the gospel normally involves the endurance of difficulty, hardship, and persecution. Paul's present bondage as well as the numerous times he had to confirm and defend the gospel (e.g., Acts 16) prove this. In Philippians 1:7–8 (and 2:30) Paul likened the Philippians' struggles in this regard to his. Also the phrase ἐν τῇ ἀπολογίᾳ καί βεβαιώσει τοῦ εὐαγγελίου clearly announces the contents of chapter 3, where both the true gospel and the true gospel lifestyle are defended against false teachers and false teaching.[29]

3. The concept of God's enabling grace for their labors is introduced here in 1:7–8 and expanded in 1:29–30. The adequacy of this grace is the main presupposition of and the basis for the exhortations to rejoice, given in 3:1 and 4:4.

4. Paul's desire for and joy at their progress is also seen. This motif is expressed frequently throughout the rest of the epistle (1:9–11, 25, 27–28; 2:2, 12–18; 3:16–17; 4:17).

These motifs are each related to the main theme like spokes of a wheel to their hub. They are bound together and find their meaning in the relationship they sustain to the main theme of partnership in the gospel.

THE PETITION: THE THEME APPLIED (1:9–11)

The contents of this prayer stand in close unity with the thematic statement in 1:5–6.[30] The passage moves from the general to the particular. Generally speaking, God will continue to work in them in order to perfect both them and their works for the gospel. But in response to God's work in them, it is imperative that they continue growing in the specific qualities of Christian virtue that Paul now prayed for.

His petition was for one specific thing—that they might develop an intelligent, discerning love. Their work on behalf of the gospel is true κοινωνία with God only to the degree that it is motivated by ἀγάπη ("self-sacrificing love").[31] If κοινωνία describes their activity, ἀγάπη is to be the motive behind the activity. In contrast are the self-seeking Christian preachers mentioned in 1:15–18, while the proper attitude and motive is exemplified by those who preach Christ from correct motives.

This love must be growing in knowledge and discernment. Brethren who are abounding in love but lacking in these two qualities can often hinder a cause. Ἐπίγνωσις probably means practical wisdom or applied knowledge. Αἴσθεσις denotes correct insight that helps one assess circumstances and people rightly.

The idea of the necessity of continuing progress ("abound still more and more") is picked up from the notion of progress clearly implied in verse 6 ("He who began" and "will perfect it").

Divine sovereignty is emphasized in verse 6, and human responsibility is seen in verse 9.

Paul gave two reasons why the Philippians ought to develop an intelligent, discerning love (v. 10). First, this will enable them to "discern (δοκιμάζειν) what is best" (τὰ διαφέροντα). In this context, τὰ διαφέροντα must be taken as the apprehending of what is the good, better, and best thing to do for the advancement of the gospel in any circumstances. Τὰ διαφέροντα refers to the ability of the informed, insightful κοινωνός ("partner") to act in a true ἀγάπη manner as he works to extend the gospel. In short, τα´ διαφέροντα gathers into one word all that is expressed and implied in verse 9 about correct attitude and correct conduct for the κοινωνός. In verses 12–26 Paul gave concrete examples of the need to "discern what is best."

Ultimately they will be judged "sincere and blameless in the day of Christ" (v. 10b). This parallels the thought of verse 6 and further defines it. Εἰλικρινεῖς ("sincere, pure") refers to moral and spiritual purity (in contrast to the motives of selfish Christian preachers [1:15–18] and false teachers [chap. 31]). Ἀπρόσκοποι ("blameless") is best taken in the active sense of "not causing stumbling,[32] referring to their effect on others. Taken this way, it clearly foreshadows the theme of Christian unity which is so important in the body of the epistle, especially in chapter 2.

In 1:11 Paul focused on the ultimate outcome for those partners whom God perfects unto the day of Christ. "Filled with the fruit of righteousness," they glorify God and contribute to His praise.

The prologue concludes with an eschatological climax. Paul and the Philippians have long passed from the earthly scene. But their works on behalf of the gospel are bearing fruit even to this day. And if Paul is to be believed, God will see to it that the partnership begun by those faithful partners will continue to bear fruit until the day of Christ, when its full harvest of righteousness is revealed to His own glory and praise.

CONCLUSION AND SUMMARY

This prologue is a true "epistolary table of contents."[33] It introduces the main theme of the epistle, indicates the manner of its development, and includes foreshadowings of the important subthemes that will be developed in relation to the main theme.

The Biographical Prologue: The Theme Exemplified (1:12–26)

This section of the letter is entitled "biographical prologue" for two reasons. First, it is obviously a biographical narrative, dealing with Paul's own circumstances. Second, it is closely related to the prologue proper in 1:3–11, in that almost every statement of this section has its conceptual genesis in 1:3–11 and expands on or illustrates an idea introduced there. In 1:12–26 Paul demonstrated how those principles for effective partnership in the gospel were working out to further the gospel in his own trying circumstances (cf. v. 7).

In the overall structure of the epistle this section bears striking resemblance to what Greco-Roman rhetoricians refer to as the *narratio* of an epistle. This is a section in which the writer stated his interest in or defended himself in relation to the subject he was writing about. This subject is introduced in an *exordium*, or epistolary introduction, which immediately preceded the *narratio*.[34] If this observation is valid, it is another indication of true epistolary structure and style in Philippians.

It is not surprising, then, to find the passage opening with a reference to the advancement of the gospel in verse 12, the topic sentence of the section. Εἰς προκοπὴν τοῦ εὐαγγελίου ("for the greater progress of the gospel") reflects the idea of the progress of the gospel introduced in verses 5–6. The second occurrence of προκοπὴν in verse 25 draws the entire section to a well-structured conclusion. In the verses in between, Paul exhibited the specific virtues mentioned in verses 9–11 and showed the readers how those virtues applied to his circumstances of imprisonment for the gospel (cf. "imprisonment," lit., "my bonds," in vv. 8 and 13).

In verses 12–18, the apostle "discerned what is best" (cf. v. 10) in regard to the advancement of the gospel. Rather than hindering the spread of the gospel, imprisonment had actually resulted in its progress. Among his unbelieving captors (v. 13), the reason for his bondage had become widely known. And besides the gospel having gained a wider audience, it also gained many more courageous preachers (v. 14)! Because of Paul's behavior in prison (which was "pure and blameless," v. 10) the majority of the believers, rather than becoming discouraged, gained a fresh confidence to speak the Word boldly, However, not all those Christians who were preaching Christ were operating from the best of motives (contrast ἀγάπη, v. 9). In verses 15–17 he wisely perceived (with ἐπίγνωσις and αἴσθεσις, v. 9) the motives and the intentions of both groups. In one group there was true κοινωνία in the work of the gospel because their work was based on love (v. 14). The other group had the opposite of the purity and blamelessness (v. 10) Paul desired for the Philippians.

Having looked at these circumstances and persons, he discerned what was of chief importance (v. 18). What mattered most was that Christ was proclaimed and nothing could rob him of the joy of that.

Next (vv. 18b–26) Paul "discerned what is best" with regard to his own desires and with regard to what was most necessary for the Philippians' progress in faith. The near future held only prospects of joy for Paul (χαρήσομαι, "I will rejoice," v. 18b). Whatever the outcome of his imprisonment—whether life or death—it would be an experience of "salvation" (σωτηρίαν, "deliverance") for him. As Hendriksen observes, "by reading not only verse 19 but also verse 20 it will be seen that for Paul salvation consisted in this—in his own words—'that Christ be magnified in my body whether by life or by death.'"[35] Paul's "deliverance," whether death or release from prison, would result in Christ being glorified.[36] The means to bring this about are the Holy Spirit and the prayers of the Philippians, who were his fellow partners (v. 7). Paul preferred to be with Christ. However, if he continued to live he had the prospect of more fruit in his ministry. And this is what finally settled the matter for him: it was more needful that he remain alive to help in their joy and progress in the faith (v. 25). The words "convinced of this" indicate a settled conclusion. Again this deliberation shows that Paul was exemplifying the ability to "discern what is best" (v. 10). Accepting what was "more necessary" (ἀναγκαιότερον) for the readers' progress (v. 24) rather than what was "very much better" (πολλῷ . . . μᾶλλον κρεῖσσον) for himself alone (v. 23) also reflects his ability to "discern what is best." Throughout this paragraph, Paul's desire to glorify Christ kept him spiritually pure (v. 10). His putting the needs of others above his own desires, even when those desires were entirely proper (to be with Christ!), served to keep him from any action that would stumble others (cf. ἀπρόσκοποι, v. 10). This could not be said of insincere preachers (vv. 17–18). In addition, the mutual fellowship pictured in verses 25–26 reflects motifs prominent in verses 5–6 and verses 7–8.

In summary, then, the apostle showed that he practiced (vv. 12–26) what he preached (vv. 3–11, esp. 9–11) concerning effective expansion of the gospel.

Verses 12–26, besides linking with the prologue, also point forward to succeeding sections in the epistle. Verses 23–26, for example, clearly foreshadow 2:5–11. Following Christ's example, Paul released any claim on privileges he rightly possessed in order to serve the needs of others more effectively. In that way, as well as by the mention of his anticipated coming to them (1:27; 2:24), this section points to what lies ahead in the epistle. These verses form a smooth and natural transition to the body of the letter which begins at 1:27.

The Body: The Theme Particularized (1:27–4:9)

The body of the epistle has three well-balanced sections: (a) an introductory and summary paragraph (1:27–30), (b) a central section (2:1–4:1), and (c) a concluding hortatory paragraph (4:29). In each of these sections, the same two subjects—unity and steadfastness—are discussed.

WALK WORTHY OF THE GOSPEL (1:27–30)

This paragraph begins with the topic sentence for the entire section of 1:27–4:9. This topic sentence is "Only conduct yourselves in a manner worthy of the gospel of Christ."[37] The subject of what constitutes a worthy walk occupies the body of the epistle.

This worthy walk consists of unity (1:27c) and steadfastness (1:28–30). Standing in one spirit, and as with one soul, they are to strive as members of the same team (συναθλοῦντες) for the furtherance of the gospel.

When they encounter opposition and persecution, they must remain courageously steadfast. Such courageous "striving together for the faith of the gospel" is possible because of the provision of grace mentioned in verses 29–30 (ἐχαρίσθη; cf. v. 7). Just as Paul could be joyful and confident of a "salvation" (deliverance) despite his unpleasant circumstances, so also could the readers experience salvation ("deliverance," v. 28).

A "worthy walk," then, means specifically the achievement of true Christian unity among themselves, and steadfastness against enemies of the gospel. Later it will be shown that this passage is important in properly interpreting 3:1, which most interpreters regard as the most problematic verse in the entire epistle (excluding 2:5–11). Also, 1:30 proves that the particular cause and type of suffering in view is suffering encountered because of their partnership in the gospel. They had seen Paul previously face this kind of trial in Acts 16 (the "conflict you saw in me") and this is the kind he faced now (you "now hear to be in me"). That the Philippians were his συγκοινωνοί in this kind of suffering for the advancement of the gospel is made clear by the words τὸν αὐτὸν ἀγῶνα ἔχοντες ("experiencing the same conflict"). This again is a development of the thematic statement in 1:5–6. Paul expressed confidence there that God would perfect both them and their works for the gospel. This may involve suffering, but where there are trials there is grace (1:7). But if their Christian character as partners blooms with the virtues mentioned in 1:9–11, then like Paul (1:12–26), they could expect the hardships they suffered for the sake of the gospel to be a "salvation" for them as well (1:29–30)![38] In their trials this was to be a continuous source of joy for them (3:1; 4:4).

This paragraph (1:27–30), then, introduces the general topic of walking worthily of the gospel. If the readers are to become more effective partners of the gospel they must walk in unity with one another and in steadfastness against opponents of the faith.

WALK IN UNITY AND STEADFASTNESS (2:1–4:1)

This central section of the epistle takes up again the two topics of unity and steadfastness. Chapter 2 discusses unity, and 3:1–4:1 is concerned with steadfastness.

Walk in unity (chap. 2). From a structural point of view, a problem in this chapter is whether verses 19–30 are in any way an extension of the line of argument in verses 1–18. Many commentators see a major break in the letter at 2:19.[39] Martin, following the form critical tradition mentioned earlier, states that this section of the letter fits a standardized form known as a "travelogue."[40] In it Paul discussed his future travel plans and how the readers fit into them. While such a section may have some transitional links with what precedes, rarely is it seen as being tied closely in thought with it.

However, evidence indicates that verses 19–30 are more closely connected with verses 1–18 than that. While verses 19–30 may be a "travelogue," they are more. They also advance the line of argument in the preceding verses. Structurally chapter 2 is a unit. And while there is a break at 2:19, it is not a break in the argument of the chapter; it is simply a transition to another link in the chain of reasoning that supports that argument.

The chapter develops as follows.

2:1–4. The readers are urged to achieve a unity based on true humility. Each one is to be concerned for the needs of others, not merely his own. This thought of self-sacrificial regard for others' needs has already been mentioned in 1:22–26 and will be contrasted with the attitude stated in 2:21. The obvious contrast between verse 4 ("look out for . . . the interest of others") and verse 21 ("they all seek after their own interests") is a link between the sections that would be difficult for a Greek reader to miss.

2:5–11. In spite of Martin's opinion to the contrary,[41] this writer is convinced that Christ is presented here as an example for the believer to follow. Christ emptied Himself of any claim to glory; He humbled Himself in order to meet the needs of helpless people. For this sacrifice God honored Him above all else in the universe. It is this humble, self-emptying, self-sacrificing attitude after which the Philippians are to pattern their relationships.

2:12–18. In the light of the preceding commands (vv. 1–4) and example (vv. 5–11), the readers are instructed to "work out" their own "salvation" (v. 12). God is the One who enables the willing and the doing of this (v. 13). What does "salvation" mean here? Positively it means achieving a unity based on imitation of the mind of Christ (vv. 1–11). Negatively it is further defined as doing "all things without murmuring and disputing" (v. 13; cf. 2:3). This is consistent with the two previous occurrences of σωτηρία in the book where the context suggests "deliverance" (1:19, 28).

If believers do this, they will be pure and spotless (cf. 1:10) and their testimony will shine like a lamp in a dark world (2:15). In verse 16, Paul took a turn in thought away from the figure suggested in 1:15. Ἐπέχοντες almost certainly must mean "hold fast" rather than "hold forth." Rather than saying they will shine as they hold forth the Word of life, he said they will shine as they hold fast the Word of life. This is related to the subject of walking worthily of the gospel. To prevent disunity from extinguishing the testimony of a church, believers must "hold fast the Word of life." That is, they must obediently achieve the sort of unity described previously. A true gospel witness demands a true gospel lifestyle. Only this wins approval in the day of Christ (2:16).

2:17–18. These verses are a hinge, a transition between verses 12–16 and verses 19–30. Here Paul himself exemplified the attitude he encouraged in verses 1–11. He was ready and willing to be poured out like a drink offering in order to further his readers' growth in faith. Paul rejoiced and invited them to do so as well (v. 18).

2:19–24. Like Paul (vv. 17–18), Timothy and Epaphroditus were worthy examples of the courageous, humble, others-serving mind of Christ.

Verses 19–24 include some exegetical connections with the immediately preceding context and with the beginning of the chapter. The εὐψυχῶ in verse 19 ("be encouraged") is natural after the χαίρω and συγχαίρω in verses 17–18. Paul wished to be made glad when he heard how things were with them. He desired to hear that they were "holding fast the Word of life" and that he had not labored in vain (v. 16). Paul sent Timothy because, like

Christ, Timothy had true concern for them; he was not concerned merely for himself (v. 20). (Cf. ἰσόψυχον here with σύμψυχοι in v. 2.) Verse 21, as mentioned, contrasts clearly with verse 4. Verse 22 mentions Timothy's proven character as shown by the fact of his συγκοινωνία ("fellow partnership") with Paul in the gospel. Thus Timothy also is an example of one who truly works out his "salvation" based on service to the Lord and to others. Timothy's service, in addition to illustrating the thought of verse 16a, also reflects the controlling idea of the body of the letter in 1:17a.

2:25–30. Like Timothy, Epaphroditus was commended because of his sacrificial service for the gospel (v. 30). That his character as a gospel worker was in view is brought immediately before the readers in verse 25 where Paul called him his "fellow-worker" and "fellow-soldier." They were to hold men such as him in the highest regard (v. 29).

In this epistle every single reference Paul made to another person is made in connection with that person's κοινωνία, his partnership in the gospel. Timothy and Epaphroditus, except for Paul himself, stand as the most prominent of these.

Walk in steadfastness (3:1–4:1). Though chapter 3 has been the traditional battleground for critics who see Philippians as a composite work, it presents almost no difficulties for the view presented here. Chapter 3 is clearly concerned with one subject— the Philippians' steadfast stance against false teaching. Verse 1 of chapter 4 is obviously a summarizing exhortation that closes the section.

Paul now turned to discuss the second major topic introduced in 1:27–30, the topic of steadfastness in the face of their opponents in the faith. This has been foreshadowed clearly in 1:7, 28–30 (esp. v. 28). If this writer has been correct in interpreting 1:27–30 as an introduction and summary statement of the subjects to follow, then chapter 3 is both natural and necessary. In chapter 3 Paul was merely following the literary blueprint sketched in 1:27–30.

Pollard has convincingly argued that chapter 3 is closely associated with chapter 2, because of parallels in terminology and concept.[42] Pollard's arguments have never been disproven despite attempts such as Martin's to weaken their relevance.[43] So both structurally and verbally chapter 3 fits comfortably in the overall arrangement of the epistle.

Three other matters must be mentioned briefly.

First, the view presented here requires that τὸ λοιπόν ("finally," 3:1) be taken as transitional.[44] This is no problem, for this usage is well attested in Greek literature and is paralleled in the New Testament (cf. 1 Thess. 4:1).

Second, the supposed roughness of transition between Philippians 3:1 and the rest of the chapter almost vanishes when it is realized that the ideas of joy and standing against opposition to the gospel have already been associated with one another earlier in the epistle. In 1:19, 28–30; 2:17–18 joy is presented as the proper reaction to such circumstances. So the readers are already prepared for the association of joy and hardship again at this point. The asyndeton of 3:2 may be striking, but the readers have already been primed to expect what follows.

Third, notice must be taken of what is probably the most serious objection to the structural scheme presented here. As stated, this writer sees chapter 3 as the fuller discussion of the second topic (steadfastness) introduced in 1:27–30. The first topic (unity) is dealt with in chapter 2. However, in 1:28–30 the emphasis is on the persecution the Philippians could expect from their enemies, not on the seductions presented by their false teachings—which is clearly the emphasis of chapter 3. Two things may be said in response. First, it may be assumed that the opponents of the gospel had something to substitute in its place. Persecution was not only physical. Second, how to face overt persecution is discussed in 4:4–9, where Paul gave a fuller exposition of how to rejoice in the Lord and the anxieties of persecution.

WALK IN UNITY AND STEADFASTNESS (4:2–9)

This concluding paragraph to the body of the letter again takes up the same two topics as the previous two sections—unity and steadfastness.

Restore unity (4:2–3). Reflecting the earlier emphasis in 1:27 and 2:1–4, Paul instructed the two women mentioned here, with the help of a coworker, to be united in the Lord. The theme of the epistle—partnership in the gospel—is mentioned in 4:3. The terms παρακαλῶ ("I urge," v. 2), τὸ αὐτὸ φρονεῖν ("to live in harmony," v. 2), and the phrase ἐν τῷ εὐαγγελίῳ συνήθλησάν μοι ("have shared my struggle in the gospel," v. 3) clearly reflect ideas introduced in 1:27–2:4.

Maintain tranquillity (4:4–9). Martin is among the few

commentators who recognize that this section does not address the subject of peace and freedom from anxiety in general, but in connection with the persecution and opposition the Philippians faced. He states, "The background is clearly that of a congregation facing opposition and threatened by danger from the hostile world. Paul proceeds to describe all the resources by which the Philippian Christians may win through."[45] The details of the text support this. Χαίρετε ἐν κυρίῳ ("Rejoice in the Lord," v. 4) recalls 3:1. Here, however, the emphasis is on the oppression caused by opponents of the gospel, not on their teaching. The term τὸ ἐπιεικὲς ("gentleness, forbearance," v. 5) presupposes pressured circumstances where the opposite response might be expected. The reference to the nearness of the coming of the Lord (v. 5) is intended as a comfort to them. This is a clear reference back to 3:20–21 where the relief and the benefits waiting for the faithful are stated. In 4:6–7, the references to anxiety and the peace of God presuppose circumstances that would normally rob them of peace and cause anxious care. The image in verse 7 is that of an armed sentry, ready to fight off any hostile intruder. Also this segment may recall 1:28–30. The prospect of "salvation" (1:28) should be a joy to them and they need not be frightened out of their composure (cf. μηδὲν μεριμνᾶτε, "be anxious for nothing" [4:6]. with μὴ πτυρόμενοι, "in no way alarmed" [1:28]). If so, this is further evidence that the subject of steadfastness is once again brought before the readers by Paul. This is not in regard to false teaching as in chapter 3, but in regard to inner anxiety and fear.

Philippians 4:8–9 serve as a conclusion to the paragraph beginning in verse 4. The reference to the God of peace reflects "the peace of God" (v. 7). Τὸ λοιπόν is best translated "finally" (cf. 3:1). However, τὸ λοιπόν also concludes the entire epistle from 1:12 up to this point. Thus the body of the epistle which began with a topic sentence in 1:27a is drawn to a summary and a well-structured close. Philippians 4:8–9, then, is a double conclusion, concluding 4:4–9 and then also summarizing all the admonition in the letter back to 1:27a. Chapter 4, verse 9 makes it clear that Paul's conduct in 1:12–26 is also to be taken into account.

CONCLUSION AND SUMMARY OF THE BODY
The body of the letter begins with a topic sentence in 1:27a.

The Philippian Christians, to be perfected in their partnership for the gospel, were to conduct themselves worthy of the gospel. Specifically two things are in view—unity with one another and steadfastness against their opponents. They need not fear, for God will supply grace (1:27–30). Chapter 2 takes up the unity motif, and chapter 3, steadfastness. The main body of the epistle then concludes with a hortatory paragraph which again addresses the same two subjects. All this is freed from any topical "loose ends" by the summarizing double conclusion of 4:8–9.

Is it true, as Eadie suggested, that "we can never know what suggested to the Apostle the order of his topics"?[46] Emphatically not. Certainly Philippians is one of the most systematically structured epistles in the New Testament.

The Epilogue (4:10–20)

The evidence of careful structure does not end with the body of the letter. Verses 10–20 of chapter 4 form an epilogue to the epistle, balancing the prologue in 1:3–10.

In general, the prologue began broadly, with Paul's remembrance of all they had done in every way to share in the work of the gospel. The epilogue is more specific, mentioning their most recent financial gift to Paul.

Dalton has superbly summarized the relationship of the prologue to the epilogue.

> . . . we seem to have evidence of an inclusion which binds the whole letter into one unit. First of all, the idea of partnership is strongly expressed at the beginning and the end. Thus in 1:5 Paul is "thankful for your partnership (κοινωνία) in the gospel"; and in 4:15 he records that "no church entered into partnership in giving and receiving except you only." This partnership is reiterated in another parallel: in 1:7 the Philippians are sharers (συγκοινωνούς) of grace with Paul; in 4:13 they are sharers (συγκοινωνήσαντες) with him in his trouble. At both beginning and end we have the same idea expressed in different ways: the long-standing partnership of the Philippians with Paul: "from the first day until now" (1:5), and "in the beginning of the gospel" (4:15). And finally the reciprocal attitude of sympathy between Paul and the Philippians is expressed in the same phrase: in 1:7 he says "it is right for me to feel this about you" (τοῦτο φρονεῖν ὑπὲρ πάντων ὑμῶν), and in 4:10, "You have revived your concern for me" (τὸ ὑπὲρ ἐμοῖ φρονεῖν).[47]

Thus the beginning and the ending of the letter have four common elements. It does seem fitting that the central idea should be that of partnership, since in fact this theme dominates the entire book.

Following the epilogue are the closing greetings (4:21–22) and benediction (4:23).

Conclusion

If the above analysis is correct, then Philippians must be considered as a masterly example of epistolary literature. A formal prologue introduces the main theme and foreshadows its development. This is followed by a biographical narrative (1:12–26) in which Paul exemplified certain qualities he had recommended to the readers in 1:3–11 and especially in verses 9–11. The body of the epistle begins with a topic sentence (1:27a) and then discusses the topics of unity and steadfastness three times. The body concludes with a summary statement in 4:8–9. The epilogue (4:10–20) artfully balances the prologue, and the closing salutation (4:21–23) balances the opening greeting in 1:1–2.

But if Philippians is an epistle with structure, this is because it is primarily an epistle with a message, a message that calls all Christians to a walk worthy of the gospel if they expect to further the work of the gospel. The power of such a walk, combined with such a message, can make an immeasurable impact in the world. Out of Macedonia, Alexander the Great once went to conquer the Eastern world but later from Macedonia the power of the gospel went out to conquer the Western world of Paul's day. The Philippians' κοινωνία εἰς τὸ εὐαγγέλιον is still bearing fruit today.

CHAPTER 15

The "Women" of 1 Timothy 3:11

Robert M. Lewis

Although at a casual glance 1 Timothy 3:11 may seem quite simple, in reality it has been a source of controversy for centuries and has been a major force in shaping the ecclesiological framework of the church, past and present. This verse, of course, has been the interpretive launching pad for the rise of a select group of women known as "deaconesses" which many consider to be a third office of the church. Alongside this interpretation stands the now common belief that this verse sets forth no additional office at all. Rather these women are select only in the sense that they are the wives of those men who are deacons and should reflect their husband's godly character.

Each of these interpretations has merit, but they should not become so standard that new suggestions cannot be offered. The purpose of this chapter is to discuss the support for and problems with the two usual views and then to offer a third suggestion which the writer feels best meets the demands of the passage.

γυναῖκας as Deacons' Wives

This first interpretation holds that these women are the wives of the male deacons being discussed in 1 Timothy 3. There is much to support this interpretation. The term γυναῖκας is the simple term for "wives." The context before and after verse 11 is specifically on male deacons. Having this verse wedged into this discourse seems clearly to indicate that these women are in some way related to those men being discussed. The marriage relationship is mentioned and the conclusion is that they are deacons' wives.

Some object by saying that no such mention is similarly made of the wives of the ἐπίσκοποι ("elders"). To counter such an objection, mention is made that only the wives of deacons could assist their husbands in actually carrying out their ministry while the elders' wives could not. Indeed the wife of an elder would be strictly prohibited (1 Tim. 2:12) from those teaching and ruling functions which he performs in the church. Concerning the deacon's wife, however, no such prohibitions exist. On the contrary, as a deacon carried out his various duties, certain situations would arise which only a woman could perform. Such functions a deacon would quite naturally turn over to his wife whose character was complementary to his own. She therefore became his assistant in the outworking of his office, and in this sense could be termed a "deaconess." Also it is argued that if Paul had some other kind of women in mind, he would have surely marked them out as such by some distinguishing phrase. The term τάς διακόνους ("the deaconesses") would have effectively eliminated any and all confusion.

This position is not without its drawbacks, however. The subject, γυναῖκας, can mean "wives" but its usage does not bind it to that meaning alone. It can just as easily be translated "widows," "brides," or "adult women" (married or unmarried). Those who translate it "wives" fail to take into account the conjunction ὡσαύτως ("likewise"). This term indicates a transition from one distinct class to another (as in verse 8). Thus three distinct groups are being discussed. If γυναῖκας were indeed the wives of deacons then in all probability καί, not ὡσαύτως, would have been used. The latter is used to emphasize distinctiveness, introducing a new subject rather than continuing (like καί) an aspect of the same subject. Along similar lines, it seems unlikely that Paul would have used γυναῖκας without some qualifier. The separation of verses 8–10 from verse 11 is intensified by the fact that there is no possessive pronoun linking γυναῖκας with the διακόνους. The phrase γυναῖκας ὑμῶν ("your wives") in the original text is necessary for one to assert confidently the translation "deacon's wives" although it still remains a viable option. To say, however, that only deacons' wives could aid their husbands in the performance of their ministries seems to force an unnecessary limitation on the text. Surely women other than one's wife could also give such assistance. And what about a deacon whose wife is tied down with a large family responsibility? To whom does he turn for womanly assistance? Surely the feminine aspects of his job are not ignored. Neither will he assume them himself with discretion thrown to the wind.

Further questions are raised concerning this interpretation because of the fact that a deacon's family life (including his wife) is dealt with specifically in verse 12 as is the elder's in verses 4–5.

As Kent says, "It seems more likely that the wives of deacons are covered by the requirement that the deacon should superintend over his own household."[1] To this, one final point may be added. If one were to ignore the evidence so far, and assume these are in fact deacons' wives, then he must also assume that *both* a deacon and his wife are elected to fulfill these service obligations. Thus an office of "deaconess" is created, open only to those women whose husbands seek the office of deacon. Women who could not fulfill these functions, for one reason or another (health, family, etc.) would probably negate their husbands' chances of obtaining the office of deacon for themselves.

γυναῖκας as Deaconesses

The second general view held in regard to the women of 1 Timothy 3:11 is that this verse presents the formal *office of deaconess*. This has long been the consensus of the majority of churches throughout the centuries and is no less true today. Why? First, this view accords well with the grammatical structure of the passage. The conjunction ὡσαύτως makes it clear that three classes are under consideration. To infuse a marital unity between verses 8–10 and verse 11 seems beyond the text. There simply is no such connection. As has been pointed out, γυναῖκας can mean any adult females, which surely it must be here.

One of the strongest arguments for this view is the very context of the passage. Paul is dealing with the subject of church offices and here has clearly marked out three distinct groups to represent the church. One must strain the flow of the passage to eliminate the women of verse 11 as a third such office. Since διάκονος came to be used for both the masculine and feminine gender, it seems natural to suppose that Paul's use of γυναῖκας in verse 11 is to avoid confusing the previous group with those being introduced here. "The reader is left to infer 'women deacons.'"[2]

To add to the grammatical evidence is the fact that at least one woman is expressly called "deacon" in the New Testament. In Romans 16:1 Phoebe is said to be a "deaconess of the church which is at Cenchrea."

There is also historical evidence which gives even further support to the meaning "office of deaconess." Major documents such as the Syrian *Didascalia Apostalorum* (third century) and the *Apostolic Constitutions* (fourth century) indicate that the church interpreted this verse to mean an office of deaconess. With such impressive evidence there is little wonder why the church in general has maintained that the women of verse 11 are "deaconesses" in the fullest sense.

Despite such evidence, however, there are some nagging doubts as to the validity of such an interpretation. Principal among these is the question that if this is indeed a full-fledged office, why is it inserted into the discussion of male deacons? Why does it not merit a paragraph all its own? As Hendriksen says:

> . . . the fact that no special and separate paragraph is used in describing their necessary qualifications, but that these are simply wedged in between the stipulated requirements for deacons, with equal clarity indicates that these women were not to be regarded as constituting a third office of the church . . . endowed with authority equal to that of deacons.[3]

What about Phoebe? Does not Romans 16:1 indicate she held the office of deaconess? Here one must be careful with the usage of the word διάκονος. In Pauline writings it occurs twenty times. It is used of civil rulers (Rom. 13:4), Christ (15:8), Paul (1 Cor. 3:5; Gal. 2:17), Timothy (1 Thess. 3:2; 1 Tim. 4:6), Epaphras (Col. 1:7), and others as well as Phoebe. If one is to make these instances technical usages as is done in the case of Phoebe, then Christ, Paul, and Timothy were deacons also. Of course the answer is that in these cases the usage is in the general sense of "servant" or "minister." If that be so, one must then ask how Romans 16:1 can be considered an *exception* to this general sense. Is there any evidence at all for a technical rendering here? Only in Philippians 1:1, where the officers of the church are formally addressed, and in 1 Timothy 3:8, 12, where the qualifications for the office of deacon are enumerated, does the technical sense seem to be called for.

One must also not confuse church history with Bible exegesis regardless of the practice followed in the church of the third and fourth centuries. This in no way ends the discussion. The issue lies not in what the early church did so much as it does in what Paul meant. And to say that Paul meant to support an office of deaconess, comparable to that of the deacon, is still suspect.

γυναῖκας as Unmarried Assistants

It has been demonstrated that the usual interpretations of 1 Timothy 3:11, "deacons' wives" and "deaconesses," are not beyond question. This is not to say that they have no validity at all. On the contrary, these are still viable options that must be considered seriously. However, another interpretation that merits consideration is the view that these are unmarried women who assist the deacons in the service functions of the church.

Grammatically, it has already been shown that ὡσαύτως is best seen as introducing a third distinct group into the discussion. Such a conjunction seems to present a drawback to the interpretation "deacons' wives." On the other hand, the conjunctive καί would have further strengthened the relationship between these women and the deacons previously discussed. But the idea that the relationship is that of husband and wife is seriously weakened with the use of ὡσαύτως. One should not, however, throw out the idea that there is no relationship at all between these two groups. Contextually one must consider the fact that verse 11 falls in the midst of a discussion on *male* deacons. Therefore the idea that verse 11 is secondary to the larger discussion yet closely related to it seems plausible. If the idea of "deacons' wives" is unfavorable, then some other *relationship* between these men and women must be sought.

The wedging of verse 11 within a discussion on deacons also seems to strengthen the argument against the interpretation "deaconesses." It would seem strange for Paul to introduce a third office of the church so briefly and then return to the former topic of male deacons without some further explanation. With the detailed qualifications for both elder and deacon so plainly spelled out, why would there be a parenthesizing of the deacons' female counterpart? If these women held a full third office of the church, why do they not merit a paragraph of their own? One might also notice that no stipulations are laid down concerning such a woman's home life or whether she should first be tested like the deacon. Some have tried to counter this by saying that since verse 11 demonstrates that a woman can be a διάκονος, the entire section on deacons (vv. 8–13) is meant to apply to women as well. Thus the implications of home life or a testing period in the discussion of deacons is to be inferred for women as well as men. If this is the case, then why did Paul not wait until the end of his discussion on deacons and then say something like "women (deaconesses) likewise are to be of such standing." And when women *are* mentioned in verse 11, Paul did not infer anything stated previously concerning deacons to these women. Rather he spelled out the qualifications for these women *even though* they are almost parallel to those of the deacon.

Since the idea that these women are related to the deacons by being deacons' wives seems questionable and since the positioning of verse 11 in the midst of the discussion on deacons seems to demand some kind of relationship between these women and the deacons, the interpretation "assistant" is offered for consideration. If it is not a marriage relationship, then it may be a working one.

Perhaps after finishing with the deacon's personal qualifications, Paul's mind flashed to those women who would assist the deacon in his office of service. Surely such women were to reproduce the same high character standards as the man under whom they serve.

If these women are indeed "assistants," then the immediate question concerns which women were eligible for this position. It has already been demonstrated that γυναῖκας can be understood to mean any adult women, married or unmarried. But to restrict the meaning of γυναῖκας here to mean unmarried women is impossible without contextual support. Hermeneutically speaking, words have no meaning apart from context and this is no less true here.

The word γυναῖκας has posed problems for every interpreter regardless of which interpretation is held. One will no doubt be forever asking, "Why did Paul use such a general term without qualification?" The addition of the possessive pronoun ὑμῶν ("your") to γυναῖκας would have ended any doubt that it was deacons' wives.

Although the male offices of deacon and elder are marked out by technical terms, it is questionable if γυναῖκας is so used. No doubt the translation "deaconess" for the word γυναῖκας (everywhere translated "woman" or "wife") came about through efforts to impose a technical sense on the word. If Paul had meant to impose such technical terminology here, τάς διάκονος ("deaconesses") was not outside his range of vocabulary. Yet he chose the general term γυναῖκας.

Can γυναῖκας be restricted to unmarried women? Two reasons seem to indicate this. The first reason is contextual; the second is historical. In verses 8–10, it should be noted that Paul began his discussion on deacons by first citing their personal qualifications. This is followed up in verse 11 by the personal qualifications of those women who are to be their assistants. Then in verse 12 the deacons' responsibilities regarding their families are spotlighted, and yet *no* such complementary qualifications are added for their feminine helpers! It is concluded that the reason no such qualifications are given is because they had no need of any. The second reason for this conclusion comes by recalling the historical setting of this letter. The backdrop of 1 Timothy seems to indicate that women were having difficulty fulfilling their womanly responsibilities especially to the home. If the women of verse 11 could be married, surely a great deal of restrictive legislation concerning the home needed to be spelled out. If anywhere, Paul needed to say "women likewise" after 1 Timothy 3:12. Yet he was strangely silent. Two reasons suggest that γυναῖκας be restricted to women who are unmarried. The fact that these women had no family responsibilities enabled them to give their undivided attention to the church.

Why would Paul allow only unmarried women to assist the deacons? For the most part one can only speculate, but some suggestions may be offered.

The first reason is that the ministry of the married women is centered in the home. In the pastoral epistles women are generally urged to return to that function for which God has especially designed them; that is, their homes, their children, and their husbands are to be their primary concern (1 Tim. 2:9–15; 5:8, 14, 16; 2 Tim. 3:14–15; Titus 2:3–5). Thus a wife serves the church primarily through her ministry in the home. One is *not* to jump to the conclusion that married women perform no service functions at all in the church. The idea suggested here is that her involvement in the church at large is to be worked around her ministry in the home (which is a "branch" of that church).

A second suggestion relates to the first in that a married woman would not be able to meet the demands of this official service position. Her duties at home would deny her the availability and/or flexibility needed to do a credible job.

No one knows how much involvement was required of the deacons and their assistants. No doubt involvement varied from church to church and person to person. To say these people served the church full-time or in their spare time or part-time is not the issue. The issue is flexibility and availability to meet the service demands of an entire church. Both the married man and the unmarried woman can meet those requirements. The married woman on the other hand, finds those same requirements troublesome. For her to be flexible in the home is to be inflexible outside of it. If the priorities are reversed, the home suffers.

Interestingly those churches following the close of the New Testament age who had the office of deaconess limited that function almost exclusively to virgins and/or widows who exemplified the character qualities required. In such churches "marriage after ordination was forbidden. . . ."[4] This is not difficult to understand in light of the duties those women were asked to perform. Early church writers picture such women as visiting the sick, distributing provisions among the poor, aiding women in baptismal ceremonies, visiting Christian women in pagan households, assisting the ill, visiting those in prison, and praying.[5] No wonder Hatch writes, "the ancient deaconess was apparently intended to make it her life work to serve the church in any way appropriate to her position. . . ."[6] A married woman of that time, without the conveniences of today, would have difficulty in keeping up with the most basic tasks of the home. Thus it was to her advantage not to have this area of service opened to her. She was not tempted to serve nor made to feel guilty in not doing so, for the option was not available.

A third suggestion is that here is an outlet for ministry of today's most neglected individuals in the church: unmarried females. The unmarried female can give her undivided attention to the service of the church. This is especially true of older widows (as in 1 Tim. 5) who would not have the burden of making a living. Thus they would have maximum availability to people and their needs.

The church of the 2d, 3d, and 4th centuries seemed to see this plainly and to capitalize on it. The widows and virgins who made up these select groups provided services beyond the range of most married women today. Thus these same ministries (visiting the sick, counseling, comforting the lonely, etc.) are today not performed for the most part by married women but by paid pastoral staffs while the church's unmarrieds sit idly by.

The simplest explanation therefore for the women of 1 Timothy 3:11 is that they are unmarried women committed unconditionally to the service of the church and who in meeting certain character qualities, have been enlisted to aid the deacons in the outworking of their office.

CHAPTER 16

Endurance in Suffering in 1 Peter

Gordon E. Kirk

Prominent in the Epistle of 1 Peter is the theme of persecution, suffering, and trials, undergirded with the resilient framework of endurance. In this short letter the apostle Peter succinctly discussed the situations, Christ's example, attitudes and actions, and purposes pertaining to believers enduring in the midst of suffering. Not leaving the believer in despair, Peter revealed the elements essential to endurance during periods of affliction.

Situations Calling for Endurance

Several times Peter wrote about situations in which his readers suffered. He referred to *trials in general* (1:6, πειρασμοί, "tests, trials"), *slander* (2:12; 3:16, καταλαλέω, "to defame, to speak evil of"), *evil* (3:9, κακός, "evil or injurious conduct"), *insult* (3:9, λοιδορίας, "verbal abuse"), and *being reviled* (3:16, ἐπηρεάζω, "to threaten or mistreat;" and 4:14, ὀνειδίζω, "to reproach or insult"). These are seen in the following verses.

"In this you greatly rejoice, even though now for a little while, if necessary, you have been distressed by various trials" (1:6).

"Keep your behavior excellent among the Gentiles, so that in the thing in which they slander you as evildoers, they may on account of your good deeds, as they observe them, glorify God in the day of visitation" (2:12).

"To sum up, let all be harmonious, sympathetic, brotherly, kindhearted, and humble in spirit; not returning evil for evil, or insult for insult, but giving a blessing instead; for you were called for the very purpose that you might inherit a blessing" (3:8–9).

"Keep a good conscience so that in the thing in which you are slandered, those who revile your good behavior in Christ may be put to shame" (3:16).

"If you are reviled for the name of Christ, you are blessed, because the Spirit of glory and of God rests upon you" (4:14).

Most of these passages point to suffering from the false accusations verbally addressed to the Christians by unbelievers. In addition, Peter speaks of their suffering as being "under sorrows" (2:19, λύπη), that is, to the point of pain or grief, and he says that by the trials they "have been distressed" (1:6, λυπηθέντες).

Peter also referred to Christians suffering "unjustly" (2:19), suffering when they do "what is right" (2:20b; 3:17), suffering "for the sake of righteousness" (3:14), suffering "as a Christian" (4:16), and suffering "according to the will of God" (4:19). In these six verses the verb "to suffer" is the general word, πάσχω.

Peter recited several specific situations in which Christians may suffer, but he at the same time compelled them to exercise submission in those circumstances. While submission in and of itself does not necessitate suffering, distressful conditions may be experienced when a Christian functions under unethical, insensitive, or unresponsive authorities. These include governmental authority (2:13–15), vocational authority (2:18–19), and marital authority (3:1).

"Submit yourselves for the Lord's sake to every human institution, whether to a king as the one in authority, or to governors as sent by him for the punishment of evildoers and the praise of those who do right. For such is the will of God that by doing right you may silence the ignorance of foolish men" (2:13–15).

"Servants, be submissive to your masters with all respect, not only to those who are good and gentle, but also to those who are unreasonable. For this finds favor, if for the sake of conscience toward God a man bears up under sorrows when suffering unjustly" (2:18–19).

"In the same way, you wives, be submissive to your own husbands so that even if any of them are disobedient to the word, they may be won without a word by the behavior of their wives" (3:1).

As seen in these verses submission in each of these situations is urged for it results in desirable consequences. In 2:13–15 submission to governmental authority ("every human institution," "a king," and "governors") is "for the Lord's sake" and can result in silencing "foolish men," apparently those who were slandering the Christians as evildoers (2:12). In 2:18–19 submission of servants to their masters—even unreasonable ones who cause unjust suffering—brings "favor" (χάρις) with God. In 3:1 submission of Christian wives to their unbelieving husbands may result in those husbands being won to the Lord by their wives' godly conduct.

Frequently, however, a Christian's suffering is simply the consequence of his own evil actions. In such situations Peter warns against claiming any special blessing from God. No credit is due the believer whose suffering results from his sin, as the following three passages indicate.

"For what credit is there if, when you sin and are harshly treated, you endure it with patience? But if when you do what is right and suffer for it you patiently endure it, this finds favor with God" (2:20).

"For it is better, if God should will it so, that you suffer for doing what is right rather than for doing what is wrong" (3:17).

"By no means let any of you suffer as a murderer, or thief, or evildoer, or a troublesome meddler; but if anyone suffers as a Christian, let him not feel ashamed, but in that name let him glorify God" (4:15–16).

Concerning the explicit exhortations found in 1 Peter 4:15–16, Wand says the following:

> In what is generally known as the Neronian Persecution, Christians did sometimes suffer (probably unjustified) on a charge of arson. It was not long before charges of cannibalism were brought against Christians, but these may have arisen out of some misunderstanding of the Eucharist. However, Christians did sometimes break the law. Both Corinthian and Ephesian Christians have to be warned against thieving (i Cor. vi 10: Eph. iv 28).[1]

It seems plausible to assume that a Christian, living during the era in which Peter penned this letter, might become disobedient to God because of the unjustified pressures and gruesome sufferings inflicted on believers by the government and society. Moffatt describes the apostle's contemporary setting.

> A Christian, especially under the influence of apocalyptic hopes, might incur the suspicion of treason by encouraging disobedience among slaves, for example, or by sympathizing with revolutionary movements, in exasperation against the persecuting authorities. The risk of an extreme left wing among Christians was not unfounded at this period. The anti-Roman tone of an apocalypse like the book of Revelation shows how the apocalyptic hope might be used to foster social discontent and political disorder.[2]

In this type of climate Peter perceived the need to warn against self-induced suffering because of disobedience and lack of submission. It is easy to be swept away by humanistic reasoning and revolutionary solutions and to retaliate against authoritative suppression. Suffering because of the name of Christ brings individual glory, but suffering because of unrighteousness and sinful activity brings disgrace to the name of Christ. Because of the oppressive nature of the Roman rule in relationship to Christians, Peter brought hope by emphasizing one major aspect of suffering: if a believer bears up under unjust treatment, he finds favor with God (2:19–25; 3:13–18; 4:12–14; 5:10). Cranfield addresses this issue of *undeserved* suffering.

> Most of the sufferings that come to us are neutral in the sense that they come to us as men, not as Christians particularly; and of course the gospel should help us to face them bravely. But sometimes we may have to suffer because we are Christians—*for righteousness' sake*—and, when that happens, says Peter, *blessed are ye*, you are to be congratulated on your high privilege. For such suffering marks a person out as an heir of the kingdom of God. It is bright with promise. Peter doubtless had in mind the saying of Christ which we have in Matt. 5:10.[3]

With this pervasive purpose in mind, Peter's succeeding statements reinforce this underlying principle.

"For this finds favor, if for the sake of conscience toward God a man bears up under sorrows when suffering unjustly. . . . But if when you do what is right and suffer for it you patiently endure it, this finds favor with God" (2:19–20).

"But even if you should suffer for the sake of righteousness, you are blessed. . . . For it is better, if God should will it so, that you suffer for doing what is right rather than for doing what is wrong. For Christ also died for sins once for all, the just for the unjust . . ." (3:14, 17–18a).

"If you are reviled for the name of Christ, you are blessed, because the Spirit of glory and of God rests upon you" (4:14).

"And after you have suffered for a little while, the God of all grace, who called you to His eternal glory in Christ, will Himself perfect, confirm, strengthen and establish you" (5:10).

Undeserved suffering results in favor with God (2:19–20), blessing (3:14; 4:14), and spiritual strength and stability (5:10).

Christ's Example of Endurance

Throughout the Book of 1 Peter, a Christological emphasis is evident. As a disciple of Jesus this fisherman's life was transformed, and before his own eyes he perceived the supreme example of the One who endured suffering. Replete within *every chapter* in this epistle is the illustration of Christ, the ultimate model of endurance.

"As to this salvation, the prophets who prophesied . . . the sufferings of Christ and the glories to follow" (1: 10–11).

"For you have been called for this purpose, since Christ also suffered for you, leaving you an example for you to follow in His steps" (2:21).

"For Christ also died for sins once for all, the just for the unjust . . ." (3:18).

"Therefore, since Christ has suffered in the flesh, arm yourselves also with the same purpose . . ." (4:1).

"Therefore, I exhort the elders among you, as your fellow-elder and witness of the sufferings of Christ, and a partaker also of the glory that is to be revealed" (5:1).

Cranfield discusses Christ's example of endurance in 1 Peter 2:21.

> Here is the supreme motive—the consciousness of an infinite indebtedness to Christ, the sense of gratitude to him for what he has done FOR YOU. These words FOR YOU (i.e., on your behalf) imply that Christ's sufferings and death were much more than an example (though that they certainly were, as the next words will emphasize). His sufferings were vicarious. . . . The words imply that the Cross provides not only the motive or reason for this meekness but also the moral strength. It provides also the pattern to be copied—*leaving you an example* (the word translated "example" denotes a copy alphabet used by children learning to write or an outline or sketch requiring to be filled in or colored; a cognate word is used in Aeschylus of the "print" of a foot). . . . The disciple is to follow in the footprints of his Lord. The Christian life is an imitation of Christ.[4]

Attitudes and Actions in Suffering

It is typical of mankind to respond negatively to pressure with an attitude of resentment and a desire for retaliation.

Christians, however, can endure suffering with a proper attitude of humility and patience. Throughout his epistle, Peter gave at least ten admonitions regarding a Christian's responses while enduring suffering.

GREATLY REJOICE AND KEEP ON REJOICING

"In this you greatly rejoice, even though now for a little while, if necessary, you have been distressed by various trials" (1:6). "But to the degree that you share the sufferings of Christ, keep on rejoicing; so that also at the revelation of His glory, you may rejoice with exultation" (4:13).

KEEP ONE'S BEHAVIOR EXCELLENT

"Beloved, I urge you as aliens and strangers to abstain from fleshly lusts, which wage war against the soul. Keep your behavior excellent among the Gentiles, so that in the thing in which they slander you as evildoers, they may on account of your good deeds, as they observe them, glorify God in the day of visitation" (2:11–12).

PATIENTLY ENDURE, DO NOT REVILE OR THREATEN, ENTRUST ONESELF TO GOD

"But if when you do what is right and suffer for it you patiently endure it, this finds favor with God. For you have been called for this purpose, since Christ also suffered for you, leaving you an example for you to follow in His steps . . . and while being reviled, He did not revile in return; while suffering, He uttered no threats, but kept entrusting Himself to Him who judges righteously" (2:20b–21, 23). "Therefore, let those also who suffer according to the will of God entrust their souls to a faithful Creator in doing what is right" (4:19).

DO NOT FEAR INTIMIDATION OR BE TROUBLED, SANCTIFY CHRIST, AND KEEP A GOOD CONSCIENCE

"But even if you should suffer for the sake of righteousness, you are blessed. And do not fear their intimidation, and do not be troubled, but sanctify Christ as Lord in your hearts, always being ready to make a defense to every one who asks you to give an account for the hope that is in you, yet with gentleness and reverence; and keep a good conscience so that in the thing in which you are slandered, those who revile your good behavior in Christ may be put to shame" (3:14–16).

ARM ONESELF

"Therefore, since Christ has suffered in the flesh, arm yourselves also with the same purpose, because he who has suffered in the flesh has ceased from sin" (4:1).

DO NOT BE SURPRISED

"Beloved, do not be surprised at the fiery ordeal among you, which comes upon you for your testing, as though some strange thing were happening to you" (4:12).

DO NOT FEEL ASHAMED

"But if anyone suffers as a Christian, let him not feel ashamed, but in that name let him glorify God" (4:16).

HUMBLE ONESELF

"Humble yourselves, therefore, under the mighty hand of God, that He may exalt you at the proper time" (5:6).

CAST ONE'S ANXIETY ON GOD

"Casting all your anxiety upon Him, because He cares for you" (5:7).

BE ON THE ALERT AND RESIST THE DEVIL

"Be of sober spirit, be on the alert. Your adversary, the devil, prowls about like a roaring lion, seeking someone to devour. But resist him, firm in your faith, knowing that the same experiences of suffering are being accomplished by your brethren who are in the world" (5:8–9).

From the very first chapter of his letter, Peter reassured believers that the hope of their salvation enables them to rejoice in spite of unfavorable circumstances. The Christian, at the approach of suffering, should not relinquish the joy he has in Christ (1:3–9). In these verses it is important to note that before Peter mentioned the difficulties and trials that will be encountered, he focused his readers' attention on a higher plane, namely, their heavenly inheritance and eschatological hope. Thus the discussion of trials is spoken of against the backdrop of the believer's position in Christ. In conjunction with such a solid foundation, the manifold temptations or "various trials" (1:6), however unpleasant, begin to be placed in perspective, and only in this context can affliction and suffering be seen in true proportion.

Compared with the promised inheritance (the eschatological hope) suffering is actually shortlived.[5] With this kind of inner stability, there is the capacity for rejoicing, entrusting, and humbling oneself under the mighty hand of God. And knowing of the promised eternal inheritance, Peter's exhortations to maintain an attitude of "rejoicing" and to produce actions of "excellence" take on new meaning.

When a believer is innocent of wrongdoing and is able to bear undeserved sufferings with the proper attitudes and actions, he demonstrates God's supernatural enabling. This extraordinary ability is characteristic of the Christian who relies on the power of God and his position in Christ.

Purposes of Endurance in Suffering

The *general purpose* of enduring, in terms of suffering, was repeatedly emphasized by Peter as the refining of one's faith. Whatever the experience, the response of one's attitudes and actions during a pressure situation is an indication of the level of his spiritual maturity. The *specific purpose* of suffering, alluded to in the first chapter, is based on the fact that the proof of one's faith far exceeds any extrinsic value. Peter stated, "that the proof of your faith, being more precious than gold which is perishable, even though tested by fire, may be found to result in praise and glory and honor at the revelation of Jesus Christ" (1:7).

> Before gold is pure it has to be tried and tested and purified in the fire. The trials which come to a person are tests of his faith, and out of them his faith can emerge stronger and clearer and firmer than ever it was before. The rigors which the athlete has to undergo are not meant to make him collapse; they are meant to make him able to develop more and more strength and staying-power. In this world trial and affliction are not meant to take the strength out of us, but to put the strength into us.
>
> In this connection there is a most suggestive fact in the language that Peter uses. He says that the Christian for the moment may well have to undergo, as the Authorized Version has it, *manifold* trials. In the Greek the word for manifold is *poikilos*, which literally means *many-coloured*. Now Peter uses that word once again and only once again, and the one other time he uses it is to describe the grace of God (1 Pet. 4:10). Our troubles maybe many-coloured, but so is the grace of God. There is no colour in the human situation which the grace of God cannot match. Whatever life is doing to us there is that in the grace of God which will enable us to meet it and to overcome it. There is a grace to match every trial, and there is no trial without its grace.[6]

The following verses point up several purposes in and results from endurance in suffering.

PROOF OF ONE'S FAITH

"In this you greatly rejoice, even though now for a little while, if necessary, you have been distressed by various trials, that the proof of your faith, being more precious than gold which is perishable, even though tested by fire, may be found to result in praise and glory and honor at the revelation of Jesus Christ" (1:6–7).

"Beloved, do not be surprised at the fiery ordeal among you, which comes upon you for your testing, as though some strange thing were happening to you" (4:12).

PROTECTION OF ONE'S INTEGRITY

"Submit yourselves for the Lord's sake to every human institution. . . . For such is the will of God that by doing right you may silence the ignorance of foolish men" (2:13, 15).

PRESENTATION OF ONE'S CALLING

"But if when you do what is right and suffer for it you patiently endure it, this finds favor with God. For you have been called for this purpose, since Christ also suffered for you, leaving you an example for you to follow in His steps" (2:20b–21).

PROMISE OF ONE'S BLESSING

"But even if you should suffer for the sake of righteousness, you are blessed" (3:14a). "If you are reviled for the name of Christ, you are blessed, because the Spirit of glory and of God rests upon you" (4:14).

PURIFICATION OF ONE'S MOTIVES

"Therefore, since Christ has suffered in the flesh, arm yourselves also with the same purpose, because he who has suffered in the flesh has ceased from sin, so as to live the rest of the time in the flesh no longer for the lusts of men, but for the will of God" (4:1–2).

PROVISION OF ONE'S EXULTATION

"But to the degree that you share the sufferings of Christ, keep on rejoicing, so that also at the revelation of His glory, you may rejoice with exultation" (4:13).

PERFECTION OF ONE'S CHARACTER

"And after you have suffered for a little while, the God of all grace, who called you to His eternal glory in Christ, will Himself perfect, confirm, strengthen and establish you" (5:10).

Reflections Concerning Peter's Theology of Endurance

It is evident that Peter was compassionate toward the early church, which was undergoing persecution. He desired to encourage and strengthen them as they faced afflictions and hardships. Two points seem to be emphasized by Peter. First, endurance in suffering can be possible only as one is able to look forward to eternal reward. Believers are able to be steadfast in the most difficult situations if they are aware of the fulfilling and righteous inheritance that awaits them. Peter wanted each believer to know that slander, insult, persecution, trouble, affliction, or any type of suffering is limited to the temporal realm, and that a future inheritance is yet to come. Hope, or something to look forward to, gives people reason for enduring hardships. Christians have the invincible promise of ultimate victory which cultivates unwavering endurance.

Second, endurance in suffering is made more tolerable through the example of Jesus Christ. Peter emphasized that if the Christian is compelled to suffer cruelly and unjustly for his faith, he is traveling the same path his Lord and Savior has already walked. The suffering Christian must always remember that he has a suffering Christ. Christ's attitudes and actions during His unjust persecution reveal the proper response to suffering that His followers are to maintain during stressful situations.

Therefore each believer during times of suffering and unjust circumstances should reiterate Peter's "grand doxology": "Blessed be the God and Father of our Lord Jesus Christ, who according to His great mercy has caused us to be born again to a living hope through the resurrection of Jesus Christ from the dead, to obtain an inheritance which is imperishable and undefiled and will not fade away, reserved in heaven for you, who are protected by the power of God through faith for a salvation ready to be revealed in the last time. In this you greatly rejoice, even though now for a little while, if necessary, you have been distressed by various trials" (1:3–6).

CHAPTER 17

Second Peter 2:1 and the Extent of the Atonement

Andrew D. Chang

A doctrinal issue that divides Christians is the question of the extent of the atonement. Did Christ die with the intention to save only the elect or was His death in some way relevant to all human beings? If one reads passages like John 3:16; 1 Timothy 2:6; 4:10 without any preconceived theological framework, the conclusion seems to be that the Bible unequivocally teaches unlimited atonement. However, if one imposes a straightjacket of his own theological bias on those and other universal passages, he may say that it is equally possible to interpret those passages from the perspective of "limited redemption." Most of those passages seem to go either way depending on one's theology. But limited redemptionists must struggle with at least a few passages to prove their view. One of these passages is 2 Peter 2:1. One limited redemptionist is of the opinion that the whole case for unlimited atonement hinges on this very verse.[1] This seems to be an oversimplification of the case; however, as Henry Alford puts it, "no assertion of universal redemption can be plainer than this."[2]

In spite of its tremendous significance, little or no scholarly attention has been directed to this passage until recently.[3]

Long took up a serious study of this passage to interpret it from the limited redemptionist viewpoint. His study seems to be cogent and his case for limited atonement very plausible. In view of this, this article seeks to point out some weaknesses in Long's arguments and to defend the unlimited atonement within the limits of 2 Peter 2:1.[4]

The Meaning of Δεσπότης

As Long correctly observes, the two key words in this verse are δεσπότης ("Master") and, more importantly, ἀγοράζω ("bought").[5]

The word δεσπότης is employed ten times in the New Testament, five of which are used of men. Four of these are clearly used in the sense of slave owner, or lord in contrast to slave (1 Tim. 6:1–2, Titus 2:9, 1 Peter 2:18). Whether 2 Timothy 2:21 falls under this category demands some discussion. Here δεσπότης is described as the one who uses different kinds of vessels for his own purpose. Σκεῦος generally means a thing or object used for any purpose,[6] but here and in other Pauline Epistles it is used metaphorically to denote certain aspects of man.[7] The context seems to show clearly that the house (2 Tim. 2:20) is analogous to the local church, the vessel to the Christians, and the δεσπότης to Christ. The owner of a household uses some vessels for honorable purposes and others for less honorable purposes. Apostates or wicked ones in the church are likened to dishonorable vessels. If a Christian frees himself from any association with apostates, he will become a useful servant for his Master.[8] Thus it is not too much to say that the nuance of slave owner is also present in 2 Timothy 2:21, at least in a metaphorical sense.[9]

The word δεσπότης is used of God the Father three times. In Luke 2:29 Simeon as God's servant referred to God as his sovereign Master. The second ascription of δεσπότης to God the Father is found in Acts 4:24. A group of Christians, hearing Peter and John's report, "lifted their voice to God with one accord and said, 'O Lord [δεσπότης], it is Thou who didst make the heaven and the earth and the sea, and all that is in them." Here the stress is obviously on God's absolute sovereignty and ownership over all His creation.[10] By virtue of His work in creation, God can claim to own the whole universe and those in it. One other reference to God the Father as δεσπότης is Revelation 6:10. Here again the idea of both Master and absolute Sovereign seems to be prominent.

The word δεσπότης is also used of Christ. Certain persons have crept in unnoticed and deny "our only Master and Lord, Jesus Christ" (τὸν μόνον δεσπότην καὶ κύριον ἡμῶν Ἰησοῦν Χριστόν, Jude 4). This construction seems to fit nicely into the Granville Sharp rule;[11] thus it can be taken that δεσπότης and κύριος ἡμῶν Ἰησοῦς Χριστός are referring to the same person. Considering Jude 3 and 4 together, one can reasonably conclude that Christ is the Master by virtue of His being the Savior. In other words the word δεσπότης is used in a soteriological context. Another ascription of δεσπότης to Christ is found in 2 Peter 2:1. Whether δεσπότης here refers to God the Father or God the Son is debated, but most scholars agree that it refers to Christ primarily because of its close parallel to Jude 4.[12] A plain reading of the passage seems to indicate that Jesus Christ paid the price to redeem even the false teachers who will surely perish. Thus the idea of slave owner is also present in this passage.

As already noted, the general meaning of the word δεσπότης is owner or lord, especially in a master-slave relationship. When the word is used of men, it denotes quite obviously the slave owner. When it refers to God the Father, it seems to emphasize God's absolute sovereignty and ownership probably by virtue of His work in creation. When it is used of Christ, the context seems to show that Christ is the slave owner by virtue of His redemption.

Long also did an extensive word study on δεσπότης. His whole point was to determine whether the word can refer to Christ as the Mediator.[13] No scholar argues that the word δεσπότης is used of Christ as the Mediator, and Long is right in this regard. However, the fact that δεσπότης does not denote the mediatorship does not lend any support to the limited atonement position. The emphasis in 2 Peter 2:1 is not on the mediatorship of Christ, but "on the redemption as a change of ownership."[14] By paying the ransom, Christ purchased everyone, including the false teachers. The same idea seems to be present in 1 Corinthians 6:19–20. Just as God the Father claims the ownership of the whole universe by virtue of His work in creation, so does Christ claim the ownership of the whole human race by virtue of His work of redemption.

The Meaning of Ἀγοράζω

The word ἀγοράζω originally meant "to frequent the forum,"[15] from which came eventually the meaning "to buy in the marketplace" and thence "to buy" in general. In Hellenistic times it was also in common use as a term for buying slaves.[16]

The Septuagint does not seem to be of much help in understanding the meaning of this word because all the references there seem to be to simple commercial purchases of such items as food (Gen. 41:27; 42:5, 7) or a threshing floor (1 Chron. 21:24). It translates the Hebrew word שָׁבַר and קָנָה primarily, with one or two occasional appearances of other verbs (e.g., חָלַק, Jer. 37:12, לָקַח, Neh. 10:31), but these shed no light on this study.[17]

In the New Testament the word ἀγοράζω is used 31 times. Twenty-five times it is used in the sense of commercial purchases, and five times it is used in a soteriological sense (1 Cor. 6:20;

7:23; Rev. 5:9; 14:3–4). One interesting observation is that when the object of purchase is nonhuman, the word ἀγοράζω is always used in the nonsoteriological sense (Matt. 13:44; 21:12; Mark 6:36; Luke 9:13; John 6:5; 1 Cor. 7:30; Rev. 13:17; 18:11; etc.). When the object is a human being, it is always used in the soteriological sense. If this is a correct observation, the word ἀγοράζω in 2 Peter 2:1 is also to be taken in the soteriological sense because the object of purchase is obviously human beings.

Long, however, argues that the word ἀγοράζω in 2 Peter 2:1 is to be understood nonsoteriologically for several reasons. The following are some of those reasons. First, he says that whenever the word ἀγοράζω is used redemptively, the purchase price is always stated or made explicit in the context. Yet in 2 Peter 2:1 the purchase price is neither stated nor implied in the context; therefore, he says, ἀγοράζω cannot be taken soteriologically.[18]

It is true that in 1 Corinthians 6:20; 7:23, and Revelation 5:9 either the technical term τιμή ("price") or reference to His "death" (implying that the blood was the price) is present along with ἀγοράζω. However, in Revelation 14:3–4 neither references are to be found and yet the context is undoubtedly soteriological.

Second, Long argues that when the word ἀγοράζω is used in the sense of redemption, it is limited to believers. Second Peter 2:1 refers to nonbelievers and therefore it cannot be used soteriologically.[19] This observation is true of all other five soteriological uses of the word ἀγοράζω, but it is wrong to impose the same conclusion on 2 Peter 2:1 without considering the passage in its own context. If one out of six uses of a word proves that its use is different, it is legitimate to establish another category. In cases of rare uses of a word even one solid reference is weighty enough to establish a new category. The use of δεσπότης in reference to Christ as the "slave owner" by virtue of His work of salvation, the use of ἀγοράζω as spiritual redemption when the object of the purchase is human beings, and the close parallel to Jude 4 seem to show that 2 Peter 2:1 is to be taken soteriologically. So it is legitimate to say that if the context allows, the word ἀγοράζω can be used of either believers or unbelievers.

Third, Long argues that ἀγοράζω is never used in the Scriptures in a hypothetical sense. Rather it is always used in a context where the purchase actually takes place in reality.[20]

When one makes a statement with a word such as "never" or "always," only one contrary bit of evidence is sufficient to disprove the argument. In Luke 14:15–24 Jesus told the story of a banquet to emphasize the truth that the Jews were rejected because of their unbelief but that the Gentiles were accepted into the kingdom because of their positive response to the invitation. A certain man gave a large banquet and invited many to come, but all made excuses. The first said, "I have bought a piece of land and I need to go out and look at it; please consider me excused" (v. 18). The second one said, "I have bought five yoke of oxen, and I am going to try them out; please consider me excused" (v. 19). And the third one said, "I have married a wife, and for that reason I cannot come" (v. 20). Geldenhuys writes of the significance of these excuses.

> Three typical examples of the kind of excuses that were made are men-
> tioned, and from this it is clear that they were merely "pretexts." They do
> not adduce any real reasons why they are unable to go. Their excuses are
> false and valueless—for one does not first buy a piece of ground and
> only afterwards goes to see what it looks like; and if one has already
> bought a yoke of oxen it is useless to go only then to try them (for the
> sale is completed); the fact that one has got married is certainly not a
> sound reason why he should not go to the supper to which he has been
> invited.[21]

If this is a correct understanding of the parable,[22] the purchases of land and oxen did not actually take place at all; yet the word ἀγοράζω is certainly used in the normal sense.

Interpretation of 2 Peter 2:1

Four interpretations of this verse have been suggested, and they can be divided into two groups—nonsoteriological interpretations and soteriological interpretations.

NONSOTERIOLOGICAL INTERPRETATIONS

Temporal deliverance view. This is the view that Peter was speaking of the false teachers not with regard to eternal redemption but with regard to the temporal physical deliverance from the pollutions of the world by virtue of their professing to be Christians (v. 20).[23]

The Bible does teach temporal deliverance, but this view does not seem to square with the teaching of 2 Peter 2:1. The text gives no evidence that these false teachers professed to be believers. Even if they were professing Christians, there is no logical connection between the physical deliverance from the pollutions of the world and the profession itself Moreover, this view hardly does justice to the meaning of the words δεσπότης and ἀγοράζω. *Sovereign creation view.* The exponents of this view hold that Peter here used the word ἀγοράζω in the sense of κτίζω and thus he wrote of Christ as the sovereign Creator and not as the Redeemer. This is the view defended by Long in his thesis and the book based on his thesis. According to him, several factors favor this view.[24] First, this view takes full note of the usage of δεσπότης in both the Old and the New Testaments.

Second, this view gives proper recognition to the usage of ἀγοράζω in both the Old and the New Testaments. In the Septuagint ἀγοράζω is never used to translate the Hebrew words גָּאַל and פָּדָה, and in the New Testament when it is used soteriologically, the technical term τιμή or its equivalent is always stated or implied in the context.

Third, the historical background and purpose of 2 Peter support this view.

Fourth, Peter's allusion to Deuteronomy 32:6 shows that Peter here emphasized that "it is the sovereign Lord who owns the false teachers because He created them and made them a covenant and privileged people in the flesh."[25] In other words,

> just as God had sovereignly acquired Israel out of Egypt . . . in order to make her a covenant nation spiritually and nationally because He had created her for this purpose, so Christ, the sovereign Lord, acquired the false teachers . . . in order to make them a part of the covenant nation of God in the flesh because He had created them, within the mystery of His providence, for the purpose of bringing glory to Himself through their foreordainment unto condemnation (cf. 2 Pet. 2:12; Jude 4).[26]

Fifth, Long also seeks to find support for his view from the context of 2 Peter 2 and its parallel to Jude 4–19.

Sixth, he argues that it is illogical to say Christ died a substitutionary death for those who are ordained to destruction.[27] These arguments appear at first glance to be plausible, but closer examination reveals that they are on shaky ground.

The first argument is to be dismissed because, as demonstrated previously, when the word δεσπότης refers to Christ it never denotes Him as the Creator. However, when it is used of God the Father, it may refer to Him as the Creator (Luke 2:29).

The second argument is inadequate to prove Long's case. The fact that the Septuagint never translates גָּאַל and פָּדָה as ἀγοράζω has little bearing on the discussion of 2 Peter 2:1. The Septuagint may occasionally shed some light on the meaning of a word in the New Testament, but it does not determine the meaning of a New Testament word. The meaning of a word is determined primarily by its usage in its context. It is also fallacious to say that when ἀγοράζω is used soteriologically, the technical term τιμή is always stated or made explicit in the context. It has already been demonstrated that this is not the case with Revelation 14:3–4.

The third argument is again insufficient. According to Long the purpose of 2 Peter is "to put its recipients [believing Jews] in mind of the need for growth in grace and spiritual knowledge"[28] and this purpose supports the sovereign creation view.

Whether the purpose of a Bible book fully determines the meaning of a particular passage is debatable, but at least it can be safely conceded that the purpose, if supplied by the broader context or stated explicitly by the author (e.g., John 20:31), helps to narrow the possible range of the meaning. However, it is wrong to say that the purpose is the sole factor in determining the verbal meaning of a passage. This would lead to many faulty conclusions. The primary determinative for the meaning of a passage is the textual particulars in a given context.[29] Even if the purpose of 2 Peter determined the meaning of 2 Peter 2:1, in what way does that purpose support the sovereign creation view? Long fails to demonstrate this in either his thesis or his book.

The fourth argument is without any ground. Any student of the Bible who has compared 2 Peter 2:1 with Deuteronomy 32:6 seriously wonders how one gets the idea that Peter here was alluding to Deuteronomy 32:6. The Nestle-Aland Greek text (25th ed.) indicates all allusions to and quotations from the Old Testament, but it does not include any Old Testament passage in reference to 2 Peter 2:1. The United Bible Societies Greek text (3d ed.) also makes no mention of this in its apparatus. The writer has consulted more than a dozen commentaries,[30] but he could find none that makes mention of this supposed allusion. Any argument based on such dubious ground carries no weight. Moreover, it is doubtful whether the Bible gives any support to the idea that God made a covenant with the wicked one like those mentioned in 2 Peter 2:1 and made them a privileged people in the flesh.

The fifth argument is inappropriate. It is true that Jude 4–19 has extensive parallels, both in language and subject matter, with 2 Peter 2. The affinities are so close that anyone who reads the passages can easily recognize them.

This, however, does not lend any support to the sovereign creation view. On the contrary, the close parallel between the two passages supports the view that Peter spoke of spiritual redemption. It has already been mentioned that Jude 4 is in parallel with 2 Peter 2:1. To understand Jude 4, one must go back to verse 3 because of the presence of the causal γὰρ ("for") in verse 4. In verse 3 Jude mentioned the common salvation which now all Christians participate in, and the faith in Jesus Christ which was delivered to the saints by the apostles. In verse 4 Jude explained the reason he was compelled to write the epistle. Certain ungodly men had denied the Master.[31] The context clearly indicates that the Master here is the Master of the common salvation and faith described in the previous verse. If this is the correct understanding of Jude 4, and Jude is in parallel with 2 Peter 2:1, it seems logical to say that Peter was speaking of the same kind of Master. In other words the Master in 2 Peter 2:1 is the Master as Savior, not the Master as Creator.

Long's sixth argument is logically inconsistent with God's character. He says, "it is illogical to say Christ died a substitutionary atonement for those who are ordained unto destruction."[32]

However, it is just as illogical, or more so, to say that the all-merciful and all-just God made provision for only some people, leaving the majority out. And it is logical and consistent to say that the all-merciful and all-just God made provision for all human beings, but that some go to hell because of their unwillingness to appropriate the provision. The Cross itself actually does not save anyone. Even the elect are under God's wrath until they personally accept what Christ has done for them on the Cross. Without the Cross no one can be saved, but with the Cross the provision was made for all to be saved. The provision is for all, but the appropriation is only for those who believe. The human response of faith is necessary if one is to be saved. Chafer stated this well.

> . . . the question here is whether the sacrifice of Christ is the only divine instrumentality whereby God *actually* saves the elect, or whether that sacrifice is a divine work, finished, indeed, with regard to its scope and purpose, which renders all men *savable*, but one applied in sovereign grace by the Word of God and the Holy Spirit only when the individual believes. Certainly Christ's death of itself forgives no sinner, nor does it render unnecessary the regenerating work of the Holy Spirit. Any one of the elect whose salvation is predetermined, and for whom Christ died, may live the major portion of his life in open rebellion against God and, during that time, manifest every feature of depravity and spiritual death.

This alone should prove that men are not severally saved by the act of Christ in dying, but rather that they are saved by the divine application of that value when they believe.[33]

The belief that God made universal provision for salvation and that some perish because of their unwillingness to accept God's provision is consistent with God's character and the teachings of the Bible.

SOTERIOLOGICAL INTERPRETATION

Christian charity view. According to this view, Peter was speaking not of the reality of the false teachers' faith but of their mere profession.[34] According to this interpretation, Peter was referring to salvation only in the sense of Christian charity, that is, he simply reported what the false teachers were saying.

This is a novel interpretation, and the text gives no support to this view. The expression "but false prophets also arose among the people" is not the reported speech, but the personal judgment Peter made for the recipients of his letter.

Spiritual redemption view. This is the view that the redeeming work of Jesus Christ extends even to the false teachers who deny the Lord and thus are never saved. Lightner notes two significant points in this passage.

> One is that the purchase price of redemption was paid by the Lord for even the false prophets and teachers, even though they quite obviously never accept it. The other important feature is that these for whom the purchase price was paid are heretics of the vilest sort, since they deny the only possible basis of salvation—the substitutionary atonement of Christ.[35]

This seems to be the best interpretation for several reasons. First, this view best explains the meaning of δεσπότης. When δεσπότης is used of Christ, it refers to Him as the Lord and Owner by virtue of His work as Savior (Jude 3–4). By paying His blood as the ransom on the cross, Christ has bought all human beings and owns them. Second, when the object of ἀγοράζω is human beings, it is always used soteriologically in the New Testament. Third, the parallel passage in Jude 4 supports the spiritual redemption view. Fourth, this view is in good harmony with God's character. If God is merciful and just, it is quite conceivable that He made at least provision for all men whether they accept it or not. Fifth, this view squares with other passages, such as John 3:16; 1 Timothy 2:6; 4:10. A plain reading of these passages seems to teach unequivocally that Christ died for all.

Conclusion

Long has made every possible effort to seek to defend the nonsoteriological sovereign creation view of 2 Peter 2:1, but it has been demonstrated that his arguments are based on strained exegesis on the one hand and on faulty theological logic on the other. All aforementioned evidences show that 2 Peter 2:1 is best explained by the spiritual redemption view. Despite some attacks this verse still remains one of the strongest in support of unlimited atonement. The main thrust of this verse is the change of ownership as a result of redemption. Christ died even for the ungodly and bought them by paying their ransom on the cross. The Cross is the *chef-d'oeuvre* of God's wisdom. By punishing His own Son instead of sinners, God's attribute of justice was satisfied; by forgiving all those who accept the provision, His attribute of love was also satisfied. God has done His work through His Son. No one can place any blame on God for his spending eternity in hell. What leads men to hell is their unwillingness to accept God's invaluable provision made for them.

CHAPTER 18

The Identity of Babylon in Revelation 17–18

Charles H. Dyer

The world is rushing toward a catastrophic period of time referred to as the Tribulation. God has sovereignly chosen to reveal many details of that period through the inspired writings of His prophets. A correct interpretation of these details is essential for a proper understanding of God's program for the future.

One key factor in interpreting God's prophetic program is the identification of the eschatological Babylon described by John in Revelation 17–18. This section occupies a significant portion of the Book of Revelation, and it provides a graphic account of God's future judgment on evil. However, one faces many problems in attempting to identify the end-time system of evil that the section presents. This chapter attempts to provide answers for these problems through an analysis of Revelation 17–18.

The relationship between chapters 17 and 18 is crucial to a proper understanding of the Babylon referred to in both. Do Revelation 17 and 18 separately describe two distinct Babylons? Or are the two chapters a unit that presents but one Babylon?

The Distinctions

Any attempt to understand the relationship between Revelation 17 and 18 must take into account several distinctions that appear between the two chapters. Primarily because of these distinctions many expositors argue for the identification of two Babylons in the chapters. Four arguments against the unity of the two chapters have been advanced by various authors.

DIFFERENT SETTINGS

The first difficulty one must face is the different settings for each of the two chapters. The chapters tell of two visions introduced by different angels. Chapter 18 begins, "After these things I saw

216

another angel coming down from heaven." The problem centers on the expression "After these things." Allen feels that this is a strong argument for making a distinction between the Babylon of chapter 17 and that of 18.

> This phrase is of great importance in Revelation 1:19 and 4:1. In the latter passage it signifies the end of the church age by the rapture of the church. The church is afterward portrayed as being in heaven, and is represented by the 24 elders. The phrase, "and after these things," is also important in Revelation 18:1, *which suggests that after the events described in Revelation 17 have run their course, the judgment of Babylon has still to occur.*[1]

Does use of the phrase "after these things" (μετὰ ταῦτα) demand a gap between the chapters? Allen cited three examples of its occurrence (1:19; 4:1; 18:1), but the phrase occurs 10 times in the Book of Revelation. Six times it occurs with a word of perception, and four times it does not. Allen implied that its occurrence in 18:1 argues for the fulfillment of chapter 18 *after* the fulfillment of chapter 17. However, the mere presence of μετὰ ταῦτα does not demand that things must occur later chronologically. It can simply be indicating the time sequence in which the visions were revealed to John.

The temporal use (as opposed to the eschatological use) of μετὰ ταῦτα in the Book of Revelation is always indicated by John's inclusion of a verb of perception ("I saw," "I heard"). In doing this he indicated that the time sequence was in his observation of the visions and not necessarily in the unfolding of future events. When John wanted to indicate a gap of time in future events, he did not include a verb of perception. The 10 occurrences are as follows:

Temporal Use

4:1a, *"After these things I looked,* and behold, a door standing open in heaven."

7:1, *"After this* (μετὰ τοῦτο) *I saw* four angels holding back the four winds of the earth."

7:9, *"After these things I looked,* and behold, a great multitude which no one could count."

15:5, *"And after these things I looked,* and the temple of the tabernacle of testimony in heaven was opened."

18:1, *"After these things I saw* another angel coming down from heaven."

19:1, "*After these things I heard,* as it were a great multitude in heaven."

Eschatological Use

1:19, "Write therefore . . . the things which shall take place *after these things.*"

4:1b, "I will show you what must take place *after these things.*"

9:12, "The first woe is past; behold two woes are still coming *after these things.*"

20:3, "So that he should not deceive the nations any longer, until the thousand years were completed; *after these things* he must be released for a short time."

The four references not associated with verbs of perception seem to indicate chronological distinctions between future events. However, those with verbs of perception only indicate the order in which the parts of the vision were viewed by John. Thus the mere presence of μετὰ ταῦτα in 18:1 does not indicate a chronological distinction between the chapters. It only shows that the events revealed to John by the second angel were shown *after* he had viewed the woman on the beast.

DIFFERENT DESTROYERS

A second alleged distinction between Revelation 17 and 18 is the apparent difference between the destroyers of Babylon. The Babylon of chapter 17 is destroyed by kings whereas the Babylon of chapter 18 is destroyed by fire.[2] The destruction of the harlot Babylon occurs in 17:16, which says, "And the ten horns [ten kings, v. 12] which you saw, and the beast, *these will hate the harlot and will make her desolate.*" The destruction of the commercial Babylon occurs in 18:8, which says, "For this reason in one day her plagues will come, pestilence and mourning and famine, and *she will be burned up with fire; for the Lord God who judges her is strong.*"

Allen agrees with this basic contrast. However, he adds another item. The destruction is a contrast not only between the 10 kings and fire, but also between a destruction by man and a destruction by God. "The great harlot is destroyed by the ten kings (Rev. 17:16); but the city of Babylon is destroyed by God, with John's description being similar to that of Isaiah and Jeremiah (Isa. 13:19–22; Jer. 51:63–64; Rev. 18:2, 8, 21)."[3]

If these distinctions are valid, then any attempt to view the chapters as a unit will be doomed to failure. However, are these distinctions consistent with the text? A careful evaluation shows that they are not. For example it is held that the harlot was destroyed by men while the Babylon of chapter 18 was destroyed by fire. This does not explain 17:16b, which says, "These will hate the harlot . . . and will burn her up with fire." Thus in reality the Babylon in both chapters is destroyed by fire.

The distinction is made between man's destruction (chap. 17) and God's destruction (chap. 18). This, however, fails to account for 17:17, which explains the destruction of the harlot by the beast and 10 kings as stemming initially from God: "For God has put it in their hearts to execute His purpose." Both chapters do ascribe the destruction to God.

Chapters 17 and 18 are more similar than many expositors believe. A chart shows that, in fact, the chapters do not have different destroyers.

	Chapter 17	*Chapter 18*
Object of destruction	"Babylon the great . . . the great city" (17:5, 18).	"the great city, Babylon" (18:10).
Instrument of destruction	"the ten horns which you saw, and the beast" (17:16).	(not given)
Means of destruction	"will burn her up with fire" (17:16).	"she will be burned up with fire" (18:8).
Source of destruction	"God has put it in their hearts to execute His purpose" (17:17).	"The Lord God who judges her is strong" (18:8).

This chart shows that the only distinction to be found is the instrument of destruction. Chapter 17 focuses on the human instrument while chapter 18 does not. If the chapters are viewed synthetically, the alleged distinctions between the destroyers vanish. In their place stands a unified whole with each chapter focusing on a different aspect of one destruction.

DIFFERENT RESPONSES

A third distinction between Revelation 17 and 18 is the different responses to the destruction that are ascribed to men. The difference is reflected in the kings of each chapter. The response of the kings in chapter 17 is recorded in verse 16. "And the ten horns which you saw, and the beast, these will *hate the harlot* and will make her desolate and naked, and will eat her flesh and will burn her up with fire."

In contrast to the hatred and destruction of Babylon by the kings of chapter 17, the kings of chapter 18 respond by mourning. "And the kings of the earth, who committed acts of immorality and lived sensuously with her, *will weep and lament over her* when they see the smoke of her burning" (18:9). In observing this different response Tenney comments, "Why should the kings both hate her and then bewail her fate at their hands? Perhaps the explanation lies in the difference between religious and commercial Babylon."[4] Thus Tenney observes the problem of a seemingly opposite reaction by the kings and attributes it to a twofold Babylonian system.

It is granted that two opposite responses are attributed to the kings of each chapter. However, there is an explanation apart from assuming two Babylons.

An alternative to postulating two Babylons is the assumption that two groups of kings are in view in the two chapters. As Ladd has observed, "The kings of the earth [in 18:9–10] are to be distinguished from the 10 kings who joined with the beast to war against the Lamb (17:12–14)."[5] Thus the kings who hate Babylon (17:16) are those 10 kings who unite with the beast to plot her overthrow. The remaining kings of the earth (18:9–10) are engaged in commerce with Babylon, so they mourn when their source of revenue is destroyed. This view is consistent with the particulars of the text and harmonizes the two chapters.

DIFFERENT CHARACTER

The final difference between the chapters is the different character of Babylon in the two chapters. Chapter 17 is said to be religious in nature while chapter 18 is more commercial. Many feel that these differences can best be explained by the existence of two Babylons in the chapters.

Allen points out the main distinction between the character of both Babylons. "In Revelation 17 'mystery Babylon' is referred to as a woman with the exception of the last verse in the chapter, but in chapter 18 the emphasis is on 'the city' or 'Babylon the great' or 'the great city Babylon' or 'the great city.' The change of language is very marked."[6]

Again it must be admitted that the basic observation is correct. Chapter 17 does focus on Babylon the harlot, while chapter 18 looks at Babylon the commercial empire. Allen concludes, "Revelation 17 sets forth a religious power centered at the seven-hilled city of Rome exerting control over all people until the Antichrist has no further use for its existence, while the city of Babylon [chapter 18] is a great commercial center controlling trade and commerce on a worldwide scale."[7]

Allen's initial observation is correct, but his conclusion is not, because he ignored the interpretive keys within chapter 17. He seems to assume that because Babylon is called a woman in chapter 17, she cannot be the city of chapter 18. This assumption needs to be examined.

Chapter 17 contains a vision with an interpretation. Babylon is referred to in the vision as a woman riding a beast. In a sense a vision is a word picture. However, the fact that something is presented in pictorial fashion does not mean that it has no concrete reality. The nation Israel is no less Israel because it is pictured as a woman in Revelation 12. Likewise Babylon is no less Babylon even though it is pictured as a harlot. The key to the vision in chapter 17 is the divine interpretation given in 17:7–18. This gives the concrete reality behind the vision. What then is the truth about the harlot? Does she represent a religious system, a spiritual prostitute? Revelation 17:18 suggests that the answer is no: "And the woman whom you saw is *the great city,* which reigns over the kings of the earth."

Allen correctly stated that chapter 17 referred to Babylon as a woman in every case with the exception of the final verse of the chapter. However, he did not note that this final verse was God's identification of the woman, and that this Babylon was definitely identified as a *city.* Therefore the entire argument falls because both chapters do contain the same character. Both are talking about a city. This may not automatically mean that the Babylons in the two chapters are identical, but it certainly cannot be used to argue against such an identification.

Four distinctions between chapters 17 and 18 have been examined. Not one of the four distinctions contains compelling evidence for making a division between the chapters. The different settings are merely temporal aspects connected with John's viewing of the visions. Supposed differences between the destroyers vanish when the chapters are viewed synthetically. The different responses by the kings are explained by the existence of two distinct groups of kings within the chapters, and the alleged different character of the chapters actually vanishes when the spotlight of God's interpretation is focused on the woman in chapter 17. All these distinctions can be answered through a synthetic examination of the two chapters.

The Specific Parallels

The first section of this chapter examined the distinctions between Revelation 17 and 18, discovering that none of the distinctions demanded two Babylons for an adequate solution. At this juncture the positive evidence for viewing the two chapters as a unit will be presented. This is found in the specific parallels between the Babylon of chapter 17 and the Babylon of chapter 18. The striking parallels between the chapters go beyond coincidence to point to a unified system. That system is identified in both chapters as a city that rules the world. This strongly suggests that the Babylon in both chapters must be identical.

To save space, the parallels are divided into four categories, each presented in chart form. Following the chart is a brief analysis of the significance of the parallels.

THE DESIGNATION

The name is the same	"Babylon the great" (17:5).	"Babylon the great" (18:2).
The identity is the same	"The woman . . . is the great city" (17:18).	"Woe, woe, the great city" (18:10).

However one wishes to interpret the Babylon of Revelation 17, he must acknowledge that the divine identification of the harlot is a city, not a mystical system. These two chapters each present a city that has the same name in the same general context. The most natural interpretation is to take the cities as identical unless there is compelling evidence to the contrary.

THE DESCRIPTION

The clothing is the same	"And the woman was clothed in purple and scarlet and adorned with gold and precious stones and pearls" (17:4).	"Woe, woe, the great city, she who was clothed in fine linen and purple and scarlet, and adorned with gold and precious stones and pearls" (18:16).
Both hold a cup	"Having in her hand a gold cup full of abominations" (17:4).	"In the cup which she has mixed, mix twice as much for her" (18:6).

Both Babylons are identified as a city, and both are described in the same fashion. Apart from the addition of fine linen in

chapter 18, both cities are arrayed with exactly the same materials.
Also both are associated with a cup that each possesses. Instead of
seeing two cities with the same name and the same description, it
is easier to assume the existence of only one city.

THE DEEDS

The relation-ship to kings is the same	"With whom the kings of the earth committed acts of immorality" (17:2).	"And the kings of the earth have committed acts of immorality with her" (18:3).
The relation-ship to the na-tions is the same	"Those who dwell on the earth were made drunk with the wine of her im-morality" (17:2).	"For all the nations have drunk of the wine of the passion of her immoral-ity" (18:3).
The relation-ship to believers is the same	"And I saw the woman drunk with the blood of the saints, and with the blood of the witnesses of Jesus" (17:6).	"And in her was found the blood of prophets and of saints and of all who have been slain on the earth" (18:24).

The Babylons in both chapters perform the same functions.
Each commits fornication with the kings of the earth and causes
all the nations of the earth to fall into a drunken stupor. Each also
persecutes God's remnant who stand in opposition to evil. It is
hard to distinguish a political Babylon from a religious Babylon
through a comparison of their deeds because the deeds are identical.

THE DESTRUCTION

The means of destruction is the same	"These will hate the harlot . . . and will burn her up with fire" (17:16).	"She will be burned up with fire" (18:8).
The source of destruction is the same	"For God has put it in their hearts to execute His purpose" (17:17).	"And God has remem-bered her iniquities . . . for the Lord God who judges her is strong" (18:5, 8).

These final similarities surround the destruction of both
Babylons. Physically both are destroyed by fire. In both instances
God is the ultimate source of destruction; His judgment is being
executed.

The parallels between the chapters are impressive. Each chapter
refers to a city with the same name. Each describes a city in the

same fashion. Each mentions a city that performs the same deeds, and each refers to a city that is destroyed in the same manner. These descriptions, going beyond mere similarity, point toward unity. Two distinct cities could hardly be described in such a similar way. It is better to view the chapters as two descriptions of the same city.

The Larger Context

The larger context in which these chapters are positioned also underscores the parallelism between the chapters. Chapters 17 and 18 are an interlude placed here to explain the destruction of Babylon the Great mentioned in Revelation 16:19. Thus both chapters would seem to be describing this one event. This also conforms to 19:1–3, in which heaven is said to rejoice over this fall of Babylon. In describing this fall those in heaven mention the harlot (cf. 19:2 with 17:1) and the smoke ascending forever (cf. 19:3 with 18:9, 18) and relate both to one judgment. Thus the larger context limits chapters 17 and 18 to such an extent that the Babylons they are describing must be considered identical.

The larger context actually begins in 14:8, which first predicts an angel flying in mid-heaven proclaiming, "Fallen, fallen is Babylon the great, she who has made all the nations drink of the wine of the passion of her immorality." Several of the phrases used here are later repeated in Revelation 17 and 18. The title "Babylon the great" is used in all three chapters; and the proclamation "Fallen, fallen is Babylon the great" is repeated in 18:2. The reference to the nations being drunk with the wine of her fornication (14:8) is also found in 17:2 and 18:3. The one proclamation is fulfilled by chapters 17 and 18, and yet there is only one Babylon in view in 14:8.

The next appearance of Babylon occurs during the outpouring of the seventh bowl in chapter 16. Part of the judgment associated with this bowl is that "Babylon the great was remembered before God, to give her the cup of the wine of His fierce wrath" (16:19). Again only one Babylon is in view. Immediately after this pronouncement John recorded the destruction of a "Babylon the great" in chapters 17 and 18. What is important is that chapters 17 and 18 are an expansion of 16:19, which seems to refer to the destruction of a city called Babylon. It is pictured as a literal city. Kuhn captures the exact relationship in these words: "The destruction of Babylon is proclaimed by an angelic voice in 14:8.

The place of the fall of Babylon in the apocalyptic drama (with the outpouring of the 7th vial) is indicated in 16:19. Then in 17:1 to 19:10 the divine expressly portrays this city and its fall in 7 visions."[8]

The larger context begins before chapters 17–18, but it does not end there. The subject of the fall of Babylon extends beyond these chapters into chapter 19. The first five verses of chapter 19 present the "Hallelujah Chorus" in heaven following the destruction of Babylon. As Ladd has noted, "The first paragraph of chapter nineteen continues the celebration of the fall of Babylon and consists of a song of thanksgiving in heaven that God had judged the great harlot."[9]

Chapter 19 begins with the phrase "After these things." Ryrie notes that "'after these things' evidently refers to the visions of the chapters immediately preceding. In 18:20 the call to rejoice was issued; here is the response to that call."[10] Thus the heavenly chorus is in response to the destruction of Babylon in chapter 18, but it looks back to the destruction in both chapters.

The first part of the heavenly praise focuses on the harlot of chapter 17. The multitude says, "Because His judgments are true and righteous; for *He has judged the great harlot* who was corrupting the earth with her immorality, and He has avenged the blood of His bond-servants on her" (19:2). In response to the angels' call to rejoice over the fall of Babylon in 18:20 the heavens do respond—with a song of praise for the judgment of the harlot. The implication is that the harlot of chapter 17 and the Babylon of chapter 18 are identical.

The song of praise continues in 19:3, which says, "And a second time they said, 'Hallelujah! Her smoke rises up forever and ever!'" This reference to the smoldering city is drawn from chapter 18, in which the kings of the earth and the shipmasters are said to look on "the smoke of her burning" (18:9, 18). The praise song in heaven over the fall of Babylon incorporates elements of both chapter 17 and chapter 18, and yet it seems to be a song celebrating just one fall and doing so in response to the command of 18:20. Again this larger context can be understood best if chapters 17 and 18 are viewed as a unit that looks forward to the destruction of a single city of Babylon.

These parallels between Revelation 17 and 18 lead to the conclusion that only one Babylon is present in the two chapters. However, the exact identity of that Babylon still needs to be determined. A more precise identification can be achieved by studying the interpretive keys within the chapters and by isolating and interpreting the Old Testament themes on which John was drawing in the chapters.

The Interpretive Keys within the Chapters

John's picture of a harlot astride a scarlet beast in chapter 17 could be entitled "Beauty on the Beast." The vision is described in the first six verses and then interpreted in the next 12 verses. Chapter 18 focuses on the response of individuals to Babylon's destruction. Within the two chapters are four interpretive keys that are crucial to the identity of Babylon.

THE DESCRIPTION OF BABYLON AS A HARLOT

The first interpretive key is the descriptive identification of Babylon in 17:1 as "the great harlot who sits on many waters." The allusion to a harlot has caused many to identify Babylon as a false religious system.

> The frequently recurring allusion to harlotry (17:1, 2, 4, 15, 16; 18:3, 7) is an echo of the Old Testament prophets, who used the term to describe the infidelity of man to God, especially in connection with idolatry. The first chapter of Isaiah denounced Jerusalem as "the faithful city become a harlot" (1:21). Jeremiah condemned Jerusalem in almost the same words: "under every green tree thou didst bow thyself, playing the harlot" (2:20), and the figure was applied later both to Israel and to Judah in this prophecy (Jer. 3). Ezekiel, in similar fashion, drew the portrait of the sisters, Oholah and Oholibah, representing Israel and Judah, who from the beginning of national existence in Egypt had been defiled with the idolatries and evils of the nations around them (Ezek. 23).[11]

Admittedly the figure of a harlot was used in the Old Testament to describe idolatry. However, Tenney overstates his case because the figure is also used in the Old Testament to show more than just religious apostasy, as Mounce notes.

> Since the harlot of the Apocalypse is a pagan city (cf. 17:18), it is more likely that a passage like Nahum 3:4 or Isaiah 23:16, 17 supplies the immediate background. In the former, the harlot is Nineveh, who betrays nations with her harlotries and her charms (cf. Rev. 17:4). Isaiah pictures Tyre as a forgotten harlot. *In the context of Revelation 17 and 18 the image is not that of religious profligacy but of the prostitution of all that is right and noble for the questionable ends of power and luxury.*[12]

Babylon is identified as a harlot. However, the reference is not to her spiritual nature. Rather the focus is on the prostitution of her values for economic gain. It is also interesting to note that the figure of a harlot was never applied to a religious system *only*. It was always used to describe a city or nation (Jerusalem, Israel, Samaria, Nineveh, or Tyre).

THE EXPLANATION OF BABYLON AS A MYSTERY

The second interpretive key centers on the name written on the harlot's forehead. More specifically, it revolves around the explanation of the word μυστήριον in 17:5. Babylon is described as a "mystery."

Two problems must be resolved before this interpretive key can be properly understood. The first is the determination of the grammatical relationship between the word μυστήριον and the title of the woman. According to Robertson μυστήριον could be taken "either in apposition with *onoma* or as part of the inscription on her [i.e., the harlot's] forehead."[13] So either John could be saying that the name on the woman is "Mystery Babylon the great" or he could be saying that the name, Babylon the great, which is written on the woman's forehead, is a mystery.

Of the two possibilities, the second offers the best explanation within the context. Whenever the woman is named elsewhere in the chapters she is simply called "Babylon" not "Mystery Babylon." Walvoord notes this when he writes, "The word *mystery* is a descriptive reference to the title, not a part of the title itself as implied by the capitalization in the Authorized Version. This can be seen by comparing the name given to the woman in 16:19 and 18:2."[14]

The second problem that must be resolved is the exact nature of the mystery. In what way is this Babylon a mystery? Many feel that the occurrence of μυστήριον means that Babylon is to be interpreted symbolically or figuratively. Robertson takes this view when he debates the grammatical usage of μυστήριον. He concludes, "In either case the meaning is the same, that the name Babylon is to be interpreted mystically or spiritually (cf. πνευματικῶς 11:8) for Rome."[15]

However, the idea of equating μυστήριον with something mystical or mysterious cannot be borne out in the New Testament usage of the word. As Vine notes, "In the N.T. it [μυστήριον] denotes, not the mysterious (as with the Eng. word), but that which, being outside the range of unassisted natural apprehension, can be made known only by Divine [*sic*] revelation, and is made known in a manner and at a time appointed by God, and to those who are illumined by His Spirit."[16]

Vine equates μυστήριον with an unrevealed secret. The word does not denote the quality or character of the truth; rather it focuses on the availability of that truth. Smalley explained the difference in this way:

> But whereas "mystery" may mean, and in contemporary usage often does mean, a secret for which no answer can be found, this is not at all the connotation of the term *mysterion* in classical and biblical Greek. In the New Testament *mysterion* signifies a secret which is being, or even has been, revealed, which is also divine in scope, and needs to be made known by God to men through His Spirit. In this way the term comes very close to the New Testament word *apokalypsis*, "revelation." *Mysterion* is a temporary secret, which once revealed is known and under- stood—a secret no longer.[17]

Calling the harlot's name a mystery does not automatically mean a spiritual or mystical system of evil as opposed to a literal or physical city. Its designation as a mystery means that the vision being given to John had not been made known before. To understand the "mystery" in the context one must examine verses 7–18, for in these verses God reveals the meaning and significance of the vision. As the angel said to John, "I shall tell you the mystery [μυστήριον] of the woman" (17:7).

THE IDENTIFICATION OF BABYLON AS A CITY

There is no lack of opinion concerning the identification of the harlot called Babylon. However, most of the identifications do not begin with the divine interpretation of the vision given at the end of chapter 17. In 17:18 the angel interpreted the harlot to John: "And the woman whom you saw is *the great city*, which reigns over the kings of the earth." Whatever else is said about the harlot, she is first a city, not an ecclesiastical system.

This divine interpretive key in 17:18 identifies the Babylon of chapter 17 as a city. It is a city of worldwide importance, for it is said to reign over the other kings of the earth. It is true that the identification can go beyond the city to the system it controls. However, the interpretation given to John focused only on the identification of Babylon as a city.

THE LOCATION OF BABYLON ON SEVEN HILLS

The beast on which the woman is sitting is described as having seven heads. When the angel interpreted this part of the vision to John he said, "Here is the mind which has wisdom. The seven heads are seven mountains, on which the woman sits, and they are seven kings; five have fallen, one is, the other has not yet come; and when he comes, he must remain a little while" (17:9–10). What are the seven hills on which the woman is sitting? The traditional understanding of the seven hills is that they refer to the city of Rome, known in John's day as the seven-hilled city.

> The seven heads of the beast are first identified as seven mountains upon which the harlot is sitting. There is little doubt that a first-century reader would understand this reference in any way other than as a reference to Rome, the city built upon seven hills. Rome began as a network of seven hill settlements on the left bank of the Tiber, and was from the time of Servius Tullius (her sixth king) an *urbs septicollis*.[18]

This view that the seven hills refer to Rome has some serious flaws. The first flaw is the assumed relationship between the woman and the hills. The seven heads are associated with the beast, not the woman. There is a distinction between the woman and the beast; and it is the beast that has the seven heads. The angel said, "I shall tell you the mystery of the woman and of the beast that carries her, which has the seven heads" (17:7). If the seven hills are Rome, then the most that can be determined is that the Antichrist's empire will be centered in the city of Rome. It does not identify the location of the harlot because she is not part of the beast.

Some might argue that the harlot is still to be associated with the city of seven hills because they are described in 17:9 as "seven mountains on which the woman sits." However, the harlot's sitting on the seven hills is a reference to her control, not her location. In 17:1 the woman is sitting on "many waters." These are interpreted in verse 15 as "peoples and multitudes and nations and tongues." The purpose of this part of the vision is not to show Babylon's location or else the city would have to be parceled out throughout the world. Rather, the harlot sitting on the waters is a reference to her control over all the nations of the world. The woman is also said to sit on the entire beast (17:3). This would go beyond just the seven heads to include the Antichrist and the kings allied with him. Again the reference is to her control, not her location. If the harlot's sitting clearly indicates control twice in the chapter, is it not inconsistent to give that same figure a different meaning when it occurs for a third time? It is far more consistent to view the harlot's sitting as indicative of her control over the seven mountains, rather than having it point to her physical location.

Even if the seven hills are taken as a reference to Rome, that identification cannot be used to associate the harlot with Rome. The woman and the seven heads are distinct; and as stated, the position of the woman indicates control, not location. However, there is evidence to believe that the seven hills could refer to something other than the city of Rome.

The identification of the seven hills as Rome is based on the assumption that John's prophecy was written exclusively for and understood by the people of John's day. This idea is open to question. Walvoord noted this problem.

> One of the common assumptions of those who reject the futurist position is that the Apocalypse is the creation of John's thinking and was understandable by him in his generation. . . . The difficulty with this point of view is twofold: (1) Prophecy, as given in the Scripture, was not necessarily understandable by the writer or his generation, as illustrated in the case of Daniel (Dan. 12:4, 9). It is questionable whether the great prophets of the Old Testament always understood what they were writing (cf. 1 Peter 1:10–12). (2) It is of the nature of prophecy that often it cannot be understood until the time of the generation which achieves fulfillment. The assumption, therefore, that the book of Revelation was understandable in the first generation or that it was intended to be understood by that generation is without real basis.[19]

To understand properly the symbolism of the seven mountains one must go beyond the Greco-Roman society in which John wrote to the Jewish heritage in which he was raised. John was a Jew, and the Book of Revelation must be interpreted in light of the Old Testament. As Jenkins has said, "The book of Revelation is the most thoroughly Jewish in its language and imagery of any New Testament book. This book speaks not the language of Paul, but of the Old Testament prophets Isaiah, Ezekiel, and Daniel."[20]

To understand the seven mountains one must go to the Old Testament to see how this symbol was used. The word "mountain" was often a symbolic reference to a kingdom or national power. The following are some examples of this usage of "mountain."

> "Now it will come about that in the last days, the mountain of the house of the Lord will be established as the chief of the mountains, and will be raised above the hills; and all the nations will stream to it" (Isa. 2:2).

> "Behold, I have made you [Israel] a new, sharp threshing sledge with

double edges; you will thresh the mountains, and pulverize them, and will make the hills like chaff" (Isa. 41:15).

"'Behold, I am against you, O destroying mountain, who destroy the whole earth,' declares the Lord, 'and I will stretch out My hand against you, and roll you down from the crags, and I will make you a burnt out mountain'" (Jer. 51:25). (The Lord is here speaking to the nation of Babylon; see Jer. 50:1. These chapters are quoted extensively in Revelation 17–18.)

"But the stone that struck the statue became a great mountain and filled the whole earth. . . . And in the days of those kings the God of heaven will set up a kingdom which will never be destroyed" (Dan. 2:35, 44). (God identified the mountain as the everlasting kingdom He will set up.)

The figure of a mountain is used in the Old Testament to refer to a kingdom. However, there is yet another reason for identifying the seven mountains in Revelation 17 as a reference to seven kingdoms. This interpretation is to be preferred because it best explains the dual identification of the seven heads as *both* mountains and kings.

If the seven mountains are applied to Rome, then there is some difficulty in relating the seven kings to the vision. Most expositors must leave out three Roman emperors (Galba, Otho, and Vitellius) to have the history of Rome fit John's chronology. However, this is not sound interpretation, for as Ladd points out, "Such a procedure is arbitrary, for Galba, Otho and Vitellius, unimportant as they may have been, were bona fide emperors and were recognized as such by ancient historians."[21]

The divine interpretation associates each head with both a mountain and a king. This can best be explained by viewing the "mountain" as a figure of speech that refers to a kingdom and the king who was ruling it. This relationship is most clearly illustrated in Daniel's interpretation of Nebuchadnezzar's dream in Daniel 2. "You [Nebuchadnezzar] are the head of gold. And after you there will arise another kingdom inferior to you" (Dan. 2:38b–39). Daniel wrote that the head of gold was a *king,* but that the breast and arms of silver were another *kingdom.* Daniel was obviously viewing the kingdom of Babylon as personified in the king that stood before him. Thus he could switch from the king to the kingdom with no inconsistency. In light of this evidence it is best to say that this key refers to seven empires and their kings rather than to the city of Rome.

The four interpretive keys within the chapters provide vital information on the identity of Babylon. Babylon is first and foremost a literal city that will dominate the world. It will be characterized as a harlot that prostitutes her moral values for material luxury. The entire city is viewed as a mystery in that her future position, relationship to the Antichrist, and ultimate destruction had not been known before John's vision. Evidently she will obtain control over seven nations, the Antichrist's growing empire, and eventually the entire earth. These keys do not unlock some mystical system of religion that will infiltrate the world. Rather, they open the door of prophecy on a brick-and-mortar city intoxicated with power and luxury. The Babylon in these chapters is one that will exist geographically and politically.

The Relationship to Jeremiah 50–51

An examination of Revelation 17–18 shows that there is but one Babylon in view. That Babylon is a city which will extend its control throughout the world. However, the city itself still needs to be identified. Chapters 17 and 18 provide little insight by themselves into the identity of the city, but through a comparison with other scriptural passages a positive identification is possible.

The key to identifying the Babylon of Revelation 17–18 is to isolate and interpret the Old Testament themes John was drawing on in these chapters. John used several Old Testament passages within these chapters, including Isaiah 13–14; 46–47; and Ezekiel 26–28. However, the central Old Testament passage on which Revelation 17–18 is constructed is Jeremiah 50–51. This is the passage to which John alluded most frequently.

THE PARALLELS BETWEEN THE PASSAGES

John's use of Jeremiah 50–51 can be observed by listing the many parallels between the passages. These parallels fall into three categories: the description, the destruction, and the response. Each category will be presented in chart form. Following the chart will be a brief analysis of the significance of those parallels.

The Description

Compared to a golden cup	"Babylon has been a golden cup in the hand of the Lord" (Jer. 51:7a).	"I saw a woman . . . having in her hand a gold cup" (Rev. 17:3–4; cf. 18:6).

Dwelling on many waters	"O you who dwell by (עַל) many waters" (Jer. 51:13).	"I shall show you the judgment of the great harlot who sits on many waters" (Rev. 17:1).
Involved with nations	"The nations have drunk of her wine; therefore the nations are going mad" (Jer. 51:7b).	"Those who dwell on the earth were made drunk with the wine of her immorality" (Rev. 17:2).
Named the same	"The word which the Lord spoke concerning Babylon, the land of the Chaldeans" (Jer. 50:1).	"Babylon the great" (Rev. 17:5). "Woe, woe, the great city, Babylon, the strong city" (Rev. 18:10).

The Babylon of Jeremiah 50–51 and the Babylon of Revelation 17–18 are described similarly. Both are described in terms of a golden cup that influences the nations that partake of its contents. Both are also said to dwell on many waters. Obviously John was employing the terminology used by Jeremiah. Jeremiah was prophesying the destruction of the literal city of Babylon, and John was prophesying the destruction of a city with the same name.

The Destruction

Destroyed suddenly	"Suddenly Babylon has fallen and been broken" (Jer. 51:8).	"For this reason in one day her plagues will come, pestilence, and mourning and famine" (Rev. 18:8).
Destroyed by fire	"Their dwelling places are set on fire" (Jer. 51:30).	"And the ten horns . . . will burn her up with fire" (Rev. 17:16). "And she will be burned up with fire" (Rev. 18:8).
Never to be inhabited	"And it will never again be inhabited or dwelt in from generation to generation" (Jer. 50:39).	"Thus will Babylon, the great city, be thrown down with violence and will not be found any longer" (Rev. 18:21).
Punished according to deeds	"Repay her according to her work; according to all that she has done, so do to her" (Jer. 50:29).	"Pay her back even as she has paid, and give back to her double according to her deeds" (Rev. 18:6).

Fall illustrated	"You will tie a stone to it and throw it into the middle of the Euphrates, and say, 'Just so shall Babylon sink down and not rise again'" (Jer. 51:63–64).	"And a strong angel took up a stone like a great millstone and threw it into the sea, saying, 'Thus will Babylon, the great city, be thrown down with violence and will not be found any longer'" (Rev. 18:21).

John and Jeremiah each described a city that is destroyed suddenly and completely. A city in full blossom is plucked up never to reappear. The destruction is meted out by God for past deeds and is pictured as a rock sinking in a body of water to rise no more.

The Response

God's people to flee	"Flee from the midst of Babylon, and each of you save his life" (Jer. 51:6). "Come forth from her midst, My people, and each of you save yourselves from the fierce anger of of the Lord" (Jer. 51:45).	"And I heard another voice from heaven, saying, 'Come out of her, my people, that you may not participate in her sins and that you may not receive her plagues'" (Rev. 18:4).
Heaven to rejoice	"'Then heaven and earth and all that is in them will shout for joy over Babylon, for the destroyers will come to her from the north,' declares the Lord" (Jer. 51:48).	"Rejoice over her, O heaven, and you saints and apostles and prophets, because God has pronounced judgment for you against her" (Rev. 18:20).

Jeremiah and John recorded the same response to the destruction of their city. Those on earth are warned to flee from the destruction that has now been promised. In heaven there is a call to rejoice, for the destruction signals God's victory over a godless city.

The ultimate identity of Babylon in Revelation 17–18 depends on John's use of Jeremiah's prophecy. Was John describing the same event or simply using "biblical language" to describe a different event? This in turn hinges on one's understanding of when Jeremiah 50–51 was or will be fulfilled. If Jeremiah 50–51 has already been fulfilled, then John was using the imagery of a past destruction to describe a different destruction that is yet future. However, if the fulfillment of Jeremiah is still future, then it would seem that John's prophecy is also viewing that same destruction.

THE FULFILLMENT OF JEREMIAH 50–51

The fulfillment of Jeremiah 50–51 is a subject of considerable debate. Several key prophecies in these two chapters need to be examined. Each prophecy will be listed and then all relevant material will be discussed under that section to see if the prophecy has been literally fulfilled.

Babylon to be destroyed suddenly: "Suddenly Babylon has fallen and been broken" (Jer. 51:8). Jeremiah's prophecy in chapters 50–51 focuses on the suddenness of Babylon's destruction. However, this was not the case when Babylon fell to the Medes and Persians. Rather than destroying Babylon, Cyrus helped rebuild portions of the city that were in a state of decay. In fact the city was made a provincial capital in the Persian Empire. The actual destruction of the city was a gradual process over several centuries.

Babylon to be destroyed completely: "For a nation has come up against her out of the north; it will make her land an object of horror, and there will be no inhabitant in it" (Jer. 50:3). "Because of the indignation of the Lord she will not be inhabited, but she will be completely desolate" (v. 13). "Come to her from the farthest border; open up her barns, pile her up like heaps and utterly destroy her, let nothing be left to her" (v. 26). "'And it will never again be inhabited or dwelt in from generation to generation.' As when God overthrew Sodom and Gomorrah with its neighbors,' declares the Lord, 'no man will live there, nor will any son of man reside in it'" (vv. 39b–40). "So the land quakes and writhes, for the purposes of the Lord against Babylon stand, to make the land of Babylon a desolation without inhabitants" (51:29).

One of the dominant themes throughout these verses is the extent of the judgment God is promising to execute on Babylon. This judgment is to be complete and permanent. When Babylon falls, she shall be "completely desolate" and "will never again be inhabited." God is, in effect, vowing to blot the very existence of Babylon from the earth.

Obviously this did not take place when Babylon fell to Medo-Persia. She remained populated and productive for centuries after her initial fall. Not much information on the city during the Middle Ages can be found, but there is information that the city has been inhabited in the modern era, at least since the 1700s.

Koldewey, a German archaeologist responsible for much of the work that has been done at Babylon, makes an interesting comment on the villages located at the ruins.

> At the bend of the Euphrates, between Babil and Kasr lie *the ruins of the former village of Kweiresh, whose population migrated elsewhere a hundred years ago.* The walls of mud brick still overtop the heaps of debris.
>
> *The modern village of Kweiresh lies close to the Kasr,* to which we must now turn our attention. The most northerly house of Kweiresh is the headquarters of our expedition . . . called by the Arabs "Kasr abid."[22]

Koldewey states first that a village definitely was in existence in his day within the ancient city of Babylon. He headquartered in this village as he excavated the nearby ruins. Koldewey also reports the existence of another village (with the same name) that had also existed within the city of Babylon a century earlier. Since he gives only an approximate date of abandonment, there is no way to determine how long that earlier city had existed in Babylon; but the permanence of the structures would suggest an extended history. Koldewey presents a detailed map of Babylon's ruins in which he shows the location of both the ancient village of Kweiresh as well as the modern village. Both are in the heart of what was once ancient Babylon.[23]

Koldewey has shown that Babylon was still inhabited at least at the time of his excavations, which took place in the early 1900s. However, what is the status of its occupation today? Several independent sources confirm the existence today of several villages *within* the walls of ancient Babylon. Included with the *Zondervan Pictorial Encyclopedia of the Bible* article on Babylon is a picture of an Arab village with the caption, "The older part of the present town within the city walls."[24] Unfortunately the name of the village pictured did not accompany the photograph. However, the accuracy of the statement was verified to this writer by Mrs. L. Glynne Dairos, assistant secretary of the British School of Archaeology in Iraq. In response to a question on the existence of any modern villages within the ancient city walls she wrote, "There are three modern settlements situated inside the walls of ancient Babylon. The government of Iraq does indeed plan to restore much of Babylon and has indeed made a start on certain buildings."[25] Wiseman also notes that a partial restoration has already begun and that the modern village of Jumjummah is located at the same site.[26]

Jeremiah predicted that when the city of Babylon fell it would never be inhabited again. However, this has never been fulfilled literally. The city of Babylon has been occupied throughout history, and even today, as noted, three settlements are within the ancient walls. The fact remains that Jeremiah's words, "She will not be inhabited, but she will be completely desolate" (50:13), are yet to be fulfilled.

Building materials never to be reused: "'And they will not take from you even a stone for a corner nor a stone for foundations, but you will be desolate forever,' declares the Lord" (Jer. 51:26). Jeremiah predicted that when Babylon would be destroyed even her stones would remain unused forever. Babylon would be destroyed so completely that not even her building materials would ever reappear. This is the ultimate in total desolation.

The history of ancient Babylon does not correspond to Jeremiah's prophecy. The materials from which ancient Babylon had been built have, in fact, been used extensively in the building of many surrounding cities. Layard even noticed that bricks mined from Babylon were so popular that men spent their lives gathering those bricks to sell to others.

> To this day there are men who have no other trade than that of gathering bricks from this vast heap and taking them for sale to the neighboring towns and villages, and even to Baghdad. There is scarcely a house in Hillah which is not almost entirely built with them; and as the traveler passes through the narrow streets, he sees in the walls of every hovel a record of the glory and power of Nebuchadnezzar.[27]

This evidence appears to be at variance with Jeremiah's prediction. However, some have sought to eliminate the difficulty by making a distinction between "stones" and "bricks." While "bricks" may have been taken from Babylon, Jeremiah predicted that no "stones" would be taken. As Stoner writes, "Bricks and building materials of many kinds have been salvaged from the ruins for cities round about, but the rocks, which were imported to Babylon at great cost, have never been moved."[28]

At first this seems to be an effective argument. However, it makes a false distinction that is alien to the culture against which Jeremiah was prophesying. There were no stone quarries near Babylon, so nearly all the buildings were made of baked brick. In fact the Babylonians considered their brick as their building stone. This can be clearly seen in the building of the tower of Babel which took place in that area. In describing the construction

Moses wrote, "And they said to one another, 'Come, let us make bricks and burn them thoroughly.' *And they used brick for stone, and they used tar for mortar*" (Gen. 11:3).

Thus the Babylonians considered their bricks to be their building stones. Jeremiah's prophecy against the use of their building materials in later construction would have been ludicrous had he been referring only to a few pieces of imported stone. The main building component in the city was burnt brick, and Jeremiah's prophecy was to show that the city would be so desolate that even its building materials would lie in waste forever. It seems far more natural to understand Jeremiah's reference to "stones" to include "bricks." This is consistent with the Genesis narrative, with the purpose of the prophecy, and with the physical characteristics of the city itself.

Once again, Jeremiah's prophecy has not found literal fulfillment in the destruction of Babylon. Babylon's bricks have been used extensively in the building of several neighboring cities. If the prophecy is to be taken literally, it must await a future fulfillment.

Believers to flee the city: "Wander away from the midst of Babylon, and go forth from the land of the Chaldeans" (Jer. 50:8). "Flee from the midst of Babylon, and each of you save his life! Do not be destroyed in her punishment" (51:6). "Come forth from her midst, My people, and each of you save yourselves from the fierce anger of the Lord" (v. 45).

In the midst of his oracle of destruction, Jeremiah turned to God's people who are dwelling under the shadow of a doomed city. These believers are urged to flee from the city so that they will not be caught in the destruction that will accompany its demise. Jeremiah predicted a "bloodbath" at Babylon's fall. The scope of destruction would be such that God's people are commanded to flee to safety before the flood of judgment strikes.

Once again there is a problem in finding a historical fulfillment for this aspect of Jeremiah's prophecy. There is no record of Jews fleeing Babylon when it fell to Medo-Persia.

> Again, mark carefully that when Cyrus took Babylon, neither Daniel, who that night prophesied to Belshazzar the end of his kingdom, nor the other Jews, fled from Babylon! As a matter of fact, Daniel was immediately elevated to the triumvirate of presidents under Darius the Median, who received the kingdom at the hand of the conqueror, Cyrus.[29]

Israel and Judah to be reunited: "'In those days and at that time,' declares the Lord, 'the sons of Israel will come, both they and the sons of Judah as well; they will go along weeping as they go, and it will be the Lord their God they will seek. They will ask for the way to Zion, turning their faces in its direction; they will come that they may join themselves to the Lord in an everlasting covenant that will not be forgotten'" (Jer. 50:4–5). "'In those days and at that time,' declares the Lord, 'search will be made for the iniquity of Israel, but there will be none; and for the sins of Judah, but they will not be found; for I shall pardon those whom I leave as a remnant'" (v. 20). "You who have escaped the sword, Depart! Do not stay! Remember the Lord from afar, and let Jerusalem come to your mind" (51:50).

Jeremiah spoke of a cause-effect relationship between the destruction of Babylon and the reestablishment of a united Israel. After Babylon is destroyed, those Jews who escaped in response to God's words will remember their God and turn toward His holy city. At that time Israel and Judah will again be reunited and will enter into an everlasting covenant with their God. God in turn will provide national redemption for His people.

This prophecy has a grandeur and majesty that far transcends any events that took place after the fall of Babylon to the Medes. First, the Jews did not turn to the Lord after a remarkable escape from "the sword." There was little or no bloodshed in the Medo-Persian conquest, and the Jews did not flee the city at that time. Second, Israel and Judah did not reunite nationally as the refugees drifted back into the land. Third, there was not a day of national repentance and forgiveness for the remnant that returned. The postexilic record is full of man's failures and God's rebukes.

These verses in Jeremiah have an eschatological significance that can find fulfillment only in the ultimate restoration of Israel and Judah just before the beginning of the millennium. Only then will these two groups be reunited in covenant relationship with their God and experience national forgiveness of sins. This part of Jeremiah's prophecy associates the destruction of Babylon with an event that is yet to occur on God's prophetic calendar.

Since none of these prophecies have been fulfilled, it must be assumed that Jeremiah 50–51 contains a prediction of a still-future destruction of the literal city of Babylon. This destruction will occur suddenly and will totally destroy the city. After this destruction the city will never be inhabited but rather will lie in ruins forever. God's people will be called forth from the city before its destruction and will be reunited in an everlasting covenant with their God.

In summary it has been shown that Jeremiah 50–51 is describing a still-future destruction of the literal city of Babylon. Jeremiah's prophecy was directed against "Babylon, the land of the Chaldeans" (50:1), and several key elements of his prophecy have never been fulfilled literally. Also this study has shown that the prophecies of John and Jeremiah are closely related. John predicted the destruction of a city with the same name as the city in Jeremiah's prophecy, having the same physical characteristics as the city in Jeremiah's prophecy, and destroyed in the same manner as the city in Jeremiah's prophecy.

These parallels lead to the conclusion that John and Jeremiah were describing the future destruction of the same city. John so identified his prophecy with the unfulfilled prophecy of Jeremiah that the association is unmistakable. Therefore the identity of the Babylon in Revelation 17–18 is the future rebuilt city of Babylon on the Euphrates. It will once again be restored and will achieve a place of worldwide influence only to be destroyed by the Antichrist in his thirst for power.

Chapter Notes

Chapter 1

1. W. Graham Scroggie, *A Guide to the Gospels* (London: Pickering & Inglis, 1967), p. 83.
2. Donald Guthrie, *New Testament Introduction* (Downers Grove, IL: InterVarsity, 1970), pp. 121–22.
3. A. T. Robertson, *A Harmony of the Gospels for Students of the Life of Christ* (New York: Harper & Row, 1950). This list is very general; further items could be included.
4. Ibid.
5. Scroggie, *A Guide to the Gospels*, pp. 349–50.
6. James Iverach, "Gospels, The Synoptics," in *The International Standard Bible Encyclopedia* (1939 ed.), 2:1282.
7. F. W. Grosheide, "The Synoptic Problem: A Neglected Factor in Its Solution," *Evangelical Quarterly* 3 (1931): 62–63.
8. Guthrie, *New Testament Introduction*, p. 129.
9. Iverach, "Gospels," 2:1282.
10. Ibid.
11. William R. Farmer, "Modern Developments of Griesbach's Hypothesis," *New Testament Studies* 23 (April 1977): 276.
12. Ibid., p. 275.
13. William R. Farmer, "The Synoptic Problem: The Inadequacies of the Generally Accepted Solution," *Perkins Journal* 33 (Summer 1980): 20–27. In this article Farmer develops five "inadequacies" of the hypothesis of Marcan priority.
14. Farmer, "Modern Developments of Griesbach's Hypothesis," pp. 283–84.
15. C. H. Pinnock, "Gospels," in *The Zondervan Pictorial Encyclopedia of the Bible*, 2:788.
16. C. Milo Connick, *The New Testament: An Introduction to Its History, Literature, and Thought* (Encino, CA: Dickenson, 1972), pp. 74–75.
17. Willi Marxsen, *Introduction to the New Testament: An Approach to Its Problems*, trans. Geoffrey Buswell (Philadelphia: Fortress, 1968), p. 118.
18. Scroggie, *A Guide to the Gospels*, p. 189.
19. B. H. Streeter, *The Four Gospels* (New York: Macmillan, 1925).
20. Connick, *The New Testament*, pp. 75–76.
21. Edward C. Hobbs, "A Quarter-Century without 'Q'," *Perkins Journal* 33 (Summer 1980): 13.

22. Guthrie, *New Testament Introduction*, pp. 133–35.
23. Ibid., p. 133.
24. Ibid., p. 135.
25. Sanders notes the problem this poses and attributes the difficulty to "the evangelists' knowledge of overlapping traditions." The only solution he can offer to the problem is to postulate the existence of additional, overlapping sources. "A theory which takes account of multiple and partially overlapping sources, despite the uncertainties inherent in such a view, may prove to be the most satisfactory overall solution" (E. P. Sanders, "The Overlaps of Mark and Q and the Synoptic Problem," *New Testament Studies* 19 [July 1973]: 464). However, there comes a time when a system must collapse under the sheer weight of its multiplicity of sources.
26. Connick, *The New Testament*, pp. 83–84. Some scholars have reacted against this wholesale use of sources because of its failure to grant any independence to the authors of the Gospels or to account for the distinctive message or argument of each book. Kingsbury notes, "In times past, the Gospel according to Matthew has often been described as an expanded and revised version of Mark. What is correct about this assessment is that it takes account of the fact that virtually the whole of Mark reappears in Matthew. . . . Nevertheless, when it comes to the matter of distinctiveness, Matthew possesses a character all its own . . ." (Jack Dean Kingsbury, "The Gospel in Four Editions," *Interpretation* 33 [January 1979]: 367).

    And yet Kingsbury is still forced to speak of Matthew "dropping Marcan references," "editing out a number of queries Jesus poses in Mark," and "modifying or omitting Marcan expressions" (ibid., pp. 368–69). Even though he recognizes the problem inherent in positing an extensive use of sources, he is still unable to break with this basic assumption. Thus he is left on the one hand arguing for the uniqueness of Matthew while on the other hand explaining away similarities by speaking of Matthew being "indebted to" Mark and explaining away differences as "an editorial revision by Matthew" (Jack Dean Kingsbury, "The Structure of Matthew's Gospel and His Concept of Salvation History," *Catholic Biblical Quarterly* 35 [October 1973]: 470).
27. William R. Farmer, *Synopticon* (Cambridge: At the University Press, 1969).
28. Samuel Davidson, *An Introduction to the Study of the New Testament*, 2 vols. (London: Longmans, Green, & Co., 1868), 1:461.
29. Birger Gerhardsson, *Memory and Manuscript: Oral Tradition and Written Transmission in Rabbinic Judaism and Early Christianity* (Lund: Gleerup, 1961).
30. Guthrie, *New Testament Introduction*, pp. 224–25.
31. Ibid.

Chapter 2

1. Merrill C. Tenney, "The Footnotes of John's Gospel," *Bibliotheca Sacra* 117 (October–December 1960): 350.
2. Ibid., 352–64.
3. John O'Rourke, "Asides in the Gospel of John," *Novum Testamentum* 21 (1979): 210–11.
4. Ibid., 216–18.
5. Ibid., 217.
6. Tenney, "The Footnotes of John's Gospel," 350.
7. Ibid.
8. Ibid.
9. Ibid., 351.
10. Ibid., 351–52 (italics his).
11. Ibid., 352, 357–58.
12. Ibid., 350.
13. Wayne C. Booth, *The Rhetoric of Fiction* (Chicago: University of Chicago Press, 1961), pp. 3–9.
14. If a place is the object of a verb of going, entering, exiting, and others, mention of it is not considered an aside and is not included in the table (see 2:12; 3:22; 6:1; 8:1; 8:2; 10:40; 11:54; 18:1). Also statements of general sequence ("the next day," "after these things") are considered aspects of narrative and do not appear in the table (see 2:1; 4:43; 13:31; 19:38).
15. Inner responses such as fear, thought, belief, and knowledge are all grouped with actions. Tenney and O'Rourke's "theological notes" would fall under the significance categories here, as they point out the theological significance of words or events. As a corollary, all Scripture citations also are included under significance.

Chapter 3

1. G. Cambell Morgan, *The Acts of the Apostles* (New York: Revell, 1924), p. 39.
2. J. W. McGarvey, *New Commentary on Acts of Apostles* (Cincinnati: Standard, 1892), p. 28.
3. In Romans 2:5 lack of repentance is linked with the heart in the phrase "impenitent heart." "Impenitent" (ἀμετανόητο) is the negative of the word "repentance" (μετάνοια).
4. See Alfred Edersheim, *The Life and Times of Jesus the Messiah,* 2 vols. (reprint, Grand Rapids: Eerdmans, 1962), 2:745–47, for a concise discussion of the baptism of proselytes.
5. The language of verse 41 implies that the three thousand converts were all baptized on the same day. There were numerous pools and reservoirs in Jerusalem which would have provided the facilities for this even by immersion. If all 120 disciples assisted in administering the ordinance, it could easily have been done in a

very short time. *Life* magazine (August 14, 1950) reported a modern instance in which 34 men immersed 3,381 converts in four hours.
6. A. T. Robertson explains the meaning of the words "unto the remission of your sins" (v. 38), and his words are here quoted lest any misinterpret the words of Peter to teach baptismal regeneration. "In themselves the words can express aim or purpose for that use of *eis* does exist as in I Cor. 2:7. . . . But then another usage exists which is just as good Greek as the use of *eis* for aim or purpose. In is seen in Matt. 10:41 . . . where it cannot be purpose or aim, but rather the basis or ground, on the basis of the name of prophet, righteous man, disciple, because on is, etc. It is seen again in Matt. 12:41 about the preaching of Jonah. . . . They repented because of (or at) the preaching of Jonah. The illustrations of both usages are numerous in the N.T. and the *Koine* generally. . . . I understand Peter to be urging baptism on each of them who had already turned (repented) and for it to be done in the name of Jesus Christ on the basis of the forgiveness of sins which they had already" (*Word Pictures in the New Testament*, 6 vols. [Nashville: Broadman, 1933], 3:35–36).
7. Richard Belward Rackham, *The Acts of the Apostles* (1901; reprint, London: Methuen, 1953), p. 33.

Chapter 4

1. Frank Stagg, *The Book of Acts: The Early Struggle for an Unhindered Gospel* (Nashville: Broadman, 1955). Also see his article "The Unhindered Gospel," *Review and Expositor* 71 (Fall 1974): 451–62.
2. H. Oliver Ohsberg, "The Principles of Church Growth," *Missionfax* (Toronto: Canadian Baptist Overseas Mission Board, April 1983), p. 2. Luke was fond of the verb προστίθημι to describe church growth (Acts 2:41, 47; 5:14; 11:24). He also used κολλάομαι in 5:13; 9:26; 17:34 (cf. 10:28) and προσκληρόομαι in 17:4 (a *hapax legomenon* in the New Testament).
3. For instance, Peter used διαφέρω ("to spread") in Acts 13:49. Acts has many references to God's sovereignty in building and extending the church: 2:39, 47; 11:21; 13:48; 16:14; 21:14; 22:10, 14. On the theme of growth as a divine mystery see E. Luther Copeland, "Church Growth in Acts," *Missiology* 4 (January 1976): 13–26 (esp. pp. 22–23). Also of note is the mention of the "Lord's hand" in the growth process (4:30–31; 11:21; cf. Luke 1:66, where it is used of John the Baptist).
4. Luke was fond of the verb ἐπιστηρίζω, which he alone used in the New Testament to describe the work of "strengthening" the spiritual life of Christians and churches (Acts 14:22; 15:32, 41; 18:23). In 16:5 Luke wrote of the churches being "strengthened in the faith" (ἐστερεοῦντο τῇ πίστει) as well as growing in numbers (ἐπερίσσευον τῷ ἀριθμῷ καθ' ἡμέραν). It is interesting as well

to note the vocabulary Luke employed to describe Paul's teaching activity in Thessalonica (διελέξατο αὐτοῖς ἀπὸ τῶν γραφῶν, διανοίγων καὶ παρατιθέμενος (17:2–3). Evidently there was a strong didactic element in Paul's message here which elicited a response (17:4; cf. 17:34 of the response in Athens).

5. Tacitus recognized the growth of the church both numerically and geographically, but he viewed Christianity as "a most mischievous superstition" (Annals 15.44), cited in C. K. Barrett, ed., *The New Testament Background: Selected Documents* (London: S.P.C.K., 1958), pp. 15–16.

6. See this writer's chapter on "Witness in the Book of Acts," in Allison A. Trites, *New Testament Witness in Today's World* (Valley Forge, PA: Judson Press, 1983), pp. 69–86.

7. Allison A. Trites, "The Prayer Motif in Luke–Acts," in *Perspectives in Luke–Acts,* ed. C. H. Talbert (Macon, GA: Mercer University Press, 1977), pp. 168–86.

8. Bruce M. Metzger, *A Textual Commentary on the Greek New Testament* (New York: United Bible Societies, 1971), p. 305.

9. Allison A. Trites, *The New Testament Concept of Witness* (Cambridge: Cambridge University Press, 1977), pp. 149–53. Cf. Huber L. Drumwright, Jr., "The Holy Spirit in the Book of Acts," *Southwestern Journal of Theology* 17 (Fall 1974): 3–17.

10. Copeland, "Church Growth in Acts," pp. 24–25.

11. Ibid., p. 25.

Chapter 5

1. C. E. B. Cranfield, *A Critical and Exegetical Commentary on the Epistle to the Romans,* 2 vols. (Edinburgh: Clark, 1977), 1:420; William Hendriksen, *Exposition of Paul's Epistle to the Romans,* New Testament Commentary (Grand Rapids: Baker, 1980), 1:273; and Ernst Käsemann, *Commentary on Romans,* trans. and ed. Geoffrey W. Bromiley (Grand Rapids: Eerdmans, 1980), p. 240.

2. Everett F. Harrison, "Romans," in *The Expositor's Bible Commentary,* 12 vols. (Grand Rapids: Zondervan, 1976), 10:95; D. Martin Lloyd-Jones, *Romans: The Final Perseverance of the Saints (8:17–39)* (Grand Rapids: Zondervan, 1975), 121; and John Knox, "The Epistle to the Romans," in *The Interpreter's Bible,* ed. George Arthur Buttrick, 12 vols. (New York: Abingdon, 1953), 9:552.

3. R. C. H. Lenski, *The Interpretation of St. Paul's Epistle to the Romans* (Minneapolis: Augsburg, 1961), p. 545.

4. Charles Hodge, *A Commentary on the Epistle to the Romans* (Grand Rapids: Eerdmans, 1950), p. 436; Lenski, *The Interpretation of St. Paul's Epistle to the Romans,* p. 545; and Henry C. Thiessen, "The Holy Spirit in the Epistle to the Romans" (Th.D. diss., Southern Baptist Theological Seminary, 1929), p. 100.

5. Hendriksen, *Exposition of Paul's Epistle to the Romans*, p. 275; Lenski, *The Interpretation of St. Paul's Epistle to the Romans*, p. 545; Lloyd-Jones, *Romans*, p. 132; and A. T. Robertson, *A Grammar of the Greek New Testament in the Light of Historical Research* (Nashville: Broadman, 1934), p. 573.

6. Thiessen, "The Holy Spirit in the Epistle to the Romans," p. 102; Lloyd-Jones, *Romans*, p. 133.

7. Lloyd-Jones, *Romans*, p. 133.

8. Gustav Stahlin, "ἀσθενής," in *Theological Dictionary of the New Testament*, 1:490–93.

9. Walter Bauer, William F. Arndt, and F. Wilbur Gingrich, *A Greek-English Lexicon of the New Testament and Other Early Christian Literature*, 2d ed., rev. Wilbur Gingrich and Frederick W. Danker (Chicago: University of Chicago Press, 1979), p. 115; Donald Grey Barnhouse, *God's Heirs* (Grand Rapids: Eerdmans, 1963), p. 141; Lloyd-Jones, *Romans*, p. 123; and F. A. Philippi, *Commentary on St. Paul's Epistle to the Romans* (Edinburgh: Clark, 1879), 2:25.

10. Abraham Kuyper, *The Work of the Holy Spirit* (1900; reprint, Grand Rapids: Eerdmans, n.d.), p. 638.

11. Barnhouse, *God's Heirs*, p. 142.

12. F. Tholuck, cited by J. P. Lange and F. R. Fay, "The Epistle of Paul to the Romans," *Commentary on the Holy Scriptures*, by John Peter Lange, 12 vols. (reprint, Grand Rapids: Zondervan, 1960), 10:276; Käsemann, *Commentary on Romans*, p. 239; and Thiessen, "The Holy Spirit in the Epistle to the Romans," p. 104.

13. Cranfield, *A Critical and Exegetical Commentary on the Epistle to the Romans*, p. 422.

14. Hendriksen, *Exposition of Paul's Epistle to the Romans*, p. 274; Lenski, *The Interpretation of St. Paul's Epistle to the Romans*, p. 546.

15. E. H. Gifford, *The Epistle of Paul to the Romans* (London: John Murray, 1886; reprint, Minneapolis: James Family, 1977); Lenski, *The Interpretation of St. Paul's Epistle to the Romans*, p. 545; and William Sanday and Arthur C. Headlam, *A Critical and Exegetical Commentary on the Epistle to the Romans*, 5th ed. (Edinburgh: Clark, 1902), p. 213.

16. Lenski, *The Interpretation of St. Paul's Epistle to the Romans*, p. 546.

17. Cranfield, *A Critical and Exegetical Commentary on the Epistle to the Romans*, p. 421.

18. Gifford, *The Epistle of Paul to the Romans*, p. 158; and Cranfield, *A Critical and Exegetical Commentary on the Epistle to the Romans*, p. 421.

19. James Denney, "St. Paul's Epistle to the Romans," in *The Expositor's Greek Testament*, ed. W. Robertson Nicoll, 5 vols. (Grand Rapids: Eerdmans, 1951), 2:651.

20. Alva McClain, *Romans: The Gospel of God's Grace* (Chicago: Moody, 1973), p. 168.
21. Karl Barth, *The Epistle to the Romans* (London: Oxford University Press, 1933), p. 316.
22. Hendricksen, *Exposition of Paul's Epistle to the Romans,* p. 275; and A. T. Robertson, *Word Pictures in the New Testament,* 6 vols. (Nashville: Broadman, 1931), 4:377.
23. Lenski, *The Interpretation of St. Paul's Epistle to the Romans,* p. 546.
24. Hendricksen, *Exposition of Paul's Epistle to the Romans,* p. 277; and Kuyper, *The Holy Spirit,* p. 637.
25. F. Godet, *Commentary on the Epistle to the Romans* (Grand Rapids: Zondervan, 1956), p. 321; and *The New Scofield Reference Bible* (New York: Oxford University Press, 1967), p. 1221.
26. Hendriksen, *Exposition of Paul's Epistle to the Romans,* p. 278.
27. Henry Alford, *The Greek Testament,* 4 vols. (reprint, Chicago: Moody, 1958), 2:397; C. K. Barrett, *Reading through Romans* (Philadelphia: Fortress, 1977), p. 44; John Calvin, *Commentary on the Epistle of Paul the Apostle to the Romans* (Grand Rapids: Eerdmans, 1948), p. 213; Harrison, "Romans," p. 96; and Knox, "The Epistle to the Romans," p. 523.
28. Lenski, *The Interpretation of St. Paul's Epistle to the Romans,* p. 548.
29. Lloyd-Jones, *Romans,* p. 137; Lenski, *The Interpretation of St. Paul's Epistle to the Romans,* p. 547.
30. Hendriksen, *Exposition of Paul's Epistle to the Romans,* p. 276.
31. Lloyd-Jones, *Romans,* p. 137.
32. Cranfield, *A Critical and Exegetical Commentary on the Epistle to the Romans,* p. 423; Gifford, *The Epistle of Paul to the Romans,* p. 158; and Hendriksen, *Exposition of Paul's Epistle to the Romans,* p. 275.
33. Hendriksen, *Exposition of Paul's Epistle to the Romans,* p. 276; and Kuyper, *The Work of the Holy Spirit,* pp. 636–37.
34. Gifford, *The Epistle of Paul to the Romans,* p. 158; Hendriksen, *Exposition of Paul's Epistle to the Romans,* p. 276; and Kuyper, *The Work of the Holy Spirit,* pp. 638–39.
35. Hendriksen, *Exposition of Paul's Epistle to the Romans,* p. 274.
36. Barrett, *Reading through Romans,* p. 44; Käsemann, *Commentary on Romans,* p. 240; and Knox, "The Epistle to the Romans," p. 523.
37. Barth, *The Epistle to the Romans,* p. 317; Denney, "St. Paul's Epistle to the Romans," p. 651; Philippi, *Commentary on St. Paul's Epistle to the Romans,* p. 27; Robertson, *Word Pictures in the New Testament,* 4:377; W. G. T. Shedd, *Commentary on Romans* (New York: Scribner's Sons, 1879; reprint, Grand Rapids: Baker, 1980), p. 261.
38. R. Haldane, *Epistle to the Romans* (New York: Robert Carter,

1847), p. 395; Kuyper, *The Work of the Holy Spirit*, p. 623; Lenski, *The Interpretation of St. Paul's Epistle to the Romans*, p. 551; H. A. W. Meyer, *Critical and Exegetical Handbook to the Epistle to the Romans* (New York: Funk & Wagnalls, 1889), p. 331; F. Tholuck, *Exposition of St. Paul's Epistle to the Romans* (Philadelphia: Sorin & Ball, 1844), p. 268; and B. Weiss, *A Commentary on the New Testament*, 5 vols. (New York: Funk & Wagnalls, 1906), 3:78.

39. J. Schneider, "στενάζω," in *Theological Dictionary of the New Testament*, 7:601.

40. Ibid., pp. 600–601.

41. With creation's groanings and the Christian's groanings, the present tense of the verb is self-evident. However, Paul used the noun στεναγμοῖς in describing the Spirit's groanings; yet even in this instance, the verbal action describing the groans is in the present tense.

42. Alford, *The Greek Testament*, 2:397; Lange and Fay, "The Epistle of Paul to the Romans," p. 277; Lenski, *The Interpretation of St. Paul's Epistle to the Romans*, p. 547; Shedd, *Commentary on Romans*, p. 261; Theissen, "The Holy Spirit in the Epistle to the Romans," p. 107.

43. Cranfield, *A Critical and Exegetical Commentary on the Epistle to the Romans*, p. 423; Hendriksen, *Exposition of Paul's Epistle to the Romans*, p. 275; and Lloyd-Jones, *Romans*, p. 135.

44. M. Black, *Romans*, New Century Bible (London: Marshall, Morgan, & Scott, 1973), p. 123; Godet, *Commentary on the Epistle to the Romans*, p. 321; Käsemann, *Commentary on Romans*, p. 240; and Knox, "The Epistle to the Romans," p. 423.

45. Cranfield, *A Critical and Exegetical Commentary on the Epistle to the Romans*, p. 423.

46. Ibid., p. 424; Käsemann, *Commentary on Romans*, p. 242; and Lenski, *The Interpretation of St. Paul's Epistle to the Romans*, p. 548.

47. Cranfield, *A Critical and Exegetical Commentary on the Epistle to the Romans*, p. 424; and Käsemann, *Commentary on Romans*, p. 242.

48. Bauer, Arndt, and Gingrich, *A Greek-English Lexicon of the New Testament and Other Early Christian Literature*, p. 866.

49. AV; NASB; NIV; RSV; TEV; Williams; and others.

50. Käsemann, *Commentary on Romans*, p. 242.

51. Sanday and Headlam, *A Critical and Exegetical Commentary on the Epistle to the Romans*, p. 214.

52. Black, *Romans*, p. 124; Cranfield, *A Critical and Exegetical Commentary on the Epistle to the Romans*, p. 424; Gifford, *The Epistle of Paul to the Romans*, p. 158; Hendriksen, *Exposition of Paul's Epistle to the Romans*, p. 278; Lenski, *The Interpretation of St. Paul's Epistle to the Romans*, p. 548; and Sanday and

Headlam, *A Critical and Exegetical Commentary on the Epistle to the Romans,* p. 214.

53. Gifford, *The Epistle of Paul to the Romans,* p. 158.

54. Cranfield, *A Critical and Exegetical Commentary on the Epistle to the Romans,* p. 424; Hendriksen, *Exposition of Paul's Epistle to the Romans,* p. 278; and Sanday and Headlam, *A Critical and Exegetical Commentary on the Epistle to the Romans,* p. 214.

55. Karl Barth, *A Shorter Commentary on Romans* (London: Oxford University Press, 1959), p. 102.

56. See the author's book, *Praying Jesus' Way* (Old Tappan, NJ: Revell, 1977), pp. 119–29.

57. Hendriksen, *Exposition of Paul's Epistle to the Romans,* p. 274.

58. Sanday and Headlam, *A Critical and Exegetical Commentary on the Epistle to the Romans,* p. 213.

59. John Murray, *The Epistle to the Romans,* New International Commentary on the New Testament (Grand Rapids: Eerdmans, 1959), p. 314.

Chapter 6

1. R. C. H. Lenski, *The Interpretation of St. Paul's Epistle to the Romans* (Minneapolis: Augsburg, 1961), p. 550.

2. Thomas Watson, *All Things for Good* (1663; reprint, Edinburgh: Banner of Truth Trust, 1986), p. 10.

3. Source unidentified.

4. John A. Witmer, "Romans," in *The Bible Knowledge Commentary, New Testament,* ed. John F. Walvoord and Roy B. Zuck (Wheaton, IL: Victor, 1983), p. 473.

5. J. N. Darby, *The "Holy Scriptures," A New Translation* (reprint, Kingston-on-Thames: Stow Hill Bible & Tract, 1949); Gerrit Verkuyl, ed., *The Modern Language Bible: The New Berkeley Version* (Grand Rapids: Zondervan, 1969); *The Twentieth Century New Testament: A Translation into Modern English* (reprint, Chicago: Moody, n.d.).

6. Frederic Louis Godet, *Commentary on Romans* (1883; reprint, Grand Rapids: Kregel, 1977), p. 322 (italics his).

7. H. A. W. Meyer, *Critical and Exegetical Hand-Book to the Epistle to the Romans* (1883; reprint, Winona Lake, IN: Alpha, 1979), p. 333.

8. Most English versions translate the particle as "and"; several omit the particle entirely.

9. J. B. Rotherham, *The Emphasized New Testament* (reprint, Grand Rapids: Kregel, 1959).

10. Lenski, *The Interpretation of St. Paul's Epistle to the Romans,* p. 550.

11. William Hendriksen, *Exposition of Paul's Epistle to the Romans,* New Testament Commentary (Grand Rapids: Baker, 1980), pp. 278–79 (italics his).

12. Lenski, *The Interpretation of St. Paul's Epistle to the Romans*, p. 551.
13. "A neuter plural subject regularly takes a singular verb" (H. E. Dana and Julius R. Mantey, *A Manual Grammar of the Greek New Testament* [reprint, New York: Macmillan, 1967], p. 165).
14. James D. G. Dunn, *Romans 1–8*, Word Biblical Commentary (Dallas, TX: Word, 1988), p. 481. See the literature cited. Also see Hans-Christoph Hahn, "Work, Do, Accomplish," in *The New International Dictionary of New Testament Theology*, 3:1152 and the references cited.
15. See United Bible Societies, *The Greek New Testament*, 3d ed. (New York: American Bible Society, 1975).
16. Hendriksen, *Exposition of Paul's Epistle to the Romans*, p. 279.
17. J. B. Rotherham, *The Emphasized New Testament; The Twentieth Century New Testament; The New Berkeley Version; The New Testament of the Jerusalem Bible;* the *New American Standard Bible;* and the *Revised Standard Version.*
18. William Barclay, *The New Testament: A New Translation* (Cleveland: Foundation, 1976), p. 324.
19. Hendriksen, *Exposition of Paul's Epistle to the Romans*, pp. 279–80.
20. Walter Grundmann, "ἀγαθός" in *Theological Dictionary of the New Testament*, 1:17.
21. Watson, *All Things for Good*, p. 11.
22. Dunn, *Romans 1–8*, p. 481.
23. Lenski, *The Interpretation of St. Paul's Epistle to the Romans*, p. 551.
24. Watson, *All Things for Good*, p. 66.
25. Lenski, *The Interpretation of St. Paul's Epistle to the Romans*, p. 550.
26. C. F. Hogg and W. E. Vine, *The Epistles of Paul the Apostle to the Thessalonians* (reprint, Grand Rapids: Kregel, 1959), p. 105.
27. John Murray, *The Epistle to the Romans*, New International Commentary (Grand Rapids: Eerdmans, 1959), p. 314.
28. Ethelbert Stauffer, "ἀγαράω," in *Theological Dictionary of the New Testament*, 1:50.
29. Lenski, *The Interpretation of St. Paul's Epistle to the Romans*, pp. 553–54.
30. Ibid., p. 555.
31. William Kelly, *Notes on the Epistle of Paul the Apostle to the Romans* (London: G. Morrish, 1873; reprint, n.d.), p. 153.
32. Meyer, *Critical and Exegetical Hand-Book to the Epistle to the Romans*, p. 335.
33. J. Behm, "προνοέω, πρόνοια," in *Theological Dictionary of the New Testament*, 4:1016.
34. Murray, *The Epistle to the Romans*, p. 318.
35. Dunn, *Romans 1–8*, p. 483.

36. Kenneth S. Wuest, *Romans in the Greek New Testament for the English Reader* (Grand Rapids: Eerdmans, 1955), p. 145.
37. W. E. Vine, *An Expository Dictionary of New Testament Words* (Westwood, NJ: Revell, 1940), 2:247.
38. Hendriksen, *Exposition of Paul's Epistle to the Romans,* p. 283 (italics his).
39. Lenski, *The Interpretation of St. Paul's Epistle to the Romans,* p. 561.
40. Dunn, *Romans 1–8,* p. 483.
41. R. Govett, *The Righteousness of God, The Salvation of the Believer: or, The Argument of the Romans* (Norwich: Fletcher and Son, 1891; reprint, Schoettle, 1981 under the title *Govett on Romans*), p. 368.
42. Vine, *An Expository Dictionary of New Testament Words,* 2:104.

Chapter 7

1. William H. Goold, ed.,*The Works of John Owen,* 16 vols (1850–1854; reprint, London: Banner of Truth Trust, 1965–), 18:481.
2. Solomon Schechter, *Some Aspects of Rabbinic Theology* (New York: Macmillan, 1923), pp. 138–42.
3. Lewis Sperry Chafer, *Systematic Theology,* 8 vols. (Dallas, TX: Dallas Seminary Press, 1948; reprint [8 vols. in 4], Grand Rapids: Kregel, 1992), 3:81.
4. O. Raymond Johnston, "Law," in *Baker's Dictionary of Theology,* p. 319.
5. John Calvin, *Institutes of the Christian Religion,* 2.11.4.
6. Ibid., 2.8.33.

Chapter 8

1. Chester E. Tulga, *Studies in Romans* (Cleveland: Union Gospel, 1939), p. 202.
2. Anders Nygren, *Commentary on Romans,* trans. Carl C. Rasmussen (Philadelphia: Muhlenberg, 1949), p. 412.
3. In Greek usage οὖν is postpositive, never used as the first word in the sentence but appended to the term with which it is used.
4. Kenneth S. Wuest, *Romans in the Greek New Testament for the English Reader* (Grand Rapids: Eerdmans, 1955), p. 204.
5. John Knox and Gerald R. Cragg, "The Epistle to the Romans," in *The Interpreter's Bible,* ed. George Buttrick, 12 vols. (New York: Abingdon Cokesbury, 1954), 9:579.
6. John Peter Lange, *Commentary on the Holy Scriptures, Critical, Doctrinal and Homiletical,* trans. and ed. with additions by Philip Schaff, 10 vols. (1869; reprint, Grand Rapids: Zondervan, n.d.), 5:381.
7. C. E. B. Cranfield, *A Critical and Exegetical Commentary on the Epistle to the Romans,* International Critical Commentary, 2 vols. (Edinburgh: Clark, 1979), 2:596.

8. Ibid.
9. Herbert L. Wallett and James M. Campbell, *The Teachings of the Books, or the Literary Structure and Spiritual Interpretation of the Books of the New Testament* (New York: Revell, 1899), pp. 130–31.
10. J. P. McBeth, *Exegetical and Practical Commentary on the Epistle to the Romans* (New York: Revell, 1937), p. 229.
11. Matthew Henry, *Commentary on the Whole Bible, New One Volume Edition*, ed. Leslie F. Church (Grand Rapids: Zondervan, 1960), p. 582b.
12. McBeth, *Exegetical and Practical Commentary on the Epistle to the Romans*, p. 230.
13. Everett F. Harrison, "Romans," in *The Expositor's Bible Commentary*, 12 vols. (Grand Rapids: Zondervan, 1976), 10:127.
14. James H. McConkey, *The Surrendered Life: Bible Studies and Addresses on the Yielded Life*, rev. ed. (Richmond, VA: Silver, 1987), pp. 23–24.
15. Robert Young, *The Holy Bible Consisting of the Old and New Covenants Translated according to the Letter and Idioms of the Original Languages*, rev. ed. (London: Pickering & Inglis, 1862).
16. Albert Barnes, *Notes on the New Testament, Explanatory and Practical*, ed. Robert Frew (reprint, Grand Rapids: Baker, 1963), p. 269.
17. Cranfield, *A Critical and Exegetical Commentary on the Epistle to the Romans*, 2:598–99.
18. Arthur S. Way, *The Letters of St. Paul, to Seven Churches and Three Friends, with the Letter to the Hebrews*, 6th ed. (London: Macmillan, 1926), p. 139.
19. H. P. Liddon, *Explanatory Analysis of St. Paul's Epistle to the Romans* (Grand Rapids: Zondervan, 1961), p. 228 (italics his).
20. Henry Alford, *The New Testament for English Readers*, 2 vols. (Boston: Lee and Shepard, 1872), 2:109.
21. Geoffrey B. Wilson, *Romans: A Digest of Reformed Comment* (London: Banner of Truth, 1969), p. 198.
22. Barnes, *Notes on the New Testament, Explanatory and Practical*, pp. 269–70.
23. Robert Jamieson, A. R. Fausset, and David Brown, *A Commentary, Critical and Explanatory, on the Old and New Testaments*, 6 vols. (New York: Revell, n.d.; reprint, Grand Rapids: Eerdmans, 1945), 5:263.
24. Cranfield, *A Critical and Exegetical Commentary on the Epistle to the Romans*, 2:601.
25. Wuest, *Romans in the Greek New Testament for the English Reader*, p. 205.
26. William R. Newell, *Romans Verse by Verse* (Chicago: Moody, 1938), p. 449.
27. William Kelly, *Notes on the Epistle of Paul to the Romans* (1878; reprint, n.p.), p. 239.

28. *The New Testament from 26 Translations* (Grand Rapids: Zondervan, 1967), p. 705, has no fewer than ten different renderings of this phrase.
29. James Reapsome, *Rozell's Complete Lessons, September 1978– August 1979* (Grand Rapids: Zondervan, 1978), p. 14.
30. W. E. Vine, *An Expository Dictionary of New Testament Words with their Precise Meanings for English Readers* (Westwood, NJ: Revell, 1940; reprint [4 vols. in 1], Nashville: Nelson, 1985), 3:253.
31. McBeth, *Exegetical and Practical Commentary on the Epistle to the Romans,* p. 232.
32. See the textual footnotes on these verses in Lange, *Commentary on the Holy Scriptures,* pp. 380–81.
33. For the textual evidence see Nestle-Aland, *Novum Testamentum Graece,* 26th ed. (Stuttgart: Deutsche Bibelstiftung, 1979).
34. John Murray, *The Epistle to the Romans,* 2 vols. (Grand Rapids: Eerdmans, 1965), 2:113.
35. J. B. Phillips, *The New Testament in Modern English* (New York: Macmillan, 1962).
36. See the renderings in *The New Testament from 26 Translations.*
37. Liddon, *Explanatory Analysis of St. Paul's Epistle to the Romans,* p. 230.
38. Vine, *An Expository Dictionary of New Testament Words,* 3:69.
39. Barnes, *Notes on the New Testament, Explanatory and Practical,* pp. 271–72.
40. M. J. Harris, "Appendix: Prepositions and Theology in the Greek New Testament," *The New International Dictionary of New Testament Theology,* 3:1187.
41. Wuest, *Romans in the Greek New Testament for the English Reader,* p. 208.
42. John Albert Bengel, *New Testament Word Studies: A New Translation,* by Carlton T. Lewis and Marvin R. Vincent, 3 vols. (Grand Rapids: Kregel, 1971), 2:137.
43. R. C. H. Lenski, *The Interpretation of St. Paul's Epistle to the Romans* (Minneapolis: Augsburg, 1961), p. 752.
44. Zeisler, cited in Jamieson, Fausset, and Brown, *A Commentary, Critical and Explanatory on the Old and New Testaments,* 2:252.
45. Robert Haldane, *Exposition of the Epistle to the Romans* (New York: Carter, 1847), p. 570.
46. Harrison, "Romans," 10:128.
47. Francis Davidson, "The Epistle to the Romans," in *The New Bible Commentary,* ed. F. Davidson, A. M. Stibbs, and E. F. Kevan (Grand Rapids: Eerdmans, 1953), p. 960.

Chapter 9

1. G. G. Findlay, "The First Epistle of Paul to the Corinthians," in *The Expositor's Greek New Testament,* 5 vols. (Grand Rapids:

Eerdmans, n.d.), 2:870; Archibald Robertson and Alfred Plummer, *A Critical and Exegetical Commentary on the First Epistle of St Paul to the Corinthians*, International Critical Commentary (Edinburgh: Clark, n.d.), p. 228; F. W. Grosheide, *The First Epistle to the Corinthians*, New International Commentary on the New Testament (Grand Rapids: Eerdmans, 1953), p. 248.

2. Charles J. Ellicott, *St. Paul's First Epistle to the Corinthians: With a Critical and Grammatical Commentary* (Minneapolis: James Family, 1978), p. 199; Robertson and Plummer, *A Critical and Exegetical Commentary on the First Epistle of St Paul to the Corinthians*, p. 228; W. Harold Mare, "1 Corinthians," in *The Expositor's Bible Commentary*, 12 vols. (Grand Rapids: Zondervan, 1976), 10:254. All these commentators see Paul introducing this topic on his own.

3. Findlay, "The First Epistle of Paul to the Corinthians," 2:871.

4. Robertson and Plummer, *A Critical and Exegetical Commentary on the First Epistle of St Paul to the Corinthians*, p. 228, first footnote.

5. See 1 Corinthians 1:4–9 and other Pauline introductions. The term used to describe such introductions is *Captatio Benevolentiae*.

6. Walter Bauer, William F. Arndt, and F. Wilbur Gingrich, *A Greek-English Lexicon of the New Testament and Other Early Christian Literature*, 2d ed., rev. F. Wilbur Gingrich and Frederick W. Danker (Chicago: University of Chicago Press, 1979), p. 423.

7. Ellicott, *St. Paul's First Epistle to the Corinthians*, p. 199; Robert Gromacki, *Called to Be Saints* (Grand Rapids: Baker, 1977), p. 133; Leon Morris, *The First Epistle of Paul to the Corinthians*, Tyndale New Testament Commentaries (Grand Rapids: Eerdmans, 1958), p. 151; Findlay, "The First Epistle of Paul to the Corinthians," 2:871.

8. Frederick Louis Godet, *Commentary on First Corinthians* (Grand Rapids: Kregel, 1977), p. 615.

9. Bauer, Arndt, and Gingrich, *A Greek-English Lexicon of the New Testament and Other Early Christian Literature*, p. 615.

10. Gordon D. Fee, *The First Epistle to the Corinthians*, New International Commentary on the New Testament (Grand Rapids: Eerdmans, 1987), pp. 491–92.

11. F. Blass and A. Debrunner, *A Greek Grammar of the New Testament and Other Early Christian Literature* (Chicago: University of Chicago Press, 1961), p. 262.

12. Bauer, Arndt, and Gingrich, *A Greek-English Lexicon of the New Testament and Other Early Christian Literature*, p. 171; Ellicott, *St. Paul's First Epistle to the Corinthians*, p. 199.

13. Bruce K. Waltke, "1 Corinthians 11:2–16: An Interpretation," *Bibliotheca Sacra* 135 (January–March 1978): 48.

14. Robertson and Plummer, *A Critical and Exegetical Commentary on the First Epistle of St Paul to the Corinthians*, p. 229; Findlay, "The First Epistle of Paul to the Corinthians."

15. See F. F. Bruce, *1 and 2 Corinthians,* New Century Bible Commentary (Grand Rapids: Eerdmans, 1971), p. 103; C. K. Barrett, *The First Epistle to the Corinthians* (New York: Harper & Row, 1968), p. 248; Fee, *The First Epistle to the Corinthians,* p. 502, n. 42.
16. V. L. Walter, "Arianism," in *Evangelical Dictionary of Theology,* ed. Walter A. Elwell (Grand Rapids: Baker, 1984), pp. 74–75.
17. John F. Walvoord, *Jesus Christ Our Lord* (Chicago: Moody, 1969), pp. 42–46.
18. For further support of this view see David K. Lowery, "The Headcovering and Lord's Supper in 1 Corinthians 11:2–34," *Bibliotheca Sacra* 143 (April–June 1986): 157.
19. Morris, *The First Epistle of Paul to the Corinthians,* p. 152; Bruce, *1 and 2 Corinthians,* p. 103.
20. Barrett, *A Commentary on the First Epistle to the Corinthians,* p. 250; Godet, *Commentary on First Corinthians,* p. 540.
21. Waltke, "1 Corinthians 11:2–16: An Interpretation," p. 49; Hurley, *Man and Woman in Biblical Perspective,* pp. 269–71; Colin Brown, "Head," in *New International Dictionary of New Testament Theology,* ed. Colin Brown (Grand Rapids: Zondervan, 1982), 2:160.
22. Robertson and Plummer, *A Critical and Exegetical Commentary on the First Epistle of St Paul to the Corinthians,* p. 229.
23. Waltke, "1 Corinthians 11:2–16: An Interpretation," p. 49; Hurley, *Man and Woman in Biblical Perspective,* pp. 269–71; Brown, "Head," p. 160.
24. Charles Talbert, *Reading Corinthians* (New York: Crossroad, 1987), p. 67.
25. David K. Lowery, "1 Corinthians," in *The Bible Knowledge Commentary, New Testament,* ed. John F. Walvoord and Roy B. Zuck (Wheaton, IL: Victor, 1983), p. 529.
26. Hurley, *Man and Woman in Biblical Perspective,* pp. 254–71; Brown, "Head," p. 160.
27. Waltke, "1 Corinthians 11:2–16: An Interpretation," p. 46; Findlay, "The First Epistle of Paul to the Corinthians," 2:870; Morris, *The First Epistle of Paul to the Corinthians,* p. 151.
28. For an elaboration of this point see Talbert, *Reading Corinthians,* pp. 66–72.
29. Wilhelm Mundle, "Hide, Conceal," in *New International Dictionary of New Testament Theology,* 2:212; Bauer, Arndt, and Gingrich, *A Greek-English Lexicon of the New Testament and Other Early Christian Literature,* pp. 29, 411.
30. Robertson and Plummer, *A Critical and Exegetical Commentary on the First Epistle of St Paul to the Corinthians,* p. 229; Waltke, "1 Corinthians 11:2–16: An Interpretation," p. 49; Brown, "Head," p. 160.
31. Blass and Debrunner, *A Greek Grammar of the New Testament and Other Early Christian Literature,* p. 294.
32. Waltke, "1 Corinthians 11:2–16: An Interpretation," p. 50; Findlay,

"The First Epistle of Paul to the Corinthians," 2:872; Brown, "Head," p. 160.

33. Daniel B. Wallace, unpublished "Grammar Notes on the New Testament," p. 150.

34. Hurley, *Man and Woman in Biblical Perspective*, p. 180.

35. Grosheide, *The First Epistle to the Corinthians;* Godet, *Commentary on First Corinthians,* p. 541.

36. Charles C. Ryrie, *The Ryrie Study Bible* (Chicago: Moody, 1978), p. 1741.

37. This understanding has been adopted in a number of recent studies, including Hurley, *Man and Woman in Biblical Perspective*, pp. 188–89, and D. A. Carson, *Showing the Spirit: A Theological Exposition of 1 Corinthians 12–14* (Grand Rapids: Baker, 1987), pp. 129–30.

38. See Hurley's outline of the passage (*Man and Woman in Biblical Perspective,* pp. 188–89).

39. For further discussion of this issue see H. Wayne House, *The Role of Women in the Ministry Today* (Nashville: Nelson, 1990).

40. For a further elaboration of this view see Wayne C. Grudem, *The Gift of Prophecy in the New Testament and Today* (Westchester, IL: Crossway, 1988).

41. Barrett, *The First Epistle to the Corinthians*, p. 252.

42. Robertson and Plummer, *A Critical and Exegetical Commentary on the First Epistle of St Paul to the Corinthians*, p. 231; Findlay, "The First Epistle of Paul to the Corinthians," 2:873; Godet, *Commentary on First Corinthians*, p. 547.

43. Godet, *Commentary on First Corinthians*, p. 548; Hurley, *Man and Woman in Biblical Perspective*, p. 174; Robertson and Plummer, *A Critical and Exegetical Commentary on the First Epistle of St Paul to the Corinthians*, p. 231.

44. Arndt and Gingrich, *A Greek-English Lexicon of the New Testament and Other Early Christian Literature*, p. 222; Ellicott, *St. Paul's First Epistle to the Corinthians: With a Critical and Grammatical Commentary,* p. 203, Findlay, "The First Epistle of Paul to the Corinthians," 2:873.

45. Hurley, *Man and Woman in Biblical Perspective*, p. 174.

46. Waltke, "1 Corinthians 11:2–16: An Interpretation," p. 51.

47. Ellicott, *St. Paul's First Epistle to the Corinthians: With a Critical and Grammatical Commentary,* p. 203.

48. Findlay, "The First Epistle of Paul to the Corinthians," 2:873.

49. Fee, *The First Epistle to the Corinthians*, p. 514.

50. Ibid.

51. Waltke, "1 Corinthians 11:2–16: An Interpretation," p. 52; Robertson and Plummer, *A Critical and Exegetical Commentary on the First Epistle of St Paul to the Corinthians*, p. 231; Findlay, "The First Epistle of Paul to the Corinthians," 2:874; Grosheide, *The First Epistle to the Corinthians*, p. 256.

52. Ellicott, *St. Paul's First Epistle to the Corinthians: With a Critical and Grammatical Commentary*, p. 204.
53. Barrett, *The First Epistle to the Corinthians*, pp. 252–53; Godet, *Commentary on First Corinthians*, p. 549.
54. F. W. Grosheide, *The First Epistle to the Corinthians*, p. 256.
55. The meaning of כְּנֶגְדּוֹ עֵזֶר in Genesis 2:18 is conveyed by "corresponding completer." The woman fits the man and completes him in his desperate situation. See the exposition of this point in Allen Ross, *Creation and Blessing: A Guide to the Study and Exposition of Genesis* (Grand Rapids: Baker, 1988), pp. 126–27.
56. Waltke, "1 Corinthians 11:2–16: An Interpretation," p. 53; Bruce, *1 and 2 Corinthians*, p. 106.
57. Lowery, "1 Corinthians," p. 529; Findlay, "The First Epistle of Paul to the Corinthians," 2:874.
58. See Fee, *The First Epistle to the Corinthians*, p. 518, for a discussion of this common occurrence in Paul's writings.
59. Findlay, "The First Epistle of Paul to the Corinthians," 2:874.
60. Bauer, Arndt, and Gingrich, *A Greek-English Lexicon of the New Testament and Other Early Christian Literature*, p. 277.
61. Hurley, *Man and Woman in Biblical Perspective*, pp. 176–77; Barrett, *1 Corinthians*, pp. 254–58; Brown, "Head," p. 161; Morna D. Hooker, "Authority on Her Head: An Examination of 1 Cor. XI. 10," *New Testament Studies* 10 (1964): 410.
62. Talbert, *Reading Corinthians*, p. 69.
63. Bauer, Arndt, and Gingrich, *A Greek-English Lexicon of the New Testament and Other Early Christian Literature*, p. 7.
64. Ibid., p. 8.
65. Ibid., p. 7.
66. Waltke, "1 Corinthians 11:2–16: An Interpretation," p. 53; Bruce, *1 and 2 Corinthians*, p. 106.
67. Robertson and Plummer, *A Critical and Exegetical Commentary on the First Epistle of St Paul to the Corinthians*, p. 233.
68. Hurley, *Man and Woman in Biblical Perspective*, pp. 269–71.
69. W. F. Moulton and A. S. Geden, *A Concordance to the Greek New Testament* (Edinburgh: Clark, 1978), pp. 9–10.
70. Waltke, "1 Corinthians 11:2–16: An Interpretation," p. 53.
71. Robertson and Plummer, *A Critical and Exegetical Commentary on the First Epistle of St Paul to the Corinthians*, p. 233.
72. See Fee's excellent discussion of the Corinthians' perspective on marriage as colored by their errant view of having arrived at an angelic state (*The First Epistle to the Corinthians*, pp. 266–357).
73. Ellicott, *St. Paul's First Epistle to the Corinthians: With a Critical and Grammatical Commentary*, p. 206; Robertson and Plummer, *A Critical and Exegetical Commentary on the First Epistle of St Paul to the Corinthians*, p. 234.
74. For the use of ὥσπερ γάρ (v. 12) to introduce an illustration see

Blass and Debrunner, *A Greek Grammar of the New Testament and Other Early Christian Literature*, p. 236.

75. E. W. Bullinger, *Figures of Speech Used in the Bible* (reprint, Grand Rapids: Baker, 1968), p. 137.

76. Blass and Debrunner, *A Greek Grammar of the New Testament and Other Early Christian Literature*, p. 262.

77. Robertson and Plummer, *A Critical and Exegetical Commentary on the First Epistle of St Paul to the Corinthians;* Findlay, "The First Epistle of Paul to the Corinthians," 2:875.

78. Bauer, Arndt, and Gingrich, *A Greek-English Lexicon of the New Testament and Other Early Christian Literature*, p. 699; James Hope Moulton and George Milligan, *The Vocabulary of the Greek New Testament* (Grand Rapids: Eerdmans, 1930), p. 534.

79. Blass and Debrunner, *A Greek Grammar of the New Testament and Other Early Christian Literature*, p. 262.

80. Findlay, "The First Epistle of Paul to the Corinthians," 2:875.

81. Grosheide, *The First Epistle to the Corinthians*, p. 260.

82. Godet, *Commentary on First Corinthians*, p. 556.

83. E.g., the Spartan warriors (Findlay, "The First Epistle of Paul to the Corinthians," 2:875).

84. Bauer, Arndt, and Gingrich, *A Greek-English Lexicon of the New Testament and Other Early Christian Literature*, p. 869.

85. Fee, *The First Epistle to the Corinthians*, p. 527.

86. Robertson and Plummer, *A Critical and Exegetical Commentary on the First Epistle of St Paul to the Corinthians*, p. 235; Morris, *The First Epistle of Paul to the Corinthians*, p. 135; Lowery, "1 Corinthians," p. 530.

87. Brown, "Head," p. 162.

88. Godet, *Commentary on First Corinthians*, p. 557; Hurley, *Man and Woman in Biblical Perspective*, p. 179.

89. Brown, "Head," p. 162.

90. Hurley, *Man and Woman in Biblical Perspective*, pp. 254–71.

91. Henry Alford, *Alford's Greek Testament: An Exegetical and Critical Commentary* (reprint, Grand Rapids: Baker, 1980), 2:568; also see Ellicott, *St. Paul's First Epistle to the Corinthians: With a Critical and Grammatical Commentary*, p. 208.

92. Blass and Debrunner, *A Greek Grammar of the New Testament and Other Early Christian Literature*, p. 189.

93. Bauer, Arndt, and Gingrich, *A Greek-English Lexicon of the New Testament and other Early Christian Literature*, p. 860; Moulton and Milligan, *The Vocabulary of the Greek New Testament*, pp. 670–71.

94. Findlay, "The First Epistle of Paul to the Corinthians," 2:876.

95. Grosheide, *The First Epistle to the Corinthians*, p. 261.

96. Robertson and Plummer, *A Critical and Exegetical Commentary on the First Epistle of St Paul to the Corinthians*, p. 235; Findlay, "The First Epistle of Paul to the Corinthians," 2:876; Godet,

Commentary on First Corinthians, p. 559; Barrett, *The First Epistle to the Corinthians*, p. 258; Waltke, "1 Corinthians 11:2–16: An Interpretation," p. 55; Ellicott, *St. Paul's First Epistle to the Corinthians: With a Critical and Grammatical Commentary*, p. 209.

97. Fee, *The First Epistle to the Corinthians*, p. 512.
98. Rick Simmons, "The Teaching of 1 Corinthians 11:2–16 and 14:34–36 on the Role of Women in Public Worship," unpublished paper, Summer 1990.
99. Ibid., p. 18.
100. Ibid., pp. 23–24.

Chapter 10

1. Hans Conzelmann, *1 Corinthians*, Hermeneia (Philadelphia: Fortress, 1975), p. 276, n. 120; and Bernard M. Foschini, "Those Who Are Baptized for the Dead: 1 Corinthians 15:29, An Exegetical Historical Dissertation," *Catholic Biblical Quarterly* 12 (1950): 260.
2. Vicarious baptism was practiced by the Marcionites (Tertullian, *Anti Marcion* 10), the followers of Cerinthus (Epiphanius, *Adv. Haer.* 28, §6), and is presently practiced by the Mormon church. The custom of the Marcionites involved an individual hiding under the body of the deceased who would answer for the corpse when the corpse was asked if he wanted to be baptized. This individual was then baptized for the dead catechumen.
3. Gordon D. Fee, *First Epistle to the Corinthians*, New International Commentary of the New Testament (Grand Rapids: Eerdmans, 1987), p. 764; and F. F. Bruce, *1 Corinthians*, New Century Bible (London: Morgan & Scott, 1971), p. 148.
4. Vicarious baptism implies a mystical view of baptism. For more on the mystical implications behind this view, see note 10.
5. The majority of suggested interpretations are based on these three general understandings, with subtle differences leading to the proliferation of interpretations.
6. W. F. Orr and J. A. Walther, *1 Corinthians*, Anchor Bible (Garden City, NY: Doubleday, 1976), p. 337; and Fee, *1 Corinthians*, p. 764.
7. Fee, *1 Corinthians*, p. 767; Orr, *1 Corinthians*, p. 337.
8. Fee, *1 Corinthians*, p. 764; and G. R. Beasley-Murray, *Baptism in the New Testament* (Grand Rapids: Eerdmans, 1974), p. 187.
9. Chrysostom *Homily* 40; Tertullian *Anti Marcion* 10; cf. Fee, *1 Corinthians*, p. 764.
10. For most commentators, vicarious baptism for the dead implies that the Corinthians held a mystical view of baptism, although the exact nature of the benefit thought to be accrued for the dead varies. Some options would include its necessity for participation in the eschatological kingdom (Fee, *1 Corinthians*, p. 767); for

participation in the resurrection (H. V. Martin, "Baptism for the Dead," *Expository Times* 54 [1942]: 193); or for salvation (Thomas Charles Edwards, *A Commentary on the First Epistle to the Corinthians* [London: Hodder and Stoughton, 1885], p. 423; and Orr and Walther, *1 Corinthians,* p. 337).

A few have suggested that vicarious baptism does not necessarily imply any benefit for the dead, but if this were the case one wonders why such a rite would have taken place (C. K. Barrett, *A Commentary on the First Epistle to the Corinthians,* Harper New Testament Commentary [New York: Harper and Row, 1968]; cf. Edwards, *A Commentary on the First Epistle to the Corinthians,* p. 424). Also the force of Paul's argument would be severely reduced if this practice had only sentimental value ("What will they do who are being baptized [as a sentimental gesture] for the dead?"). As a result, most commentators who espouse vicarious baptism hold that the practice involved a mystical view of baptism on the part of the Corinthians in which baptism was thought to have some measure of saving efficacy (e.g., Henry Leighton Goudge, *The First Epistle to the Corinthians* [London: Methuen, 1903], p. 149; Heinrich A. W. Meyer, *Meyer's Commentary on the New Testament,* trans. William P. Dickson [reprint, Winona Lake, IN: Alpha, 1980], p. 365; Jean Héring, *The First Epistle of Paul to the Corinthians,* trans. A. W. Heathcote and P. J. Allcock [London: Epworth, 1962], p. 169; and David K. Lowery, "1 Corinthians," in *The Bible Knowledge Commentary, New Testament,* ed. John F. Walvoord and Roy B. Zuck [Wheaton, IL: Victor, 1983], p. 544).

The problem with this position is that neither Paul nor any other New Testament writer hinted of a practice in which one's baptism could be substituted for another's baptism. The clear teaching in the New Testament is that baptism has a personal character, with each individual being called to identify himself personally with Christ in obedience to His command (Matt. 28:18–20).

Pauline teaching makes it clear that baptism lacks saving efficacy. Paul taught with great vigor that personal faith alone is the sole condition for justification (Rom. 3:28, 10:8–9; Gal. 2:16, 3:6, 8; Eph. 2:8–9). Baptism is simply an act of faith symbolizing a believer's identification and union with Christ in His death and resurrection (Rom. 6:3; Col. 2:12; Donald Guthrie, *New Testament Theology* [Downers Grove, IL: InterVarsity, 1981], p. 755; and George Eldon Ladd, *Theology of the New Testament* [Grand Rapids: Eerdmans, 1967], p. 548). In addition Guthrie suggests that Paul corrected the Corinthians for holding a superstitious view of baptism when he declared in 1 Corinthians 1:17, "For Christ did not send me to baptize, but to preach the gospel" (*New Testament Theology,* p. 755).

In light of Paul's teaching on baptism it is implausible that he would have referred to a practice so contrary to a fundamental aspect of his theology without commenting on it. This is especially true in 1 Corinthians, in which Paul sought to correct various errors in the church. The examples of believers taking each other to court and the issue of headcoverings seem insignificant in comparison to the error of vicarious baptism for the dead. Some have argued that Paul elsewhere referred to practices with which he did not agree. Often cited is Paul's appeal to dining in the temple of an idol in 1 Corinthians 8:10 (Leon Morris, *1 Corinthians,* Tyndale New Testament Commentaries [Grand Rapids: Eerdmans], p. 215; Charles Hodge, *An Exposition of the First Epistle to the Corinthians* [New York: Nisbet, 1868], p. 337; and Murray J. Harris, "Prepositions and Theology in the Greek New Testament," in *New International Dictionary of New Testament Theology,* 3:1208). In this case, however, Paul prevented any misunderstandings by specifically denouncing this practice in the course of his argument (1 Cor. 10:20). One would expect him to have done the same in 15:29 if he were referring to a practice of vicarious baptism.

11. Fredrick Godet, *Commentary on First Corinthians* (1889; reprint, Grand Rapids: Kregel, 1977), p. 818.
12. Ibid.. Godet counters this objection by listing examples of martyrs in the New Testament such as Stephen and James, concluding that there were many other cases of martyrdom that are not known. This argument from silence is doubtful in light of historical data suggesting that the church was experiencing a period of relative peace in Achaia at that time (Earle Cairns, *Christianity through the Centuries* [Grand Rapids: Zondervan, 1982], p. 90; and F. F. Bruce, *The Spreading Flame* [Grand Rapids: Eerdmans, 1982], pp. 21, 140).
13. Jerome Murphy-O'Connor, "Baptized for the Dead; 1 Cor. 15:29: A Corinthian Slogan?" *Revue Biblique* 88 (October 1981): 534.
14. Ibid., Walter Bauer, William F. Arndt, and F. Wilbur Gingrich, *A Greek-English Lexicon of the New Testament and Other Early Christian Literature,* 2d ed., rev. F. Wilbur Gingrich and Frederick W. Danker (Chicago: University of Chicago Press, 1979), p. 838.
15. Murphy-O'Connor suggests that the group in Corinth that was denying the resurrection was influenced by the pre-Gnostic views of Philo ("Baptized for the Dead," p. 536).
16. In addition the diatribe form of 1 Corinthians 15 is maintained. Verse 29 is a general statement referring to the troubles evangelists face, whereas verses 30–32 provide specific examples of these sufferings by referring to Paul's troubles in Ephesians and elsewhere (ibid., p. 533).
17. Fee, *1 Corinthians,* p. 765.
18. Carson lists three characteristics of a slogan: "They are short, they

are usually followed by sustained qualification, and the Pauline response is unambiguous and does not require the addition of words or phrases to make sense of the text" (D. A. Carson, *Showing the Spirit* [Grand Rapids: Baker, 1987], p. 55). For example the slogans in 6:12–13; 7:1b; and 8:1b meet these three criteria.

19. Paul would be saying in essence, "I agree that I am suffering for the spiritually dead (i.e., the unenlightened)," which would reinforce the Corinthians' gibe.

20. Paul usually used an adversative to distinguish the slogan from his response to it (1 Cor. 6:12, 13; 7:1; Fee, *1 Corinthians,* p. 765).

21. Ibid.

22. A. T. Robertson and Alfred Plummer, *A Critical and Exegetical Commentary on the First Epistle of St. Paul to the Corinthians,* International Critical Commentary (Edinburgh: Clark, 1975), p. 359; G. G. Findlay, "St. Paul's First Epistle to the Corinthians," in *The Expositor's Greek Testament,* ed. W. Robertson Nicoll, 4 vols. (Grand Rapids: Eerdmans, 1976), 2:931; R. C. H. Lenski, *The Interpretation of I and II Corinthians* (Minneapolis: Augsburg, 1963), p. 690; John F. MacArthur, *1 Corinthians* (Chicago: Moody, 1984), p. 425; and J. K. Howard, "Baptism for the Dead; A Study of 1 Corinthians 15:29," *Evangelical Quarterly* 37 (July–September 1965): 140.

23. M. Raeder, "Vikariatstaufe in I Kor. 15:29?" *Zeitschrift für die neutestamentliche Wissenschaft* 46 (1956): 256–60; and J. Jeremias, "Flesh and Blood Cannot Inherit the Kingdom of God," *New Testament Studies* 2 (1955–1956): 155.

24. F. Blass and A. Debrunner, *A Greek Grammar of the New Testament and Other Early Christian Literature,* trans. Robert W. Funk (Chicago: University of Chicago Press, 1961), p. 121; and Bauer, Arndt, and Gingrich, *A Greek-English Lexicon of the New Testament and Other Early Christian Literature,* p. 839.

25. Jeremias, "Flesh and Blood Cannot Inherit the Kingdom of God," p. 155.

26. Findlay, *1 Corinthians,* p. 931.

27. See the discussion below on ὑπέρ; and Fee, *1 Corinthians,* p. 763, n. 11.

28. Jeremias, "Flesh and Blood Cannot Inherit the Kingdom of God," p. 156; Raeder, "Vikariatstaufe in I Kor. 15:29?" pp. 258–60; Rudolf Schnackenburg, *Baptism in the Thought of St. Paul,* trans. G. R. Beasley-Murray (New York: Herder and Herder, 1964), p. 102.

29. Jeremias, "Flesh and Blood Cannot Inherit the Kingdom of God," p. 155.

30. This sense is evident in 2 Corinthians 1:6 and may be present in Philippians 2:13 and 1 Corinthians 15:3 (Blass and Debrunner, *A Greek Grammar of the New Testament and Other Early Christian Literature,* p. 121; Conzelmann, *1 Corinthians,* p. 276; Beasley-

Murray, *Baptism in the New Testament,* p. 186; cf. Bauer, Arndt, and Gingrich, *A Greek-English Lexicon of the New Testament and Other Early Christian Literature,* p. 839; cf. H. E. Dana and Julius R. Mantey, *A Manual Grammar of the Greek New Testament* [New York: Macmillan, 1957], pp. 111–12).

31. Meyer, *Meyer's Commentary on the New Testament,* p. 367.
32. That is, "What will they do who are being baptized to take the place of dead believers?" (A. G. Moseley, "Baptized for the Dead," *Review and Expositor* 49 [1952]: 57–61; and S. Lewis Johnson, Jr., "1 Corinthians," in *The Wycliffe Bible Commentary* [Chicago: Moody, 1962], p. 1257).
33. See Philemon 13; cf. H. Riesenfeld, "ὑπέρ," in *Theological Dictionary of the New Testament,* 8:513.
34. Edwards, *A Commentary on the First Epistle to the Corinthians,* p. 422. In addition this designation could rightly apply to all believers since all new believers are in a sense replacing the previous generation of believers. Paul, however, used the third person in this verse to indicate that he had a specific group of individuals in mind as opposed to all believers ("what will they do") (Meyer, *Meyer's Commentary on the New Testament,* p. 367).
35. Evans, *1 Corinthians,* p. 364; Moseley, "Baptized for the Dead," pp. 57–58; and Albert Barnes, *Barnes' Notes on the New Testament* (reprint, Grand Rapids: Kregel, 1962), p. 793.
36. Bauer, Arndt, and Gingrich, *A Greek-English Lexicon of the New Testament and Other Early Christian Literature,* p. 839.
37. Robertson and Plummer, *A Critical and Exegetical Commentary on the First Epistle of St. Paul to the Corinthians,* p. 359; and Edwards, *A Commentary on the First Epistle to the Corinthians,* p. 432.
38. Tertullian commented on this passage on two occasions and espoused the interpretation of Christian baptism for their dead or dying bodies (*Anti Marcion* 10; cf. *De Resurrectione Carnis* 48; cf. K. C. Thompson, "1 Cor. 15:29 and Baptism for the Dead," *Studia Evangelica* 2 [1964]: 654). Chrysostom argued that Paul was referring here to Christian baptism for their own dying bodies (*Homily* 40). The other Greek fathers generally espoused a similar interpretation (Evans, *1 Corinthians,* p. 373; Philip Schaff, ed., *Nicene and Post Nicene Fathers,* vol. 12: *St. Chrysostom—Homilies on I & II Corinthians* [Grand Rapids: Eerdmans, 1956], pp. 244, n. 3; 245.).
39. John Calvin, *I and II Corinthians,* trans. John Pringle (Grand Rapids: Baker, 1979), p. 38; John Albert Bengel, *Gnomon of the New Testament,* trans. James Bryce, 7th. ed., 3 vols. (Edinburgh: Clark, 1873), 3:329. There is some evidence of deathbed conversion in the early church (Calvin, *I and II Corinthians,* p. 37; Chrysostom, *Homily* 40).
40. O'Neill proposes accepting the reading αὐτῶν τῶν νεκρῶν (codex

69) for τῶν νεκρῶν in order to support his suggestion that in verse 29 the meaning of νεκρός approaches that of the Hellenistic form τα νέκρα, "corpses": "What do those hope to achieve who are baptized for their dying bodies?" (O'Neill, "1 Corinthians 15:29," p. 311). The major problem with this suggestion is that this reading occurs only in codex 69 and that O'Neill's deduction from this variant is tenuous (i.e., from "corpses" to "their own dead bodies"), which he himself admits. For further criticism of this view, see Fee, *1 Corinthians*, p. 766.

41. Bauer, Arndt, and Gingrich, *A Greek-English Lexicon of the New Testament and Other Early Christian Literature*, pp. 534–35.
42. Thompson, "1 Cor. 15:29 and Baptism for the Dead," p. 647; Foschini, "Those Who Are Baptized for the Dead"; and F. J. Badcock, "Baptism for the Dead," *Expository Times* 54 (1942–43): 330.
43. Foschini, "Those Who Are Baptized for the Dead," pp. 278–79.
44. Thompson, "1 Cor. 15:29 and Baptism for the Dead," p. 651.
45. Ibid., p. 649; Foschini, "Those Who Are Baptized for the Dead," p. 278.
46. For example Foschini suggests that his punctuation breaks the connection between baptism and the prepositional phrase "for the dead" (ibid.). However, his interpretation still hinges on the understanding of ὑπέρ (i.e., the second question could still be, "Is it for the benefit of the dead?"). In addition Foschini's proposal that ὑπέρ is equivalent to εἰς ("into") is doubtful; this nuance is evident only in classical Greek (Bauer, Arndt, and Gingrich, *A Greek-English Lexicon of the New Testament and Other Early Christian Literature*, p. 838). Foschini strains to argue for this use by appealing to a few extrabiblical sources ("Those Who Are Baptized for the Dead," p. 281).
47. Fee, *1 Corinthians*, p. 11.
48. The subordinating conjunction ἐπεὶ is probably functioning as an apodosis in an elliptical condition where the protasis is suppressed (A. T. Robertson, *A Grammar of the Greek New Testament in the Light of Historical Research*, 4th ed. [Nashville: Broadman, 1934], p. 1025). The probable ellipsis in this case would be the first-class conditional statement, "If all that I, Paul, have just said is not true, then what will they do" (Lenski, *The Interpretation of I and II Corinthians*, p. 688; and Fee, *1 Corinthians*, p. 763).
49. During the classical period the word βαπτίζω was used in the literal (active) sense of "to suffer shipwreck," "to perish," or "to drown." In the Septuagint the word occurs only four times and both the literal and figurative senses are present (cf. Lev. 6:28; Isa. 21:4). In the Koine Greek period the usage of the word βαπτίζω continued with both the literal (active) and figurative (passive) meanings, with the active sense of "to immerse" becoming especially prevalent. In a few cases the literal meaning was applied

to the sacred washings of the mystery religions. However, the figurative sense continued as βαπτίζω is used to refer to "going under" with respect to sleep or intoxication and "perishing" (A. Oepke, "βάπτω, βαπτίζω," in *Theological Dictionary of the New Testament,* 1:536; and G. R. Beasley-Murray, "βαπτίζω," in *New International Dictionary of New Testament Theology,* 1:144).

50. This view requires a change in the meaning of νεκρῶν within the verse under question (see discussion on νεκρός).

51. Godet, *1 Corinthians,* p. 818.

52. Paul used βαπτίζω 13 times (10 times in 1 Cor.). He utilized the word literally with reference to initiatory baptism eight times (six times in 1 Cor.), excluding the two occurrences in 15:29. In the remaining three occurrences Paul used this term in a non-standard way with reference to a believer being identified with Christ in His death (Rom. 6:3), the Israelites being identified with Moses (1 Cor. 10:2), and believers being immersed by the Spirit of God (1 Cor. 12:13).

53. In other words this interpretation is less repetitive, since verses 29 and 30 do not both refer to the apostles' suffering.

54. W. Harold Mare, "1 Corinthians," in *The Expositor's Bible Commentary,* 12 vols. (Grand Rapids: Zondervan, 1977), 10:287.

55. Fee, *1 Corinthians,* p. 763, n. 15.

56. Murphy-O'Connor, "Baptized for the Dead," pp. 536–37; cf. Fee, *1 Corinthians,* p. 765.

57. Calvin, *1 Corinthians,* p. 36; O'Neill, "1 Corinthians 15:29," p. 310; and Bengel, *Gnomon of the New Testament,* p. 330.

58. R. Bultmann, "νεκρός," in *Theological Dictionary of the New Testament,* 4:893; cf. Matthew 8:22; John 5:21; Ephesians 5:14.

59. Bauer, Arndt, and Gingrich, *A Greek-English Lexicon of the New Testament and Other Early Christian Literature,* pp. 534–35.

60. O'Neill, "1 Corinthians 15:29," pp. 310–11.

61. Blass and Debrunner, *A Greek Grammar of the New Testament and Other Early Christian Literature,* p. 133.

62. Anarthrous constructions (i.e., the dead in general) are found in verses 12, 13, 15, 16, 20, 21, and 29, whereas articular constructions (i.e., the Christian dead) are found in verses 29, 35, 42, and 52 (Raeder, "Vikariatstaufe in I Kor. 15:29?" pp. 258–59; Jeremias, "Flesh and Blood Cannot Inherit the Kingdom of God," p. 155; and Howard, "Baptism for the Dead," p. 140.

63. Beasley-Murray, "βαπτίζω," 1:146.

64. Fee, 1 Corinthians, p. 767; Goudge, *The First Epistle to the Corinthians,* pp. 149–50; and C. K. Barrett, *A Commentary on the First Epistle to the Corinthians* (New York: Harper and Row, 1968), p. 364.

65. The distinction between the two ideas becomes blurred at times since the idea of representation can include substitution and vice versa. For example in the passages relating to Christ's vicarious

sacrifice, Christ is presented as both the substitute and representative
(Harris, "Prepositions and Theology in the Greek New Testament,"
3:1196–97).

66. Fee, *1 Corinthians,* p. 763; Maximilian Zerwick, *Biblical Greek,*
trans. and ed. Joseph Smith (Rome: Pontificii Instituti Biblici,
1963), p. 529; George B. Winer, *Greek Grammar of the New
Testament* (Edinburgh: Clark, 1870), p. 479; C. F. D. Moule, *An
Idiom Book of New Testament Greek,* 2d ed. (Cambridge:
Cambridge University Press, 1953), p. 64; and Dana and Mantey,
A Manual Grammar of the Greek New Testament, p. 111.

67. Fee, *1 Corinthians,* p. 764; Conzelmann, *1 Corinthians,* p. 227;
Beasley-Murray, *Baptism in the New Testament,* p. 187; and
Riesenfeld, "ὑπέρ," 8:512–13.

68. Fee, *1 Corinthians,* p. 764.

69. That is, "What will they do who are being baptized to take the
place of dead believers?" (Johnson, "1 Corinthians," p. 1257).

70. Blass and Debrunner, *A Greek Grammar of the New Testament
and Other Early Christian Literature,* p. 121; Lenski, *1 Corinthians,*
p. 690; see 2 Corinthians 12:8; Romans 15:9; cf. Bauer, Arndt,
and Gingrich, *A Greek-English Lexicon of the New Testament and
Other Early Christian Literature,* p. 839; and Riesenfeld, "ὑπέρ,"
8:514.

71. Cf. Acts 5:41. Here ὅτι is used in the place of ὑπέρ in a parallel
construction.

72. Riesenfeld, "ὑπὲρ," 8:514–15.

73. Bauer, Arndt, and Gingrich, *A Greek-English Lexicon of the New
Testament and Other Early Christian Literature,* p. 132.

74. Harris, "Prepositions and Theology in the Greek New Testament,"
3:1196–97; and Fee, *1 Corinthians,* p. 763.

75. The causal sense is particularly evident in Acts 9:16 and 21:13,
since ὑπέρ is substituting for ὅτι in the parallel construction found
in Acts 5:41 (Riesenfeld, "ὑπέρ," 8:514).

76. Jeremias, "Flesh and Blood Cannot Inherit the Kingdom of God,"
p. 156.

77. Beasley-Murray highlights the rarity of this usage (*Baptism in the
New Testament,* p. 186). Blass and Debrunner suggest that this
sense is found in Philippians 2:13 (*A Greek Grammar of the New
Testament and Other Early Christian Literature,* p. 231). However,
Riesenfeld and Harris translate the only other occurrence of ὑπέρ
in 1 Corinthians 15 with a final sense: "for the expiation of our
sins," verse 3 (Riesenfeld, "ὑπέρ," 8:514; and Harris, "Prepositions
and Theology in the Greek New Testament," 3:1197).

78. That is, "baptized in order to be united with their deceased Christian
relatives at the resurrection" (Jeremias, "Flesh and Blood Cannot
Inherit the Kingdom of God," p. 156).

79. Schnackenburg gives the example of 1 Corinthians 15:3 and
Galatians 1:4, where the statement "Christ died for our sins" is

interpreted to mean "Christ died in order to redeem us from our sins" (*Baptism in the Thought of St. Paul*, p. 102).

80. Martin Luther, *Luther's Works*, ed. Hilton Oswald, trans. Martin Bertram (St. Louis; Concordia, 1973), vol. 28: *I Corinthians 7–15*, pp. 146–54. This view is also suggested with reservation by F. W. Grosheide, *1st Epistle to the Corinthians*, New International Commentary on the New Testament (Grand Rapids: Eerdmans, 1974), p. 373.

81. Bauer, Arndt, and Gingrich, *A Greek-English Lexicon of the New Testament and Other Early Christian Literature*, p. 838; and Riesenfield, "ὑπέρ," 8:507–8.

82. A. T. Robertson, *A Grammar of the Greek New Testament in the Light of Historical Research* (Nashville: Broadman, 1934), p. 632; and Barnes, *Barnes' Notes on the New Testament*, p. 793. This nuance also occurs with a person as the object as in John 1:30 (Riesenfeld, "ὑπὲρ," 8:514).

83. Robertson and Plummer, *A Critical and Exegetical Commentary on the First Epistle of St. Paul to the Corinthians*, p. 359; and Edwards, *A Commentary on the First Epistle to the Corinthians*, p. 423.

84. Fee, *1 Corinthians*, p. 763.

85. See n. 10.

Chapter 11

1. For example, Edwin Hatch, *The Influence of Greek Ideas and Usages upon the Christian Church* [London: Williams & Norgate, 1890); Richard Reitzenstein, *Hellenistic Mystery Religions: Their Basic Ideas and Significance* (Pittsburgh: Pickwick, 1978). For a discussion on proper methodology in studying the mystery religions see Bruce Metzger, "Methodology in the Study of the Mystery Religions and Early Christianity," in *Historical and Literary Studies, Pagan, Jewish, and Christian*, vol. 8: *New Testament Tools and Studies* (Grand Rapids: Eerdmans, 1968), pp. 1–24. Bruce Metzger's *A Classified Bibliography of the Graeco-Roman Mystery Religions 1924–1973* (forthcoming) will be an important tool for mystery religion research.

2. Walter Schmithals, *Gnosticism in Corinth*, trans. John E. Steely (Nashville: Abingdon, 1971), pp. 141–301. That there are elements of Gnosticism at Corinth is certain, but this is due not to accepting a system of beliefs but to the intermixing of ideas in the Hellenistic Age. All the developed systems of thought in the first-century Mediterranean world are the children of one mother—Hellenistic syncretism. Yamauchi discusses Gnosticism versus incipient Gnosticism in the first century A.D. (Edwin M. Yamauchi, *Pre-Christian Gnosticism* (Grand Rapids: Eerdmans, 1973]). The weakness of Yamauchi's work is the lack of interaction with primary Gnostic sources.

3. Bruce says, "It would be anachronistic to call these [enthusiasts at Corinth] 'men of the Spirit' Gnostics: that is a term best reserved for adherents of the various schools of Gnosticism that flourished in the second century A.D." (F. F. Bruce, *Paul: Apostle of the Heart Set Free* (Grand Rapids: Eerdmans, 1977], p. 261).

4. Carl Clemen, *Religions of the World*, trans. A. K. Dallas (London: Harrap, 1931), p. 342; cf. Carl Clemen, *Der Einfluss der Mysterienreligionen auf das aelteste Christentum* (Giessen: Töpelmann, 1913), p. 86.

5. Karl Heussi, *Kompendium der Kirchengeschichte* (Tübingen: Mohr, 1957), p. 75.

6. P. D. Pahl, "The Mystery Religions," *Australian Theological Review* 20 (June 1949): 20.

7. A. S. Geden, *Mithraism* (London: Macmillan, 1925), p. 4; cf. also for this view Kenneth Scott Latourette, *A History of Christianity* (New York: Harper & Brothers, 1953), p. 259.

8. Albert Schweitzer, *Paul and His Interpreters*, trans. G. W. Montgomery (New York: Macmillan, 1950), p. 189.

9. Karl Pruemm, "Mystery Religions, Greco-Oriental," in *New Catholic Encyclopedia*, pp. 163–64.

10. Metzger, "Methodology in the Study of the Mystery Religions and Early Christianity," p. 11.

11. Frederick C. Grant, "Greek Religion in the Hellenistic-Roman Age," *Anglican Theological Review* 33 (1951): 26.

12. S. A. Cook, F. E. Adcock, and M. P. Charlesworth, *The Augustan Empire: 44 B.C.–A.D. 70*, vol. 10 of *The Cambridge Ancient History* (Cambridge: Cambridge University Press, 1963), p. 504.

13. P. Gardner, "Mysteries," in *Encyclopaedia of Religion and Ethics*, n.d., 9:81.

14. H. J. Rose, *Religion in Greece and Rome* (New York: Harper & Brothers, 1959), p. 278.

15. Williston Walker, *A History of the Christian Church* (New York: Scribner's Sons, 1970), p. 56.

16. George Frazer, *The Golden Bough* (New York: Macmillan, 1963), p. 450.

17. Peter Hoyle, *Delphi* (London: Cassel, 1967), p. 76.

18. Martin P. Nilsson, "The Baachic Mysteries of the Roman Age," *Harvard Theological Review* 46 (October 1953): 175–85.

19. Cleon L. Rogers, "The Dionysian Background of Ephesians 5:18," *Bibliotheca Sacra* 136 (July–September 1979): 249–57.

20. Oscar Broneer, "Paul and the Pagan Cults at Isthmia," *Harvard Theological Review* 44 (1971): 182.

21. Pruemm, "Mystery Religions, Greco-Oriental," p. 161.

22. Hoyle, *Delphi*, p. 73.

23. Oscar Broneer, "Corinth," *Biblical Archaeologist* 14 (1951): 84.

24. Apollo was worshiped as the Pythian god at the shrine of Delphi (known also as Pytho). He was especially associated with oracles

(F. F. Bruce, *Commentary on the Book of Acts* [Grand Rapids: Eerdmans, 1954], p. 332).

25. Bruce, *Paul: Apostle of the Heart Set Free*, p. 260.
26. Edith Hamilton, *The Greek Way* (New York: Time, 1930), p. 275.
27. Gardner, "Mysteries," 9:77.
28. In addition to the sources given in this article see Samuel Dill, *Roman Society: From Nero to Marcus Aurelius* (New York: World, 1956); Pruemm, "Mystery Religions, Greco-Oriental," pp. 153–64; also the thorough bibliography in *Sourcebook of Texts for the Comparative Study of the Gospels*, ed. David L. Dungan and David R. Cartlidge, 3d ed. (Missoula, MT: Scholars, 1973).
29. W. R. Inge, "Ecstasy," in *Encyclopedia of Religion and Ethics*, 5:158.
30. Fredrick C. Conybeare, "Gift of Tongues," in *Encyclopedia Britannica*, 1911 ed., 27:10.
31. H. A. A. Kennedy, *St. Paul and the Mystery Religions* (London: Hodder & Stoughton, n.d.), pp. 280–81.
32. Eduard Lohse, *The New Testament Environment*, trans. John E. Steely (Nashville: Abingdon, 1976), p. 240.
33. "They represent them, one and all, as a kind of inspired people and as subject to Bacchic [Dyonysian] frenzy, and, in the guise of minister, as inspiring terror at the celebration of the sacred rites by means of wardances accompanied by uproar and noise and cymbals and drums and also by flute and outcry. . . ." This was stated by Strabo. (Richard Kroeger and Catherine Kroeger, "Pandemonium and Silence at Corinth," *Reformed Journal* 28 [June 1978]: 7).
34. Alexander Rattray Hay, *What Is Wrong in the Church?* vol. 2: *Counterfeit Speaking in Tongues* (Audubon, NJ: New Testament Missionary Union. n.d.), p. 26.
35. Cited from Kroeger and Kroeger, "Pandemonium and Silence at Corinth," p. 7.
36. Ibid., pp. 9–10.
37. Martin P. Nilsson, *A History of Greek Religion*, 2d ed. (New York: Norton, 1964), p. 205.
38. Kennedy, *St. Paul and the Mystery Religions*, p. 160.
39. Robert H. Gundry, "'Ecstatic Utterance' (N.E.B.)?" *Journal of Theological Studies* 17 (October 1966): 299–307.
40. Charles R. Smith, *Tongues in Biblical Perspective* (Winona Lake, IN: BMH, 1973), p. 26.
41. Gundry, "Ecstatic Utterance (N.E.B.)?" p. 305 (italics added).
42. Cited from D. W. B. Robinson, "Charismata versus Pneumatika: Paul's Method of Discussion," *Reformed Theological Review* 21 (May–August 1972): 49–50.
43. Hay, *What Is Wrong in the Church?* p. 43.
44. Hurd lists several slogans possibly used by the Corinthians which Paul quoted from their letter to him. To each of these Paul gave a

swift correction (John Hurd, *The Origin of I Corinthians* [New York: Seabury, 1965], p. 67):
> 6:12; 10:23 "All things are lawful."
> 6:13 "Food is meant for the stomach and the stomach for food."
> 7:1 "It is well for a man not to touch a woman."
> 8:1 "All of us possess knowledge."
> 8:4 "An idol has no real existence. There is no God but one."
> 8:5–6 "For although there may be so-called gods in heaven or on earth (as indeed there are many 'gods' and many 'lords') yet for us there is one God, the Father, from whom we exist and one Lord, Jesus Christ, through whom are all things and through whom we exist."
> 8:8 "Food will not commend us to God. We are no worse off if we do not eat, and no better off if we do."
> 11:2 "We remember you in everything and maintain the traditions even as you delivered them to us [reversing the pronouns]." Those statements that seem to be from the Corinthians are 6:12 (10:23); 6:13; 7:1; 8:1; 11:2. The NIV indicates that most of these are statements that Paul quotes. Also the un-Pauline use πνευματικὸς in 1 Corinthians 12:1; 14:1–5; and 14:37 indicates a similar device. Especially is this true in 12:1, which Paul immediately follows with a correction.

45. Πνευματικοί in 1 Corinthians 12–14 is always in a speaking context (cf. 1 Cor. 12:1; 14:1, 37). Also there is obviously a contrast between πνευματικά and προφητεύητε in 14:1 and the connected contrast between γλώσση and προφητεύων in the following two verses. Pearson is typical of seeing πνευματικῶν of 12:1 as equal to χαρισμάτων in 12:4 (Birger Albert Pearson, *The Pneumatikos-Psychikos Terminology in I Corinthians* (Missoula, MT: Society of Biblical Literature, Dissertation Series no. 12, 1973], p 50). Ellis narrows the term to prophetic gifts of inspired speech and discernment and not simply equivalent to χαρίσματα (E. Earle Ellis, *Prophecy and Hermeneutics in Early Christianity* [Grand Rapids: Eerdmans, 1978], pp. 24, 68).

46. Howard M. Ervin, *These Are Not Drunken as Ye Suppose* (Plainfield. NJ: Logos International, 1968), p. 125.

47. Frederick Dale Bruner, *A Theology of the Holy Spirit* (Grand Rapids: Eerdmans, 1970), pp. 286–87.

48. John Stanley Gerlicher, "An Exegetical Approach to First Corinthians Twelve to Fourteen" (Th.M. thesis, Western Conservative Baptist Seminary, 1966), pp. 24–25.

49. In *Contra Celsum* (written about A.D. 246) Origen noted that the Orphites asked those who would enter their churches to curse Jesus (F. Godet, *Commentary on the First Epistle of Paul to the Corinthians*, trans. A. Cusin, 2 vols. [Grand Rapids: Zondervan, 1957], 2:187).

50. Anthony David Palma, "Tongues and Prophecy—A Comparative Study in Charismata" (S.T.M. thesis, Concordia Theological Seminary, 1966), p. 72. See also William F. Orr and James Arthur Walter, *1 Corinthians*, Anchor Bible (Garden City, NY: Doubleday, 1976), p. 278.
51. Ervin, *These Are Not Drunken as Ye Suppose*, p. 200.
52. This writer takes ἕκαστος here in the distributive sense.
53. James Moffatt, *The First Epistle of Paul to the Corinthians*, Moffatt New Testament Commentary (New York: Harper & Brothers, n.d.), p. 211.
54. Ervin, *These Are Not Drunken as Ye Suppose*, p. 200.

Chapter 12

1. John Calvin, *The Epistles of Paul the Apostle to the Galatians, Ephesians, Philippians and Colossians*, trans. T. H. L. Parker, Calvin's New Testament Commentaries 11, ed. David W. Torrance and Thomas F. Torrance (1556; reprint, Grand Rapids: Eerdmans, 1965), pp. 4–7.
2. Martin Luther, *Commentary on Galatians*, trans. Erasmus Middleton, ed. John P. Fallowes (London: Harrison Trust, 1850; reprint, Grand Rapids: Kregel, 1979), p. 2.
3. Ferdinand C. Baur, *Ausgewählte Werke in Einzelausgaben*, ed. K. Scholder (reprint, Stuttgart: Frommann, 1963), 1:49.
4. Ferdinand C. Baur, *Paul, His Life and Works*, trans. E. Zeller, 2 vols. (London: Williams and Norgate, 1875), 1:113, 129–30.
5. Walter Schmithals, *Paul and the Gnostics*, trans. John E. Steely (Nashville: Abingdon, 1972), p. 13.
6. For example, Helmut Koester, *Introduction to the New Testament*, vol. 2: *History and Literature of Early Christianity* (New York: de Gruyter, and Philadelphia: Fortress, 1982), pp. 118–19.
7. For example, Werner Georg Kümmel, *Introduction to the New Testament*, rev. English ed., trans. Howard Clark Kee (Nashville: Abingdon, 1975), pp. 298–301.
8. For example, George Howard, *Paul: Crisis in Galatia*, Society for New Testament Monograph Series 35 (Cambridge: Cambridge University Press, 1979), pp. 1–19.
9. For example, Ronald Y. Fung, *The Epistle to the Galatians*, New International Commentary on the New Testament (Grand Rapids: Eerdmans, 1988), pp. 13–19.
10. For example, J. Louis Martyn, "A Law-Observant Mission to Gentiles: The Background of Galatians," *Scottish Journal of Theology* 38 (1985): 307–24, and John M. G. Barclay, "Mirror-Reading a Polemical Letter: Galatians as a Test Case," *Journal for the Study of the New Testament* 31 (1988): 73–93.
11. Johannes Munck, *Paul and the Salvation of Mankind* (Richmond, VA: Knox, 1959), pp. 87–134.

12. Ibid., p. 87.
13. Ibid., pp. 87–89.
14. A. E. Harvey, "The Opposition to Paul," *Studia Evangelica* 4 (1968): 319–32.
15. Ibid., p. 324.
16. Ibid., pp. 327–29.
17. Wilhelm Lütgert, *Gesetz und Geist: Eine Untersuchung zur Vorgeschichte des Galaterbriefes.* Beiträge zur Förderung christlicher Theologie, vol. 22, book 6 (Gütersloh: Bertelsmann, 1919).
18. Luther, *Commentary on Galatians,* pp. 325–29.
19. Lütgert, *Gesetz und Geist,* p. 16.
20. Ibid., p. 9.
21. Ibid., pp. 27–28.
22. Ibid., pp. 14–19.
23. James H. Ropes, *The Singular Problem of the Epistle to the Galatians,* Harvard Theological Studies 14 (Cambridge: Harvard University Press, 1929).
24. Ibid., p. 38.
25. Douglas K. Fletcher, *The Singular Argument of Paul's Letter to the Galatians* (Ph.D. diss., Princeton Theological Seminary, 1982), p. 42.
26. Ropes, *The Singular Problem of the Epistle to the Galatians,* p. 10.
27. As noted by Bernard H. Brinsmead, *Galatians—Dialogical Response to Opponents,* Society of Biblical Literature Dissertation Series 65 (Missoula, MT: Scholars, 1982), p. 10.
28. Walter Schmithals, *Paul and James,* trans. Dorothea M. Barton, Studies in Biblical Theology, no. 46 (Naperville, IL: Allenson, 1965), pp. 103–17; idem, *Paul and the Gnostics,* pp. 13–64; and idem, "Judaisten in Galatien?" *Zeitschrift für die neutestamentliche Wissenschaft* 74 (1983): 27–58.
29. Schmithals, *Paul and the Gnostics,* p. 59, n. 134.
30. Ibid., p. 17.
31. Ibid., p. 18.
32. Willi Marxsen, *Introduction to the New Testament,* trans. G. Buswell (Philadelphia: Fortress, 1968), p. 53. In fairness to Marxsen, it should be noted that he changed his view in the fourth edition of *Einleitung in das Neue Testament* (Gütersloh: Mohr, 1978), pp. 56–71 to one similar to Hans Dieter Betz (to be discussed shortly).
33. See Edwin D. Hirsch, Jr., *Validity in Interpretation* (New Haven, CT: Yale University Press, 1967), pp. 19–23.
34. Frederic R. Crownfield, "The Singular Problem of the Dual Galatians," *Journal of Biblical Literature* 64 (1945): 491–500.
35. Ibid., pp. 492–93.
36. Ibid., p. 493, and Schmithals, *Paul and the Gnostics,* pp. 44–46.
37. Heinrich Schlier, *Der Brief an die Galater,* 5th ed.,

Kritischexegetischer Kommentar über das Neue Testament 7 (Göttingen: Vandenhoeck & Ruprecht, 1971).
38. Ibid., pp. 21–24.
39. Brinsmead, *Galatians—Dialogical Response to Opponents,* pp. 164–78.
40. For example, David E. Aune, "Review of *Galatians—Dialogical Response to Opponents,*" *Catholic Biblical Quarterly* 46 (1984): 145–47; E. A. Russell, "Convincing or Merely Curious? A Look at Some Recent Writing on Galatians," *Irish Biblical Studies* 6 (1984): 156–76; and Barclay, "Mirror-Reading a Polemical Letter: Galatians as a Test Case," pp. 81–83.
41. Dieter Georgi, *Die Geschichte der Kollekte des Paulus für Jerusalem,* Theologische Forschung, vol. 38 (Hamburg: Evangelischer, 1965), p. 35.
42. Schmithals, *Paul and the Gnostics,* p. 14.
43. Georgi, *Die Geschichte der Kollekte des Paulus für Jerusalem,* p. 35.
44. Klaus Wegenast, *Der Verstandnis der Tradition bei Paulus und in den Deuteropaulinen,* Wissenschaftliche Monographien zum Alten und Neuen Testament, no. 8 (Neukirchen: Neukirchener, 1962), p. 39.
45. For example, Schmithals, *Paul and the Gnostics,* pp. 51–55.
46. Hans Dieter Betz, *Galatians: A Commentary on Paul's Letter to the Churches in Galatia,* Hermenia (Philadelphia: Fortress, 1979), p. 154.
47. This view was first set forth in Hans Dieter Betz, "2 Cor. 6:14–7:1: An Anti-Pauline Fragment?" *Journal of Biblical Literature* 92 (1973): 88–108, and in idem, "Spirit, Freedom, and Law: Paul's Message to the Galatian Churches," *Svensk exegetisk årsbok* 39 (1974): 154–55.
48. Betz, *Galatians: A Commentary on Paul's Letter to the Churches in Galatia,* pp. 14–25.
49. Ibid., p. 273.
50. Fletcher, *The Singular Argument of Paul's Letter to the Galatians,* pp. 82–83.
51. Schlier, *Der Brief an die Galater,* pp. 20–24.
52. Barclay, "Mirror Reading a Polemical Letter: Galatians as a Test Case," pp. 74–79.
53. Ibid., pp. 79–83.
54. Ibid., pp. 84–86.
55. David T. Gordon, "The Problem at Galatia," *Interpretation* 41 (1987): 33–34.
56. E. W. Bullinger, *Figures of Speech Used in the Bible Explained and Illustrated* (London: Messrs. Eyre and Spottiswoode, 1898; reprint, Grand Rapids: Baker, 1968), p. 388.
57. Hans D. Betz, "The Literary Composition and Function of Paul's Letter to the Galatians," *New Testament Studies* 21 (1975): 355.

58. Betz, *Galatians: A Commentary on Paul's Letter to the Churches in Galatia,* p. 39.
59. Ibid., p. 313.
60. J. Louis Martyn, "Apocalyptic Antinomies in Paul's Letter to the Galatians," *New Testament Studies* 31 (1985): 410–24.
61. Brinsmead, *Galatians—Dialogical Response to Opponents,* pp. 58–67.
62. Martyn, "Apocalyptic Antinomies in Paul's Letter to the Galatians," p. 421.
63. Schmithals, *Paul and the Gnostics,* p. 41.
64. Betz, *Galatians: A Commentary on Paul's Letter to the Churches in Galatia,* pp. 16–23.
65. Ibid., p. 25.
66. Ibid.
67. Ibid.
68. Ibid.
69. Robert Jewett, "Agitators and the Galatian Congregation," *New Testament Studies* 17 (1971): 200–201.
70. R. McL. Wilson, "Gnostics—in Galatia?" *Studia Evangelica* 4 (1968): 358–67, and Jewett, "Agitators and the Galatian Congregation," pp. 199–200. They both point out that the meager information about these late 1st-century and early 2d-century syncretists represents a later stage of development in Gnosticism and should not be read back into the mid-1st century. Also the later Gnostic interest in circumcision as a symbol of transcendence over the bodily sphere is not comparable to the Judaizers' emphasis of it as an ethnic identifier essential for salvation.
71. See R. Travers Herford, ed., *The Ethics of the Talmud: Sayings of the Fathers,* 3d ed. (Cincinnati: Jewish Institute of Religion, 1945; reprint, New York: Schocken, 1962), p. 70, and I. Abrahams, *Studies in Pharisaism and the Gospels, First and Second Series* (Cambridge: Cambridge University Press, 1917, 1924; reprint, New York: KTAV, 1967), pp. 4–14.
72. Translation from Philip Blackman, ed. and trans., *Mishnayoth,* 7 vols., 2d ed. (New York: Judaica, 1977), 4:508.
73. Jacob Neusner, ed. and trans., *Scriptures of the Oral Torah* (San Francisco: Harper & Row, 1987), p. 71.
74. For example, Abrahams, *Studies in Pharisaism and the Gospels,* p. 7, and M. B. Lerner, "The Tractate Avot," in *Literature of the Sages, Part One,* ed. Shmuel Safrai, Compendia Rerum Iudaicarum ad Novum Testamentum, vol. 2.3a (Philadelphia: Fortress, 1987), pp. 265–66.
75. Several writers accurately see the continuity in Paul's argument from Galatians 1–4 to 5–6 in addressing the fleshliness of the Judaizers. These include Howard, *Paul: Crisis in Galatia,* pp. 11–17; Brinsmead, *Galatians—Dialogical Response to Opponents,* pp. 164–92; and D. J. Lull, *The Spirit in Galatia: Paul's Interpretation*

of PNEUMA as Divine Power, Society of Biblical Literature Dissertation Series 49 (Chico, CA: Scholars, 1980), pp. 113–30.

76. Barclay, "Mirror-Reading a Polemical Letter: Galatians as a Test Case," pp. 86–90, and idem, *Obeying the Truth: A Study of Paul's Ethics in Galatians,* Studies of the New Testament and Its World, ed. John Riches (Edinburgh: Clark, 1988), pp. 36–74.

77. Barclay, "Mirror-Reading a Polemical Letter: Galatians as a Test Case," p. 86.

78. Ibid., p. 87.

79. For example, Jewett, "Agitators and the Galatian Congregation," pp. 209–12.

80. Ibid., pp. 204–8.

81. Barclay, "Mirror-Reading a Polemical Letter: Galatians as a Test Case," p. 88.

82. Fung, *The Epistle to the Galatians,* pp. 6–7.

83. Martyn, "A Law-Observant Mission to Gentiles: The Background of Galatians," p. 323.

84. Ibid., pp. 310–12.

85. For example, C. K. Barrett, "The Allegory of Abraham, Sarah, and Hagar in the Argument of Galatians," in *Essays on Paul* (Philadelphia: Westminster, 1982), pp. 154–70, and Daniel H. King, "Paul and the Tannaim: A Study in Galatians," *Westminster Theological Journal* 45 (1983): 361–69.

86. Kirsopp Lake, "Paul's Controversies," in *The Beginnings of Christianity,* ed. F. J. Foakes Jackson and Kirsopp Lake, 5 vols. (London: Macmillan, 1920–1933; reprint, Grand Rapids: Baker, 1979), 5:215.

87. Joseph B. Tyson, "Paul's Opponents in Galatia," *Novum Testamentum* 10 (1968): 252–54.

88. Munck, *Paul and the Salvation of Mankind,* pp. 87–100, 130–34.

89. For example, Martyn, "A Law-Observant Mission to Gentiles: The Background of Galatians," p. 313.

90. John Knox, *Chapters in a Life of Paul,* rev. ed., ed. Douglas R. A. Hare (Macon, GA: Mercer University Press, 1987), p. 68.

91. Robert Jewett, *A Chronology of Paul's Life* (Philadelphia: Fortress, 1979), foldout page.

92. Gerd Luedemann, *Paul, Apostle to the Gentiles: Studies in Chronology,* trans. E. Stanley Jones (Philadelphia: Fortress, 1984), pp. 262–63.

93. Harold W. Hoehner, "A Chronological Table of the Apostolic Age," 2d rev. ed. (1989), from "Chronology of the Apostolic Age" (Th.D. diss., Dallas Theological Seminary, 1965), pp. 1–4.

94. The Western text of Acts 15:1–5 makes the Pharisaic identity even stronger with several extensive additions. See Bruce M. Metzger, *A Textual Commentary on the Greek New Testament* (New York: United Bible Societies, 1971), pp. 426–28.

95. E. Earle Ellis, "'Those of the Circumcision' and the Early Christian

Mission," *Studia Evangelica* 4 (1968): 391. See also F. F. Bruce, "The Church of Jerusalem in the Acts of the Apostles," *Bulletin of the John Rylands University Library of Manchester* 67 (1985): 641–61.
96. King, "Paul and the Tannaim: A Study in Galatians," pp. 349–61.
97. Ibid., p. 351.
98. Ibid., pp. 352–54.
99. Ibid., p. 354.
100. The epistemological and hermeneutical maxim of "simplicity" is worth noting at this point. It is that the "simplest" hypothesis fitting the facts is the best hypothesis. This goes back to William of Ockham (1285–1349), author of "Ockham's Razor," which is widely paraphrased as "entities are not to be multiplied beyond necessity" (W. F. Bynum, E. J. Browne, and Roy Porter, eds., *Dictionary of the History of Science* [Princeton: Princeton University Press, 1981], pp. 386–87). While fully recognizing the complexities of persons and communities, the principle of simplicity can still be applied in a nonreductionist manner. In hypothesizing about the identity of Paul's opponents in Galatia, the traditional Judaizer identity is the simplest hypothesis and yet allows for the human complexities associated with the clash of cultures and traditions. There is no need to multiply other entities or identities.

Chapter 13

1. The suggestion for this study postulating a Dionysian background for Ephesians 5:18 was provided in reading the erudite commentary of Marcus Barth, *Ephesians: Translation and Commentary on Chapters 4–6*, Anchor Bible (Garden City, NY: Doubleday, 1974), p. 580.
2. For example, on crucifixion, see Martin Hengel, *Crucifixion in the Ancient World and the Folly of the Message of the Cross* (Philadelphia: Fortress, 1977); on slavery, see S. Scott Bartchy, *First Century Slavery and First Corinthians 7:21* (Missoula, MT: Scholars, 1973).
3. Homer *Iliad* 6.13; 14. 325; *Odyssey* 11. 324; 24.74.
4. See Martin P. Nilsson, *Geschichte der griechischen Religion* (Munich: Beck, 1955), 2:352–53.
5. See ibid., 1:564–68, 578–82; Ulrich von Wilamowitz-Moellendorf, *Der Glaube der Hellenen* (Darmstadt: Wissenschaftliche, 1973), A. 2:60; and *Oxford Classical Dictionary*, 2d ed., s.v. "Dionysus," pp. 352–53.
6. See Hjalmar Frisk, *Griechisches Etymologisches Worterbuch* (Heidelberg: Winter-Universitatsverlag, 1973), 1:396; Nilsson, *Geschichte der griechischen Religion*, 1:567–68; and Wilamowitz-Moellendorf, *Der Glaube der Hellenen*, 2:62.
7. Ibid., 2:62; and Frisk, *Griechisches Etymologisches Worterbuch*, 2:42.

8. The opposition of Pentheus, king of Thebes, to Dionysus is considered to be "hubris" (shameful, arrogant treatment) and he is horribly punished by the deity (Euripides *The Bacchanals*). Note also the Roman Senate decree of 186 B.C., "Senatusconsultum de Bacchanalibus," prohibiting the cult. See Carlton T. Lewis and Charles Short, *A Latin Dictionary* (Oxford: Clarendon, 1969), p. 218.

9. It was particularly Olympias, the mother of Alexander the Great, who spread the wild orgies of the women who worshiped Dionysus in Macedonia (see Plutarch *Lives, Alexander* 2.5–6; and Wilamowitz-Moellendorf, *Der Glaube der Hellenen*, 2:61–62).

10. Charles Edson, "Cults of Thessalonica," *Harvard Theological Review* 41 (July 1948): 164. Edson even suggests that "the temple of Dionysus in Roman Thessalonica stood at or near the site of the Theodosian church of the Akheiropoietos" (ibid., p. 179).

11. See Martin P. Nilsson, "The Bacchic Mysteries of the Roman Age," *Harvard Theological Review* 46 (October 1953): 184.

12. See, for example, Aristophanes *The Archarnians*, 245; Thucydides *History of the Peloponnesian War* 2.15; and *Lexikon der Antike, Religion-Mythologie* (Munich: Deutscher Taschenbuch Verlag, 1976), s.v. "Dionysia," by F. R. Walton, 1:213–14.

13. Pausanias *Description of Greece* 2:6.

14. Plutarch *Lives, Antony* 24.3. For further evidence of the worship in Ephesus as found in inscriptions, see Nilsson, *Geschichte der griechischen Religion*, 2:359–62.

15. See ibid., 2:358–67; and Eduard Lohse, *The New Testament Environment* (Nashville: Abingdon, 1976), pp. 235–36. Schmitz observes, "The worship of Dionysus was almost universal among Greeks in Asia as well as in Europe" (*A Dictionary of Greek and Roman Antiquities* [London: Murray, 1872], s.v. "Dionysia," by Leonhard Schmitz, p. 412).

16. See David Flusser, "Paganism in Palestine," in *The Jewish People in the First Century* (Assen/Amsterdam: Van Gorcum, 1976), 2:1067–68, 1083–84.

17. Goldstein has suggested that the "abomination of desolation" consisted of three meteorite cult-stones, representing the God of the Jews, the queen of heaven, and the divine son Dionysus (Jonathan A. Goldstein, *I Maccabees*, Anchor Bible [Garden City, NY: Doubleday, 1976], p. 224; also see pp. 125–60, esp. 143–57). He also suggests that the pig sacrificed was in honor of Dionysus (ibid., p. 158).

18. 2 Maccabees 6:7; also see Flusser, "Paganism in Palestine," 2:1068–69.

19. See, for example, Wilamowitz-Moellendorf, *Der Glaube der Hellenen*, 2:72–74.

20. "The men prophesied like insane persons, with ecstatic bodily movements" (Livy *Ab urbe cundita* 24.13, cited in Lohse, *The*

New Testament Environment, p. 235; also see Nilsson, *Geschichte der griechischen Religion*, 2:350; 1:58–59; and Nilsson, "Bacchic Mysteries," pp. 179–80.

21. See ibid., pp. 185–86; Plutarch *Lives, Antony* 50.3. Caligula impersonated, among other deities, the god Dionysus (Dio Cassius *Roman History* 59.6; Philo *Embassy to Gaius* 78–79). Wilamowitz-Moellendorf points out that the movement arose from the lower class of society and these remained true to their god (*Der Glaube der Hellenen*, 2:71).

22. Note, for example, Euripides *The Bacchanals*; Aristophanes *The Archarnians* 245, 280; for sculpture and painting see David Soren, "The Fogg Kleophrades Vase under the Ultraviolet Light," *Bulletin of the American Society of Oriental Research* 228 (October 1977): 29–46; and Mary C. Sturgeon, "The Reliefs on the Theater of Dionysus in Athens," *American Journal of Archaeology* 81 (1977): 31–53. Note her discussion of and bibliography on such motifs as "The Birth of Dionysus," "Entrance of Dionysus into Athens," "Sacred Marriage of Dionysus and the Basilinna," and "The Enthronement of Dionysus." For music, note the so-called Dithyrembos, a song of the theater concerning Dionysus (*Oxford Classical Dictionary*, s.v. "Dithyram," p. 356; and Jacob Burckhardt, *Griechische Kulturgeschichte* [Munich: Deutscher Taschenbuch Verlag, 1977], 3:191–92).

23. See, for example, Nilsson, *Geschichte der griechischen Religion*, 1:35–38.

24. For a description of these male and female figures, half-clad, carrying musical instruments, wearing ivy wreaths, and having animal features, see *Oxford Classical Dictionary*, s.v. "Satyrs and Sileni" and "Maenads," pp. 636, 956.

25. For example, one of the temple gates in Jerusalem was decorated with golden grapevines from which huge grape clusters hung (Josephus *Jewish Wars* 5.210). Plutarch gives quite an elaborate "Proof" that the Jews worshiped Dionysus. He appeals to such things as vines and ivy used in the Feast of Tabernacles (Plutarch *Table-Talk* 4.6). For a discussion of these and other possible associations, see Goldstein, *I Maccabees*, pp. 129–30, and Flusser, "Paganism in Palestine," 2:1068–69. Also see Tacitus *Histories* 5. 5.

26. Note especially Plutarch *Table-Talk* 1; 3.1; etc.

27. See Plutarch *Lives, Antony*, 60.2. The Latin phrase "Bacchanalia vivere" means "to live in the manner of the Bacchantes," that is, "to live riotously and wantonly" (Lewis and Short, *A Latin Dictionary*, p. 218). Compare the expression κοριναθιάζεσθαι, "to live an immoral life."

28. For example as a vegetation god, he had to do with fertility, or in the mystery religions he was connected with Demeter or Osiris (Nilsson, *Geschichte der griechischen Religion*, 1:582–603; 2:359;

Strabo *Geography* 10.3.10; and Plutarch *Moralia: Isis and Osiris* 362.

29. "The sexual associations of the cult of Dionysus were a commonplace of conversation and the comic theater" (Goldstein, *I Maccabees*, p. 133).

30. See Aristophanes *The Archarnians*, 245–75; and Nilsson, *Geschichte der griechischen Religion*, 1:590–94.

31. For this common occurrence, see E. R. Dodds, "Maenadism in the Bacche," *Harvard Theological Review* 33 (July 1940): 155–76; Euripides *The Bacchanals* 116, 134, 137, 380, 510; and Nilsson, *Geschichte der griechischen Religion*, 1:585–90.

32. See Dodds, "Maenadism," pp. 156, 164–66.

33. See H. Lewy, *Sobria Ebrietas: Beiheft der Zeitschrift für die neutestamentliche Wissenschaft* (Berlin: de Gruyter, 1929), pp. 43–44; *Real-lexikon für Antike und Christentum*, 10 vols. (Stuttgart: Anton Hiersemann, 1950–78), s.v. "Ekstase," by F. Pfister, 4 (1959): 944–87; *Lexikon der Antike, Religion-Mythologie*, s.v. "Enthusiasmus," by B. Lohse, 1:227–28.

34. For example Pentheus was forced to do the will of Dionysus (Euripides *The Bacchanals* 910–1150), and Dionysus forced Hephaistos to return to Olympus "by intoxicating him and leading him back in a frenzied Bacchic procession" (Soren, "The Fogg Kleophrades Vase," p. 31; cf. Homer *Iliad* 18.398).

35. For a detailed discussion of this, see Lewy, *Sobria Ebrietas*, pp. 45–50; Plutarch *Moralia: Obsolescence of Oracles* 432; and Euripides *The Bacchanals* 298.

36. Lewy, *Sobria Ebrietas*, pp. 50–51: Bacchus was to the Romans the "god of poets" because of his intoxicating and inspiring acts (Lewis and Short, *A Latin Dictionary*, p. 218).

37. Wilamowitz-Moellendorf, *Der Glaube der Hellenen*, 2:68; and Euripides *The Bacchanals* 142, 300, 700.

38. See esp. Nilsson, "Bacchic Mysteries," pp. 175–202; and Nilsson, *Geschichte der griechischen Religion*, 1:599–601; and 2:358–59.

39. Wilamowitz-Moellendorf, *Der Glaube der Hellenen*, 2:68.

40. Werner Foerster, "ἄσωτος, ἀσωτία," in *Theological Dictionary of the New Testament*, 1:506. One interesting fact is that the related term Σαώτης was applied to Dionysus as a descriptive title (Frisk, *Griechisches Etymologisches Worterbuch*, 2:844).

41. Foerster, "ἄσωτος, ἀσωτία," 1:506.

42. Ibid., p. 507. In addition to the extrabiblical passages mentioned by Foerster, also see Josephus *Jewish Wars* 4.651; Philo *De Sobrietate* 40; and Philo *De Praemius et Poenis* 52.

43. Note the contrastive ἀλλά.

44. See G. Mussies, *The Morphology of Koine Greek* (Leiden: Brill, 1971), pp. 272–73. Also see W. F. Bakker, *The Greek Imperative* (Amsterdam: Hakkert, 1966).

45. For a discussion of the preposition ἐν used like the dative and

with an instrumental force with the passive πληρόω see Robert Helbing, *Die Kasussyntax der Verba bei den Septuaginta* (Göttingen: Vandenhoeck & Ruprecht, 1928), pp. 145–47.

46. Philo *Embassy to Gauis* 78–79.
47. Barth, *Ephesians*, p. 580.
48. Ibid.

Chapter 14

1. Robert Jewett, "The Epistolary Thanksgiving and the Integrity of Philippians," *Novum Testamentum* 12 (1970): 49.
2. For instance, Jewett sees each section of the letter bound to the other by an apocalyptic conception of a suffering messianic apostle and community whose composure in persecution heralds the coming destruction of their enemies at the παρουσία as well as their own perfected salvation in that day (ibid., p. 51).
3. Some popular works have suggested Christian unity as the main theme: Robert Gromacki, *Stand United in Joy* (Grand Rapids: Baker, 1980); Frank Stagg, "Philippians," in *The Broadman Bible Commentary*, ed. Clifton J. Allen, 12 vols. (Nashville: Broadman, 1972), 11:178–216; and Howard Vos, *Philippians: A Study Guide* (Grand Rapids: Zondervan, 1975). See also Gerald Blazek, "Unity through Humility in Philippians" (Th.M. thesis, Dallas Theological Seminary, May 1977). The main objection to this view is that while unity is an important subtheme, it is not comprehensive enough to unify the entire epistle. This is most obvious in chapter 3 where the threat to the congregation is not presented as a threat primarily to their unity. Rather, the threat is to the maturity and perfection of the believers at Philippi. Failure to meet this threat would render them unable "to walk worthy of the gospel of Christ" (1:27). Also this view fails to note the thematic statement in the prologue of the epistle.
4. Ernst Lohmeyer, *Der Briefe an die Philipper* (Göttingen: Vandenhoeck & Ruprecht, 1954). His attempt to unity the epistle around the theme of martyrdom has been criticized both theologically and exegetically and has attracted almost no scholarly following.
5. Marvin Vincent, *A Critical and Exegetical Commentary on the Epistles to the Philippians and to Philemon* (Edinburgh: Clark, 1897), p. xxxi (italics added).
6. John Eadie, *A Commentary on the Greek Text of the Epistle of Paul to the Philippians* (Edinburgh: Clark, 1896), p. xxxi.
7. William Hendriksen, *Exposition of Philippians* (Grand Rapids: Baker, 1962), pp. 37–38.
8. Note, for example, Ralph P. Martin's first commentary on Philippians (*The Epistle of Paul to the Philippians: An Introduction and Commentary*, Tyndale New Testament Commentaries [Grand

Rapids: Eerdmans, 1959], p. 43). See also J. J. Muller, *The Epistles of Paul to the Philippians and to Philemon* (Grand Rapids: Eerdmans, 1955), p. 21; and H. A. W. Meyer, *Critical and Exegetical Handbook to the Epistles to the Philippians and Colossians, and to Philemon*, 4th ed., trans. John C. Moore, rev. and ed. Wm. P. Dickson, preface and supplementary notes by Timothy Dwight (New York: Funk & Wagnalls, 1889), p. 4.

9. The various forms this view has taken over the years are summarized concisely by Jewett ("The Epistolary Thanksgiving and the Integrity of Philippians," pp. 40–49). Ralph P. Martin in his most recent commentary covers the same ground and updates his discussion of the book (*Philippians*, New Century Bible [London: Oliphants, 1976], pp. 10–22).

10. While the issue is much too complicated to be discussed fully here, this writer feels that all these theories are subject to one basic criticism: they fail to explain the final form of the letter. The structure is a problem if the letter is a unit and is Pauline. The structure is still a problem if it is the work of an editor. What motive—doctrinal, practical, or ecclesiastical—can account for an editor's pasting it together the way he has? To say that it is all right for an editor to construct a document with an enigmatic structure, but not for an original author to do so, is not acceptable reasoning. H. A. A. Kennedy's observation is still valid today: "There must be some strong basis for such an hypothesis [i.e., as editorial redaction] derivable from the Epistle itself" ("The Epistle to the Philippians," in *The Expositor's Greek Testament*, 5 vols. [Grand Rapids: Eerdmans, 1951), 3:409).

11. Martin, *Philippians*, pp. 10–22.

12. John Lee White, *The Form and Function of the Body of the Greek Letter: A Study of the Letter-Body in the Non-Literary Papyri and in Paul the Apostle*, Society of Biblical Literature Dissertation Series (Missoula, MT: Scholars, 1972).

13. Robert W. Funk, "The Letter: Form and Function," in *Language, Hermeneutic, and the Word of God* (New York: Harper and Row, 1966), pp. 250–74. White basically accepts Funk's categorization of the structural elements of a Pauline letter (*The Form and Function of the Body of the Greek Letter*, pp. 43–45). His subsequent conclusions refine some of Funk's observations, but do not really modify them greatly.

14. Martin notes his acceptance of White's scheme and its adaptation to the "overall structure" of Philippians (*Philippians*, p. 63). The form criticism of Paul's letters began with Adolf Deissmann's comparisons of Paul's epistles to the common letters of the papyri. Deissmann was emphatic that the letters of Paul were in every way "common letters" and not to be considered "epistles" or "epistolary." Paul Schubert reacted against Deissmann's absolute dichotomizing of "letter" and "epistle" (*Form and Function of the*

Pauline Thanksgivings [Berlin: Topelmann, 1939]) and this same direction is followed by Funk and White. See also J. T. Sanders, "The Transition from Opening Epistolary Thanksgiving to Body in the Letters of the Pauline Corpus," *Journal of Biblical Literature* 81 (1962): 348–62.

15. White, *The Form and Function of the Body of the Greek Letter*, p. 75.

16. Schubert, *Form and Function of the Pauline Thanksgivings*, p. 77, nn. 1 and 2.

17. For instance, Martin, following White, breaks up the close-knit argument and unity of 1:12–26 in a way few if any exegetes would agree with. Also the labeling of 1:19b–2:18 as "theological argument" and chapter 3 as "paraenesis" seems arbitrary. A good deal of paraenesis is in 1:19b–2:18 as well as theological argument in chapter 3. Further evidence that Philippians defies this scheme is seen in the fact that scholars who basically accept Funk's schema cannot agree on what is "hortatory" and what is not. With Martin, Ronald Russell sees chapter 3 as paraenetical ("Pauline Letter Structure in Philippians," *Journal of the Evangelical Theological Society* 25 [September 1982]: 303–5). However, W. G. Doty feels that no exclusively "hortatory" section can be identified in the letter, whether in chapter 3 or elsewhere (*Letters in Primitive Christianity* [Philadelphia: Fortress, 1973], p. 43, chart).

18. Martin, *Philippians*, pp. 57–58, 63.

19. Schubert, *Form and Function of the Pauline Thanksgivings*, p. 24.

20. Ibid., p. 27.

21. Hans Conzelmann, "εὐχαριστέω, εὐχαριστία, εὐχάριστος," in *Theological Dictionary of the New Testament* 9 (1974): 412.

22. Schubert contends that this type of Pauline thanksgiving characteristically consists of seven formally constructed cola (*Form and Function of the Pauline Thanksgivings*, pp. 56–62). However, it seems that Schubert must stretch the syntax too far to support this.

23. This writer does not agree with Martin (*Philippians*, pp. 63–64),who like Schubert sees ὑμῶν as a subjective genitive. Seen this way, it is the Philippians' remembrance of Paul, not his remembrance of them, which is the basis of his thanks.

24. Good examples are J. B. Lightfoot, *St. Paul's Epistle to the Philippians* (London: Macmillan, 1913), p. 84; Martin, *The Epistle of Paul to the Philippians*, p. 61; Eadie, *Philippians*, p. 11; Vincent, *Philippians*, p. 8; Meyer, *Philippians*, p. 14. But see Dwight's notes for conclusions approaching those drawn in this chapter (in Meyer, *Philippians*, pp. 47–48).

25. The reference to κοινωνία should not be restricted to the gift the readers had sent to Paul. Nor does it here mean "fellowship" in the personal and subjective sense. That motif is not referred to until in verses 7–8. Here the term should be taken in the sense of "partnership" in a common enterprise. This usage is well attested

and is well suited for use in a prologue where general topics were introduced which were more fully developed later in the epistle. For a defense of a view similar to the one presented here, see George Panikulam, *Koinōnia in the New Testament—A Dynamic Expression of Christian Life* (Rome: Biblical Institute Press, 1979), pp. 80–86. Both in his view of the scope of the term κοινωνία and in his view of the relationship of verse 6 to verse 5, Panikulam is close to the view suggested here.

26. Jewett, "The Epistolary Thanksgiving and the Integrity of Philippians," p. 53.
27. Meyer, *Philippians*, p, 14.
28. Meyer's exegesis of verses 7–8 is enlightening, especially his recognition that grace here is grace to defend, confirm, and suffer for the gospel (*Philippians*, p. 16). See also Dwight's comments about the particular force of the verses (in Meyer, *Philippians*, pp. 48–49).
29. How Schubert could miss this borders on the incredible (*Form and Function of the Pauline Thanksgivings*, p. 77, n. 2).
30. From a form critical point of view Schubert also argues for the close connection of verses 9–11 with the verses before (ibid., 67, 71).
31. Dwight catches the precise meaning of ἀγάπη in this context: "The meaning of ἀγάπη is, accordingly, love as connected with κοινωνία, that love which brought the Philippians into fellowship for the furtherance of the gospel. The reference does not seem to be . . . simply to their love to one another, but to Christian love which, existing as a power in each individual soul, led them to work together as the opportunity and call for such working came to them" (in Meyer, *Philippians*, p. 49).
32. Dwight perceptively comments, "The prominence of the thought of κοινωνία εἰς τὸ εὐαγγέλιον in the paragraph . . . favors though it does not fully prove the transitive sense" (ibid., p. 50).
33. Jewett, "The Epistolary Thanksgiving and the Integrity of Philippians," p. 53.
34. See H. Betz, *Galatians: A Commentary on Paul's Letter to the Churches in Galatia* (Philadelphia: Fortress, 1979), pp. 14–15, 58–62.
35. Hendriksen, *Philippians*, p. 74.
36. Taken this way, σωτηρίαν bears the meaning it frequently has in the Septuagint—the general sense of "deliverance." The context must then supply the modal definition of the deliverance. For a view almost identical to this writer's view, see Zane C. Hodges, *The Gospel under Siege* (Dallas: Redencion Viva, 1981), pp. 90–94. The view of Meyer (*Philippians*, pp. 29–30) is, as far as it goes, compatible with the view presented here. It might also be noted that if the clause is a quotation from Job 13:16, then further support is given to this view.

37. T. E. Pollard sees 1:27a as stating Paul's primary concern in writing to the Philippians ("The Integrity of Philippians," *New Testament Studies* 13 [1966]: 65).
38. Again Dwight notes, "πάσχειν and the 30th verse . . . make it clearly manifest that the writer has especially in mind the furtherance of the gospel by the Philippians, in, and notwithstanding, experiences similar to his own, i.e., persecution, etc." (in Meyer, *Philippians*, p. 58): cf. Martin's comments on v. 30 (*Philippians*, p. 85).
39. For example, Hendriksen, *Philippians*, p. 39; Lightfoot, *Philippians*, p. 69; Müller, *Philippians*, p. 18; Vincent, *Philippians*, pp. 72, 75; and Martin, *Philippians*, p. 57.
40. Martin, *Philippians*, pp. 116–17.
41. Ibid., pp. 91–93. In this commentary Martin's entire discussion of 2:5–11 reveals that he has not changed his opinion since the publication of his major work *Carmen Christi: Philippians ii. 5–11 in Recent Interpretation and in the Setting of Early Christian Worship* (Cambridge: Cambridge University Press, 1967).
42. Pollard, "The Integrity of Philippians."
43. See Martin, *Philippians*, p. 18.
44. See C. F. D. Moule, *The Epistle to the Philippians* (reprint, Grand Rapids: Baker, 1981), p. 56. Moule notes that τὸ λοιπόν marks the transition between the two major topics of the epistle—unity and a firm stance for the gospel.
45. Martin, *Philippians*, p. 154.
46. Eadie, *Philippians*, p. xxxi.
47. William J. Dalton, "The Integrity of Philippians," *Biblica* 60 (1979): 101.

Chapter 15

1. Homer Kent, *The Pastoral Epistles* (Chicago: Moody, 1958), p. 141.
2. Ibid.
3. William Hendriksen, *I-II Timothy and Titus*, New Testament Commentary (Grand Rapids: Baker, 1957), p. 132.
4. Edwin Hatch, *The Organization of the Early Christian Churches* (London: Longmans, Green, 1918), p. 185.
5. Charles Ryrie, *The Place of Women in the Church* (New York: Macmillan, 1958), p. 97.
6. Hatch, *The Organization of the Early Christian Churches*, p. 187.

Chapter 16

1. J. W. C. Wand, *The General Epistles of St. Peter and St. Jude*, Westminster Commentaries (London: Methuen, 1934), p. 119.
2. James Moffatt, *The General Epistles James, Peter, and Judas*, Moffatt New Testament Commentary (New York: Harper and Bros., n.d.), p. 158.

3. Charles E. B. Cranfield, *I & II Peter and Jude*, Torch Bible Commentaries (London: SCM, 1960), p. 98.
4. Ibid., pp. 83–84 (capitalization and italics his).
5. Ibid., p. 41.
6. William Barclay, *The Letters of James and Peter*, Daily Study Bible (Philadelphia: Westminster, 1960), pp. 209–10.

Chapter 17

1. Gary D. Long, *Definite Atonement* (Philadelphia: Presbyterian and Reformed, 1977), p. 68.
2. Henry Alford, *Alford's Greek Testament*, 4 vols. (Grand Rapids: Baker, 1980), 4:402.
3. According to the writer's survey of *New Testament Abstracts* indexes since its beginning (1956), not even a single article was devoted to the discussion of this passage with regard to the extent of the atonement.
4. For some of these insights the writer is indebted to Charles C. Ryrie, "Soteriology and Evangelism" (unpublished class notes, Dallas Theological Seminary, Fall 1980).
5. Long, *Definite Atonement*, p. 70; "Theological Proof for Definite Atonement" (Th.M. thesis, Dallas Theological Seminary, 1969), p. 87.
6. W. L. Lane, "Vessel, Pot, Potter," in *New International Dictionary of New Testament Theology*, 3:913.
7. Christian Maurer, "σκεῦος," in *Theological Dictionary of the New Testament*, 7:362.
8. Cf. A. T. Hanson, *The Pastoral Epistles*, New Century Bible Commentary (Grand Rapids: Eerdmans, 1982), pp. 138–39.
9. This point is also admitted by Gary Long who says that in all these five instances the word δεσπότης "is used of men in a master-servant relationship" ("Theological Proof for Definite Atonement," p. 89).
10. Ibid. Also see W. E. Vine, *An Expository Dictionary of New Testament Words* (London: Oliphants, 1940), 3:46.
11. Daniel B. Wallace, "Selected Notes on the Syntax of New Testament Greek" (class notes, Dallas Theological Seminary, 1980), p. 103.
12. Alford, *Alford's Greek Testament*, 4:402; Horst Balz and Wolfgang Schrage, *Die Katholischen Briefe* (Göttingen: Vandenhoeck & Ruprecht, 1973), p. 134; Charles Bigg, *The Epistles of St. Peter and St. Jude*, International Critical Commentary (New York: Charles Scribner's Son, 1909), p. 272; Edwin A. Blum, "2 Peter," in *The Expositor's Bible Commentary* (Grand Rapids: Zondervan. 1981),12:276; Joseph Chaine, *Les epitres Catholiques* (Paris: Librairie Lecoffre, 1939), p. 59; Charles R. Erdman, *The General Epistles* (Philadelphia: Westminster, 1919), p. 98; Joseph Felten,

Die zwei Briefe des heiligen Petrus und der Judas brief
(Rogensburg: G. J. Manz, 1929), p. 190; Raymond C. Kelcy, *The
Letters of Peter and Jude* (Austin: Sweet, 1972), p. 136; René
Leconte, *Les epitres Catholiques* (Paris: Les Éditions du Cerf,
1961), p. 141; R. C. H. Lenski, *The Interpretation of the Epistles
of St. Peter, St. John and St. Jude* (Minneapolis: Augsburg, 1966),
p. 305; Karl Hermann Schelkle, *Die Petrusbriefe/Der Judasbrief*
(Freiburg: Herder, 1976), p. 204; J. W. C. Wand, *The General
Epistles of St. Peter and St. Jude* (London: Methuen, 1937), p.
163.

13. Long, *Definite Atonement*, pp. 70–71; Long, "Theological Proof
    for Definite Atonement," pp. 86–93.
14. I. Howard Marshall, "The Development of the Concept of
    Redemption," in *Reconciliation and Hope*, ed. Robert Banks (Grand
    Rapids: Eerdmans, 1974). p. 159.
15. Leon Morris, *The Apostolic Preaching of the Cross* (Grand Rapids:
    Eerdmans, 1965), p. 53.
16. D. H. Field, "Buy, Sell, Market," in *New International Dictionary
    of New Testament Theology*, 1:267.
17. Cf. Morris, *The Apostolic Preaching of the Cross*, p. 53.
18. Long, "Theological Proof for Definite Atonement," p. 101.
19. Ibid.
20. Ibid.
21. Norval Geldenhuys, *The Gospel of Luke*, New International
    Commentary on the New Testament (Grand Rapids: Eerdmans,
    1979), p. 393; also see Leon Morris, *The Gospel according to St.
    Luke*, Tyndale New Testament Commentaries (Grand Rapids:
    Eerdmans, 1974), p. 234.
22. J. Howard Marshall, for example, states that "the purchase may
    well have been arranged on condition of a later inspection and
    approval" and that the use of ἀνάγκη "implies the legal obligation
    of the purchaser to complete the sale" (*Commentary on Luke*, New
    International Greek Testament Commentary [Grand Rapids:
    Eerdmans, 1978], p. 589). This may be a possible interpretation,
    though unlikely, but even in this case the actual complete purchase
    did not take place when the excuse was made.
23. Long, "Theological Proof for Definite Atonement," p. 107; Long,
    Definite Atonement, p. 75.
24. Long, "Theological Proof for Definite Atonement," pp. 108–16:
    Long, *Definite Atonement*, pp. 76–78.
25. Long, "Theological Proof for Definite Atonement," pp. 111–12.
26. Long, *Definite Atonement*, p. 77.
27. Long, "Theological Proof for Definite Atonement," pp. 115–16;
    Long, *Definite Atonement*, pp. 77–78.
28. Long, "Theological Proof for Definite Atonement," p. 109.
29. For further discussion on this subject, see Geoffrey W. Bromiley,
    "The Interpretation of the Bible," in *The Expositor's Bible*

Commentary, 1:62; Norman L. Geisler, "How Stressing the Intention (Purpose) of the Author Leads to Unorthodox Conclusions" (address presented at luncheon seminar, Dallas Theological Seminary, 1983); E. D. Hirsch, Jr., *Validity in Interpretation* (New Haven, CT: Yale University Press, 1967), pp. 44–51; Moisés Silva, *Biblical Words and Their Meaning* (Grand Rapids: Zondervan, 1983), pp. 137–69.

30. See note 12 for references. In addition, see Michael Green, *The Second Epistle General of Peter and the General Epistle of Jude*, Tyndale New Testament Commentaries (Grand Rapids: Eerdmans, 1968), pp. 93–95; J. N. D. Kelly, *A Commentary on the Epistle of Peter and Jude* (New York: Harper & Row, 1969), pp. 326–28; Stephen W. Paine, "The Second Epistle of Peter," in *The Wycliffe Bible Commentary* (Chicago: Moody, 1962), p. 1459: E. M. Sidebottom, *James, Jude, 2 Peter*, New Century Bible Commentary (Grand Rapids: Eerdmans, 1967), p. 113; and David H. Wheaton, "2 Peter," in *The New Bible Commentary* (Grand Rapids: Eerdmans, 1970), p. 1254.

31. Cf. Edwin A. Blum, "Jude," in *The Expositor's Bible Commentary*, 12:388.

32. Long, "Theological Proof for Definite Atonement," p. 115; Long, *Definite Atonement*, p. 77.

33. Lewis Sperry Chafer, *Systematic Theology*, 8 vols. (Dallas: Dallas Theological Seminary, 1948; reprint [8 vols. in 4], Grand Rapids: Kregel, 1993), 3:193 (emphasis his).

34. Blum, "2 Peter," p. 276; Long, "Theological Proof for Definite Atonement," p. 104; Long, *Definite Atonement*, p. 74.

35. Robert P. Lightner, *The Death Christ Died: A Case for Unlimited Atonement* (Schaumburg, IL: Regular Baptist, 1967), p. 75.

Chapter 18

1. Kenneth W. Allen, "The Rebuilding and Destruction of Babylon," *Bibliotheca Sacra* 133 (January–March 1976): 25 (italics added).

2. Martin Otto Massinger, "Babylon in Biblical Prophecy" (Th.D. diss., Dallas Theological Seminary, 1967), p. 165.

3. Allen, "The Rebuilding and Destruction of Babylon," p. 26.

4. Merrill C. Tenney, *Interpreting Revelation* (Grand Rapids: Eerdmans, 1957), p. 85.

5. George Eldon Ladd, *A Commentary on the Revelation of John* (Grand Rapids: Eerdmans, 1972), p. 235.

6. Allen, "The Rebuilding and Destruction of Babylon," p. 26.

7. Ibid.

8. Karl Georg Kuhn, "βαβυλών," in *Theological Dictionary of the New Testament*, 1 (1964): 514.

9. Ladd, *A Commentary on the Revelation of John*, p. 244.

10. Charles C. Ryrie, *Revelation* (Chicago: Moody, 1968), p. 100.

11. Tenney, *Interpreting Revelation*, pp. 83–84.

12. Robert H. Mounce, *The Book of Revelation* (Grand Rapids: Eerdmans, 1977), p. 307 (italics added).
13. A. T. Robertson, *Word Pictures in the New Testament,* 6 vols. (Nashville: Broadman, 1933), 6:430.
14. John F. Walvoord, *The Revelation of Jesus Christ* (Chicago: Moody, 1966), p. 246.
15. Robertson, *Word Pictures in the New Testament,* 6:430.
16. W. E. Vine, *An Expository Dictionary of New Testament Words,* s.v. "Mystery," 3:97.
17. S. S. Smalley, "Mystery," in *The New Bible Dictionary,* 1974 ed., p. 856.
18. Mounce, *The Book of Revelation,* pp. 313–14.
19. Walvoord, *The Revelation of Jesus Christ,* pp. 22–23.
20. Ferrel Jenkins, *The Old Testament in the Book of Revelation* (Grand Rapids: Baker, 1976), p. 22.
21. Ladd, *A Commentary on the Revelation of John,* p. 229.
22. Robert Koldewey, *The Excavations at Babylon,* trans. Agnes S. Johns (London: Macmillan, 1914), p. 22 (italics added).
23. Ibid., fig. I.
24. D. J. Wiseman, "Babylon, OT," in *Zondervan Pictorial Encyclopedia of the Bible,* 1975 ed., 1:445.
25. L. Glynne Dairos, Assistant Secretary of the British School of Archaeology in Iraq, to Charles H. Dyer, 15 August 1978. Personal files of Charles H. Dyer, Lanham, Maryland.
26. D. J. Wiseman, "Babylon," in *International Standard Bible Encyclopedia,* 1979 ed., 1:390.
27. Austen H. Layard, *Discoveries among the Ruins of Nineveh and Babylon* (New York: Harper & Brothers, 1875), pp. 431–32.
28. Peter W. Stoner, *Science Speaks: An Evaluation of Christian Evidences* (Chicago: Moody, 1963), p. 94.
29. Willam R. Newell, *The Book of Revelation* (Chicago: Moody, 1935), p. 267.